MEL COUSINS

The Irish Social Welfare System

LAW AND SOCIAL POLICY

THE ROUND HALL PRESS

This book was typeset
in 10.5 on 11.5 Times by
Carrigboy Typesetting Services for
THE ROUND HALL PRESS LTD
Kill Lane, Blackrock, Co. Dublin, Ireland.

and in North America by
THE ROUND HALL PRESS
c/o ISBS, 5804 NE Hassalo St, Portland, OR 97213

© Mel Cousins 1995

A catalogue record for this book
is available from the British Library.

ISBN 1-85800-055-6 hbk
ISBN 1-85800-039-4 pbk

Printed in Ireland by
Betaprint Ltd, Dublin

For Maureen and Hannah

Contents

The Arthur Cox Foundation

Arthur Cox, solicitor, classical scholar and former President of the Incorporated Law Society of Ireland, was associated with the setting up of many Irish companies, not least the E.S.B. He was a specialist in company law and was a member of the Company Law Reform Committee which sat from 1951 and reported to the Government in 1958, ultimately giving rise to the Companies Act, 1963. When he decided to retire from practice as a solicitor in 1961 a number of his clients, professional colleagues and other friends, in recognition of his outstanding contribution to Ireland and his profession, thought that a fund should be established as a tribute to him which fund would be used to encourage the writing and publication of legal textbooks. There was a generous response to this appeal.

After his retirement he studied for the priesthood and was ordained in 1963. He went to Zambia to do missionary work. He died there in 1965 as a result of a car accident.

The Foundation was established to honour Arthur Cox and was for many years administered by Mr Justice John Kenny in conjunction with the Law Society. In paying tribute to the memory of Arthur Cox it is appropriate that tribute should also be paid to Mr Justice John Kenny, who died on 25 March 1987. John Kenny was a close personal friend of Arthur Cox and, like Arthur Cox, graced with distinction his own profession of barrister, as a chancery practitioner, and both the High Court and Supreme Court, as a judge. John Kenny was the encouraging force behind the publication of a number of Irish legal textbooks. Without his quiet drive and enthusiasm there would have been no Foundation. To both Arthur Cox and John Kenny we pay tribute.

The Law Society, as the continuing trustee of the Foundation, is pleased to have been able to assist in the publication of Mel Cousins' book

Michael V. O'Mahony
President
The Incorporated Law Society of Ireland
November, 1994

Introduction

'This society turns everything it touches into a potential source of progress *and* of exploitation, of drudgery *and* satisfaction, of freedom *and* of oppression.'
Herbert Marcuse, *One Dimensional Man.*

THE IMPORTANCE OF SOCIAL WELFARE

The Irish social welfare system currently accounts for one third of current government spending:

• in 1995 over £4,000 million will be spent on social welfare;

• about one and a half million people out of a population of three and a half million benefit from social welfare income-support payments;

• over one and a third million workers are insured under the social insurance scheme;

• almost half a million families receive child benefit for over one million children.

Yet despite the enormous importance of the social welfare system in Irish society, there has been relatively little written on the development of the system as a whole, particularly when one looks at the range of publications in other areas of social policy such as education and health.[1] This book aims to take a preliminary step to redress this imbalance. It analyses the development of the social welfare system in Ireland, with particular emphasis on developments in the twentieth century, and looks at several aspects of the social welfare system which are of particular importance at this stage in its development.

It may be that the complexity of the social welfare system accounts for this comparative lack of informed discussion and debate. Yet as Peter Baldwin points out the development of social welfare 'conceals questions of utmost importance under matters that may at first seem merely technical and abstruse . . . the battles behind the welfare state lay bare the structure and conflicts of modern society' (1990, p. 1).

9

CONTRADICTIONS, CONTROL AND CRISIS

This book highlights several important aspects of the Irish system and, in particular, the contradictions which are created by the development of the welfare state. On the one hand, there can be no doubt that the social welfare system provides financial support to many people who do not have other means of support and raises a large proportion of the population above the poverty line. Yet, on the other, one of the most important aspects of the system is the control which it exercises over the claimant population (and indeed over an even broader group of people), whether this be at a macro level though the management of an economic crisis by increased payments of social welfare to those affected by unemployment and poverty, or at a micro level through, for example, the control of signing on times for travellers or the control of women's sexual and emotional relationships through the cohabitation rule. Indeed the provision of support is almost inextricable linked with that of control: Rosanvallon (1988, p. 210) argues that 'in "welfare" society relations of mutual support between people assume the form of reified relations between individuals and "the system"' (see Foucault, 1988; Habermas, 1987).[2]

This analysis of the development of the Irish system also suggests that the social welfare system has played an important role in the management of economic and societal crises – and incipient crises (Habermas, 1987). The argument here is rather the reverse of the much discussed 'crisis of the welfare state'. Rather than the growth of the welfare system leading to crises in the economic system, it is argued that crises (in the sense of periods of instability or turning points) in the economy and in society – such as, for example, Ireland's transition from a mainly agricultural to an industrial society – are, in part, managed through developments in the social welfare system.

Thus the book seeks to emphasise both the positive and the negative aspects of the Irish system and also seeks to explain how they have developed in order that we can better see the society from which they have developed. It argues that the social welfare system is a reflection of the economic, political, ideological and cultural structures and conflicts in Irish society: a mirror *of* power in the sense that it reflects the existing power structures and a mirror *with* power in that it tends to freeze the picture of society which it sees until structural changes force a refocussing of its gaze.

This book does not claim to be, in any sense, a comprehensive account of the Irish social welfare system and makes only passing reference to some of the most important areas of policy, including payments to the elderly, the unemployed and people with disabilities. Rather it is hoped that the publication of these initial studies may stimulate further and more comprehensive debate of this area of fundamental importance in Irish society.

OUTLINE AND ACKNOWLEDGEMENTS

Chapters 1 and 2 outline the development of the social welfare system and analyse the forces at play behind that development. Chapter 3 looks at how the social welfare system interacts with changes in the paid labour force, in particular the growth of atypical working patterns.

Much of the emphasis in this book is on the ways in which the social welfare system reflects and reinforces the existing construction of gender roles in Irish society. The treatment of households is considered in chapter 4 while chapters 5 and 6 look at two specific types of payments to households where major reforms have recently been introduced: payments to lone parents and financial support to carers (the vast majority of claimants in both groups being women). Chapter 7 examines the major structural changes which have been made in the social welfare system as a result of the implementation of the EU directive on equal treatment for men and women, while chapter 8 considers the social welfare provisions for women during pregnancy and maternity.

The next two chapters consider aspects of the administrative structure of the system with chapter 9 looking at the development of adjudication and appeal structures since the establishment of the first income support systems under the Poor Law in 1847 and chapter 10 examining the operation of the administrative procedures in relation to one specific and contentious aspect: the recovery of overpaid welfare. Finally chapter 11 summarises the trends which have become apparent in the preceding chapters and discusses the possible future development of the social welfare system in the context of economic and demographic change and of an advance toward a closer European Union.

In terms of terminology: Ireland refers to the Republic of Ireland and, for the sake of convenience, I have throughout referred to the European Union (formerly the European Economic Community and then the European Communities) as the EU. The term 'social welfare' as used in Ireland normally refers to range of income support payments administered by the Department of Social Welfare and I have also referred, where appropriate, to the much smaller range of income-support payments operated under the auspices of the Department of Health. Unless otherwise stated the figures for Department of Social Welfare payments are taken from the Department's Annual Reports and, from 1983, from the annual *Statistical Information on Social Welfare Services*.

I would like to thank, in particular, Gerry Whyte and Larry Bond of Trinity College who commented on earlier drafts of this book. The usual disclaimer applies. Earlier versions of chapters 3, 4, 5 and 8, and 10 have appeared in the *International Labour Review*, the *Journal of Social Welfare and Family Law*, *Administration*, and the *Irish Journal of Sociology* respectively.

CHAPTER ONE

The Development of the Social Welfare System in Ireland

In this chapter we look at the main developments in the Irish social welfare system from its earliest stages to the 1990s. We go on, in chapter 2 to analyse these developments in more detail. Thus, in broad terms, this chapter looks at *how* the system has developed whereas chapter 2 discusses *why* the system has developed in this way. We first summarise briefly the main features of the current system and some of the main trends in its development.

The Irish social welfare system currently includes three types of benefits: social insurance (or contributory) schemes, social assistance (or means tested) schemes and a universal child benefit. Almost all benefits are paid at a flat (subsistence) rate with increases for adult and child dependants. Most social welfare schemes are administered by the Department of Social Welfare, although the residual means tested supplementary welfare allowance is administered by the eight regional health boards on behalf of the Department. In addition there are a number of health and disability related payments administered by the Department of Health and the regional health boards.

The first statutory system of social welfare in Ireland was the means tested Poor Law (1838). Subsequently a range of social welfare schemes introduced in the United Kingdom at the end of the nineteenth and in the early twentieth century also applied to Ireland. These included the first social insurance scheme introduced in 1911.[1] Thus at the time of Independence in 1921–22, the basis of the current social insurance and social assistance system already existed in Ireland. Developments since then have consolidated and expanded the social insurance system and introduced new social assistance schemes in order to take people off the unpopular Poor Law. In 1975, the old Poor Law (by then renamed 'home assistance') was abolished and replaced by supplementary welfare allowance. Economic recession in the 1980s has seen a renewed emphasis on the importance of means tested payments, although the social insurance scheme has continued to expand at the same time with its extension to cover the self-employed (1988) and part-time workers (1991).

THE DEVELOPMENT OF THE SYSTEM TO THE TWENTIETH CENTURY

Early developments (600–1838) Early Irish law (Brehon Law) did not provide for any collective system of social welfare.[2] However, it did impose a

12

legal responsibility on the kin group to care for its members who were insane, aged or suffering from physical disability (Kelly, 1988). The kin group consisted of the descendants through the male line of the same great-grandfather. Early Irish law also included provisions imposing liability on individuals to provide support to persons incapacitated by them as a result of an unlawful attack. This was known as sick-maintenance. The original Irish laws were suppressed as the English gained control over an increasing proportion of Ireland, and after about 1600 the Brehon Laws largely disappeared and were replaced by English legislation.

In 1634, summoned by the then Viceroy (appointed by the King of England), the Irish Parliament passed an Act for the erecting of Houses of Correction and for the Punishment of Rogues, Vagabonds, Sturdy Beggars and other Lewd and Idle Persons (Powell, 1992). This provided that houses of correction were to be built in each county where persons could be set to work. The groups to which this Act applied included mendicant scholars, gypsies and labourers unwilling to work for reasonable wages. This Act also provided that 'an able bodied rogue' who had deserted his family would be sent to a house of correction until support had been provided. Thus the onus of support had shifted from the Celtic kin group to the common law concept of the more immediate family. The houses of correction soon fell into disuse and the government sought other means of controlling the poor. In 1701, vagrancy was made a transportable offence in Ireland. As a vagrant was not allowed to contest the charge of vagrancy, this meant that any poor homeless person could be transported. However, it appears that this draconian measure was also not implemented strictly. In 1771–72, the Irish Parliament enacted legislation to set up houses of industry. These were intended to provide shelter for the 'aged, infirm and industrious' and to provide a prison for the 'profligate, idle and refractory'. This was in effect a model for the workhouses which later appeared under the Poor Law. However, unlike the situation in the UK, no Poor Law existed in Ireland prior to 1838 and the relief of the poor was the sole responsibility of charitable organisations, including church bodies.

The introduction of the Poor Law (1838–97)   In England, the Poor Law had existed since the sixteenth century. In 1834, the English Poor Law system was extensively revised and, following the establishment of several Commissions and Inquiries to investigate the matter, it was decided to establish a broadly similar system of Poor Law in Ireland (Nicholls, 1856; Powell, 1992).[3] The Poor Law system was based on the principle of 'less eligibility', i.e. the conditions for those in receipt of Poor Law must be worse than those of the poorest labourer. As a result of the very impoverished conditions of Irish workers in the early nineteenth century, it was insisted that support would only be provided to those prepared to enter a workhouse and it was intended that 'outdoor relief' would not be provided. One of the arguments put forward by those who objected to the extension of the English system of Poor Law to Ireland was that the conditions of Irish workers were so bad that it would be impossible to achieve the principle of 'less eligibility'. Thus, it was feared that the Poor Law would undermine the Irish economy as it would be at least as attractive to exist on the Poor Law as to work.

Powell (1992, p. 52) argues that the introduction of the Poor Law was a response to a recognition that the agricultural system was incapable of supporting the increasing population and that a transformation of the Irish peasantry into wage labour was ultimately necessary. The Poor Law was to support this period of transition. In the event, the introduction of the Poor Law in Ireland was followed almost immediately by a series of famines in the 1840s culminating in the Great Famine of 1846–48. The Poor Law was not intended to cope with the extent of poverty caused by the famine and it is estimated that a million people died and a million emigrated during the famine years. The famine was followed by a long term pattern of emigration such that the population dropped from over 6.5 million people in 1841 (in the part of Ireland which now constitutes the Republic) to below 3 million in the 1920s. However, one consequence of the famine was that, in 1847, the Poor Law was amended to allow outdoor relief to be paid. This remained a feature of poor law relief in Ireland.

DEVELOPMENTS IN THE TWENTIETH CENTURY

UK laws applied to Ireland (1897–1921) In the period until Ireland became independent of the UK in 1921–22, the developing UK social welfare system generally applied to Ireland. Thus the Workmen's Compensation Act[4] of 1897 applied as did the non-contributory old age pension established in 1908 (Carney, 1985). The majority of benefits under the National Insurance Act, 1911 (including unemployment, sickness and maternity benefit) also applied, although medical benefit (i.e. treatment by a general practitioner and other medical expenses) was not extended to this country as a result of the opposition of the Catholic Church and sections of the Irish medical profession (Barrington, 1987). The Church argued that the national insurance system as a whole was not appropriate to Irish conditions, which were agricultural rather than industrial. The opposition of the medical profession appears to have been largely based on a claim for higher remuneration. Barrington argues that this outcome favoured doctors with large private practices who feared a loss of paying patients. She also points out that the approach of the Catholic Church 'illustrates the way in which the bishops viewed the issues raised by the Bill through predominantly rural and capitalist eyes and from the standpoint of the farmer and the small trader' (1987, p. 50). The failure to extend medical benefit to Ireland began a trend whereby primary health care did not develop as an insurance-based scheme unlike most other countries in Europe.

Although much UK legislation was applied to Ireland, it must be remembered that circumstances in Ireland were quite different to those which applied in England and Wales. Ireland as a whole had not experienced large-scale industrialisation and a large proportion of the population was engaged in agriculture. In 1926, 44 per cent of the male working population was engaged in farming other than in an employed capacity (i.e. as employers, self-employed or assisting relatives) compared to only 32.5 per cent manual employees (Rottman et al. 1982).[5] Friendly societies developed relatively slowly and it has been estimated that in the early twentieth century there were only about 40,000 members of such societies (Barrington, 1987). Thus the social welfare schemes which applied to employees only, such as the workmen's compensation scheme and the national insurance system, had a significantly different impact in Ireland than in England.

Independence and after (1922–44)   Following Independence, Ireland was governed by a conservative Cumann na nGaedheal government until 1932. During this period there was little development in social welfare and, in fact, the amount of the old age pension was reduced by ten per cent in 1924. The Democratic Programme of the First Dáil had called for the abolition of the 'odious, degrading and foreign poor law system', but the Poor Law system was retained, although indoor relief was largely abolished and outdoor relief was renamed 'home assistance' (O'Cinnéide, 1970). In addition the administrative structure of the Poor Law was extensively reformed (see chapter 9).

The National Insurance Act, 1911 had been based on the assumption of a male breadwinner supporting his dependent wife and children. Reflecting the generally lower rates of women's earnings, different rates of unemployment and sickness benefit were paid to men and women. The earnings of married women were assumed to be of secondary importance and even lower rates of benefit were generally paid to such women. In 1929, the government reinforced this assumption of women's dependency by providing that a woman's membership of the insurance scheme terminated on marriage. In return women received a once-off marriage benefit.

It was not until the Fianna Fáil government came to power in 1932 that significant developments occurred in the area of social welfare. First, in response to the unemployment crisis in the 1930s, an unemployment assistance scheme was introduced in 1933. This meant that one group of people (unemployed people without entitlement to unemployment benefit or whose entitlement had expired) no longer had to rely on the Poor Law for support. Second, a widow's and orphan's pension scheme was introduced in 1935. This followed the introduction of a similar scheme in the UK in 1925 and the report of a Committee on Widows and Orphans Pensions (1933). The Irish scheme provided for an insurance-based pension but a means-tested pension was also introduced, because of the narrow scope of the social insurance scheme (with only 32 per cent of the male population of insurable age actually covered by social insurance). Thus a further group of people were removed from the scope of the Poor Law.

The benefits provided under the national insurance scheme were administered by a range of non-profit making organisations, including friendly societies which had already been involved in the provision of such benefits. The operation of these bodies was overseen by the government-appointed Irish Insurance Commissioners. Only bodies approved by the Commissioners were allowed to administer the benefits. In 1933 there were about 474,000 insured persons affiliated to 65 approved societies. The societies enjoyed a large degree of autonomy in financial matters and, while there were common rates of contributions, benefits varied from one society to another. The variations in benefits and the administrative difficulties and costs generated by the multiplicity of societies subsequently led to their amalgamation into the National Health Insurance Society in 1933. This approach had been recommended by the Committee of Inquiry into Health Insurance and Medical Services (1925). In 1936, the Catholic Bishop of Clonfert, Bishop Dignan, was appointed Chairman of the Society.

In 1939, the Poor Law was further revised and renamed 'public assistance'. However, it remained a locally administered discretionary payment, and the rates of assistance and administrative practices varied greatly from one area to another.

In 1944, following the report of an inter-departmental committee in 1942, a children's allowance for families with three or more children was introduced (Lee, 1989, p. 277 *et seq.*). This led to a significant increase in the level of social welfare spending (figure 1). The introduction of children's allowance followed a trend evident in other European countries to provide a family allowance in the post-war period. In total, 11 European countries introduced family allowances in the period between 1921 and 1944, including Austria

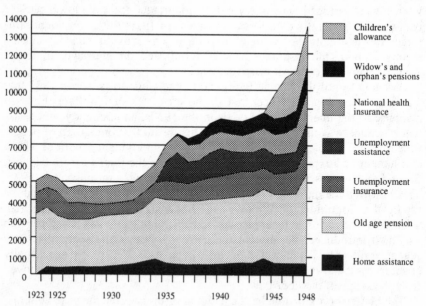

Figure 1: Social Welfare Expenditure 1923–48 (£'000)

SOURCE: Department of Social Welfare, *Social Security*. NOTES: (1) No figures on home assistance payments are available for 1923. (2) The data used in figures 1 to 4 are drawn from different sources and thus are not comparable in all respects.

(1921), Belgium (1930), France (1932), Italy (1937), Spain and Hungary (1938), Netherlands (1939) and Portugal (1942). The purpose of the payment was declared to be to assist in the 'alleviation of want in large families' rather than any pro-natalist policy (92 *Dáil Debates* 23 *et seq.*). The interdepartmental committee had recommended that, as in several other countries, the payments should be insurance-based (with non-contributory payments for those not covered by insurance). However, the government decided to opt for a universal payment in respect of all children (although the income tax child dependent allowances were reduced where children's allowance was payable).[6] Seán Lemass, the Minister responsible, explained that the decision not to have an insurance-based scheme was based on the fact that it would be impossible to collect contributions from self-employed persons and other non-employees and that, as a result, these groups would not benefit from an insurance-type scheme. The decision to opt for a universal scheme may also have been influenced by the publication in the UK of the Beveridge report (1942), which was cited in the Dáil debates during the discussion of the new payment. In fact, in this case Ireland anticipated the UK, which did not introduce such a payment until the following year.

The trends in expenditure over this period are shown in figures 1 and 2. As can be seen, expenditure increased sharply in the mid 1930s following the introduction of the unemployment assistance and widow's and orphan's pensions schemes and again in the early 1940s with the establishment of children's allowances. Expenditure as a proportion of national income was about 3 per cent in the second half of the 1920s and the early thirties.[7] It subsequently rose to almost five per cent by the late 1930s, reflecting the

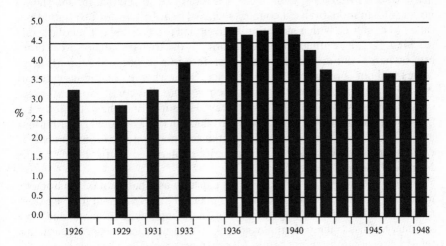

Figure 2: Social Welfare Expenditure as a percentage of
National Income 1926–48

SOURCE: As figure 1; Duncan, 'Social Income of the Irish Free State 1926–1938' XVI *JSSISI* 1;
White Paper on National Income and Expenditure 1938–1944.

increased spending by the Fianna Fáil government. This subsequently declined
to about 3.5 per cent by 1945 as social welfare spending failed to keep pace
with the sharp increase in national income. As can be seen from table 1,
means-tested payments dominated the system in its early years with over two
thirds of social welfare expenditure being means-tested as opposed to one
third by way of social insurance payments. However, by 1945 this had been
reduced to about 60 per cent, although the shift was towards the universal
children's allowance (14 per cent) rather than to social insurance payments.

In summary, following an initial period of austerity up to 1932, there was a
development in social welfare either in response to a crisis situation (unemployment) or for particular categories of claimant who were seen as deserving
(widows, orphans and large families). The commitment to the 'deserving' poor
can be seen in the new Constitution adopted in 1937, article 45 of which sets out
non-binding principles of social policy including a commitment by the state to
contribute, where necessary, 'to the support of the infirm, the widow, the orphan
and the aged'. The structure of the Irish welfare system began to diverge from
the UK system during this period, although where schemes were introduced
in Ireland UK provisions tended to be used as a guide.

Post-war expansion (1945–54)   This period began with the publication of
several Irish responses to the Beveridge report and proposals for expansion of
the Irish system. These included an article by a prominent Catholic theologian
and future bishop, Rev. Cornelius Lucey, who, while commenting favourably
on the report's proposals for the UK, did not support its application in Ireland
(Lucey, 1943). While accepting the necessity to plan for a more comprehensive social welfare system in the near future, he argued that Ireland should
not turn to an industrialised country such as Great Britain for inspiration but
rather to countries with a more similar economic position and to Catholic social
teaching. Dr Lucey argued that the majority of the Irish population were property owners – not employees – and therefore in a position to support themselves without compulsory state insurance. Somewhat in contradiction to this
point, he went on to argue that many were so poor that compulsory insurance
contributions would lead to bankruptcy. He supported the retention of a
(modified) means-tested system, the introduction of pay-related contributions
and benefits and the administration of the scheme by a vocational body (i.e.
consisting of representatives of the various interested parties) such as the
National Health Insurance Society.

Shortly after this, Dr Dignan, in his capacity as Chairman of the Society,
published a plan for Social Security (Dignan, 1945). He argued for the extension of social insurance to all employees (including public servants) and, on a
voluntary basis, to the self-employed. Like Rev. Lucey, he supported earnings-
related contributions and benefits. All schemes were to be amalgamated under
the control of one vocational body responsible to a Minister for Social
Security but with a wide degree of autonomy. This proposal was influenced
by Catholic social teaching (including the principle of subsidiarity) and by the
experience of Catholic European countries rather than the British experience

(Kaim-Caudle, 1967). The vocational aspects of the proposals were also in line with the proposals of the government-appointed Commission on Vocational Organisation (1943). However, the government did not respond favourably either to the proposals or to the fact that Dr Dignan had taken it upon himself to make them and, when his period as Chairman of the National Health Insurance Society ended in 1945, he was replaced by a civil servant (Whyte, 1980).

Up to 1947, the administration of the social welfare system was the responsibility of a range of different departments including the Departments of Local Government (old age pensions), Industry and Commerce (unemployment insurance and workmen's compensation), the Revenue Commissioners (old age pensions) and the National Health Insurance Society (sickness and maternity benefits). In 1947 a unified Department of Social Welfare was established which took over responsibility for the majority of social welfare schemes. Following the establishment of the Department, a White Paper on social welfare policy was published in 1949 (Department of Social Welfare, 1949). This proposed the extension of social insurance to all employees and the establishment of a range of new benefits, including a retirement pension. While it followed the recommendation of the Dignan proposals on several issues, it differed in opting for a centralised system of control through the Department of Social Welfare and for flat-rate benefits and contributions. Thus it followed the solutions proposed by the Beveridge report in these areas. The White Paper discussed the possibility of relating benefits to wages but, echoing the Beveridge report, it argued that flat-rate benefits were preferable. This was based on the argument that the state should only insist on basic standard of protection, that earnings-related benefits might provide a 'moral danger' and impose intolerable financial pressures on contribution levels, that earnings-related benefits would be complicated and, finally, that it was desirable to leave room for voluntary private insurance. The White Paper also argued against extending social insurance to the self-employed as many farmers were too poor to afford the contributions and the collection of contributions would create great administrative difficulties.

The proposals contained in the White Paper were introduced by the then coalition government (made up of a very wide spectrum of parties) in the Social Welfare Bill, 1950 (124 *Dáil Debates* 1069 *et seq*.). However, the government fell before the bill was passed. Many of the proposals were accepted by the new Fianna Fáil government in the Social Welfare Act 1952 (130 *Dáil Debates* 616 *et seq*.). This unified the various existing schemes and introduced a new maternity allowance. Equal rates of benefit for single men and women were also introduced, but married women still received lower rates and many other areas of gender discrimination remained. At this time, children's allowance became payable for the second child in the family. However, the proposal to extend social insurance to all employees was not accepted and employees earning above a set amount were excluded from insurance. Although civil and public servants were insured under the general social insurance scheme, they paid reduced contributions and were entitled to limited benefits on the grounds that they had general security of employment and had occupational pension schemes. The retirement pension was not introduced at that time, although a contributory old age pension payable at age 70 was subsequently introduced in 1961.

Thus, in terms of the scope of the social insurance scheme, the Irish scheme, unlike that in the UK, excluded (or substantially excluded) the higher paid non-manual workers (middle classes), the self-employed and civil servants from coverage and from liability to pay contributions. The exclusion of the self-employed can be seen as recognising the interests of the better-off members of that group in that they did not have to pay contributions while the poorer members received tax-funded social assistance payments. The exclusion of the non-manual workers recognised their lower exposure to insurable risks, while the partial inclusion of civil servants (with their low level of exposure to insurable risks and separate occupational schemes) emphasises both the extent to which the scheme recognised the interests of specific advantaged groups by excluding them from liability to pay social insurance contributions and the *étatist* policy of the Irish state in providing generous welfare benefits to its civil servants (Esping Andersen, 1990, p. 59). In his speech on the second stage of the 1952 Bill, the Minister for Health and Social Welfare, James Ryan, accepted that the scope of the Irish social insurance scheme was not comprehensive and stated that 'I cannot see either the justice or necessity for the inclusion of classes that can never benefit': he could not approve of what he described as 'hidden' taxation on such classes by the imposition of social insurance contributions (130 *Dáil Debates* 633). Thus in contrast to the relative universality of the UK system post-Beveridge, the Irish system remained essentially fragmented and showed little commitment to inter-class solidarity.

Not surprisingly, given the different proposals put forward by prominent Catholic churchmen, exponents of Catholic social teaching did not welcome the White Paper or the subsequent bill (Dignan, 1950; Whyte, 1980, p. 179). There was opposition in particular to the proposed abolition of the National Health Insurance Society and the centralisation of control within the Department of Social Welfare and to the fact that the scheme did not apply to the self-employed. However, the hierarchy as a body did not come out against the proposals and by 1952 the Fianna Fáil government encountered little opposition in introducing the legislation.

Thus the 1952 Act integrated and improved the existing social insurance scheme and provided a national social welfare system under the central administration of the Department of Social Welfare (although at a time when services were being unified in one department, the Department of Health established two 'health related' income maintenance payments under its own auspices: infectious diseases maintenance allowance (1947) and disabled persons maintenance allowance (1954)). The influence of the Beveridge report can clearly be seen in the adoption of flat-rate contributions and benefits and, again, UK provisions tended to be used as a model for the introduction of schemes in Ireland, e.g. maternity allowance. In the period between 1947 and 1954, social welfare expenditure as a percentage of GDP grew from 4.5 per cent to 5.9 per cent, with a 'growth pause' in 1950 and 1951 followed by rapid growth to the mid 1950s (Maguire, 1987, p. 464, see figure 3). The expansion of social insurance and the extension of children's allowance resulted in a shift away from assistance payments; by 1955 less than half of expenditure was on means tested payments (table 1). In 1953, 59 per cent of those in employment were insured under the social welfare scheme (52 per cent for all benefits: Maguire, 1987). However, no national means-tested payment was established during this period; the old Poor Law (now home assistance) remaining in force.

Consolidation (1954–64) Following the activity of the previous decade, the period from the mid 1950s to the mid 1960s was one of consolidation. The mid to late 1950s saw a period of economic depression in Ireland which did not begin to change until after the publication of the Programme for Economic Expansion (Ireland, 1958). The only major developments during this period were the introduction of a contributory old age pension in 1961 and the extension of children's allowance to the first child in 1963. The policy during this period is perhaps best described in the Second Programme for Economic Expansion, which stated that 'the policy adopted in the first and second programmes is to improve social welfare services in line with improvements in national production and prosperity'. The Programme declared that such increases 'must have regard to the extent to which national resources make such increases possible and desirable' (Ireland, 1964, p. 258).

During this period, expenditure as a percentage of GDP remained fairly static with a increase from 5.9 per cent in 1954 to 6.2 per cent in 1965 (Maguire, 1987, p. 464, see figure 3). This conceals a drop in expenditure both in real terms and as a proportion of GDP in 1958 and 1959, with spending as a proportion of GDP not returning to 1957 levels until the early 1960s. The introduction of the contributory old age pension marked a sharp increase in the importance of social insurance payments, with expenditure of social insurance growing from 28 per cent of spending in 1955 to 46 per cent in 1965. Social assistance now accounted for less than 30 per cent of all spending. The importance of state funding declined from 76 per cent in 1955 to 68 per cent in 1965 with a consequent rise in the level of employers and employees contributions arising from the shift to insurance payments (tables 2 and 4).

Economic development (1965–79) The Irish economy improved substantially in the period from the early 1960s until the 1970s. This period corresponded with a significant expansion in the social welfare scheme. The change in government policy can be seen in the Third Programme for Economic and Social Development published in 1969 (Ireland, 1969). In contrast to the cautious approach of the Second Programme, this set out an extensive list of promised reforms including the introduction of pay-related benefits, and of retirement and invalidity pensions. In the same period, the emphasis of the Catholic social movement shifted away from concern about excessive state intervention towards calling for increased state action in many poverty-related areas (Whyte, 1980, chapter XI). However, this did not mean that there was unanimous support in the Catholic hierarchy for an expanded welfare state, and several eminent Catholic theologians remained firmly opposed to 'excessive' state intervention in social welfare (Newman, 1987).

In 1966, the workmen's compensation scheme was finally abolished and, following the report of a Commission on Workmen's Compensation (1962), an occupational injuries scheme was adopted which was largely similar to the industrial injuries scheme in the UK. A range of new social insurance payments was also established including a retirement pension payable at age 65 (1970), an invalidity pension for persons with a long-term incapacity (1970), a death grant (1970) and a deserted wife's benefit (1973). In 1974, social insurance was extended to all private sector employees (except part-time workers). This resulted in an increase in the numbers insured as a proportion of those in employment from 73 per cent (66 per cent insured for all benefits) in 1973 to 85 per cent (73 per cent for all benefits) in 1975 (Maguire, 1987). The eligibility age for the old age pension was reduced from 70 to 66 years between 1973 and 1977. A pay-related benefit scheme was introduced in 1974 payable with unemployment, maternity and disability benefits. This followed the intro-duction of earnings-related supplements in the UK in 1966. However, the earning related pension for long-term pensions introduced in the UK in 1975 was never followed in Ireland although a Green Paper on a National Income Related Pension scheme was published in 1976.

In the area of social assistance or means-tested payments, several new payments were introduced, particularly in the area of payments to lone mothers (1970–74). Many of these payments has been recommended by a government-appointed Commission on the Status of Women (1972). A limited payment towards the costs of caring for elderly and invalided persons was also estab-lished (1968). In 1975, the remnants of the old Poor Law were finally abolished and a new national means-tested scheme (supplementary welfare allowance) was established. This supplemented rather than replaced the existing categorical payments to the unemployed, widows, etc. While the legislation established a legal right to benefit in some cases, the administration of the payment remained at a local level and much of the old discretionary approach to this payment remained.

As we have seen, the self-employed were generally not covered for contin-gencies such as unemployment and disability under the social welfare system. However, some self-employed persons on low incomes were allowed to claim unemployment assistance if their income was below the relevant threshold. In rural areas, occupiers of land over a certain value were automatically disqualified for unemployment assistance, regardless of means, from March to October, as were all men without dependants in rural areas from June to October (when it was assumed that seasonal farm work would be available). In 1965, following an Inter-departmental Committee Report which indicated that the means test acted as a disincentive to increased output by small holders, a scheme of notional assessment was introduced in the poorest farming areas. The farmer's entitlement was assessed not on the actual income but on a notional basis according to the value of the farmland owned (see McCashin, 1975–76). Thus a farmer could increase income without a decrease in assistance. The numbers in receipt of 'smallholders assistance' increased to over 30,000 by 1976. Concern at the increase in numbers led to restrictions on the scheme in the late 1970s (Curry, 1980).

Over this period, the emphasis continued to shift towards social insurance payments which accounted for over half of spending by 1975 and over 55 per cent by 1980 (table 1). This was due in part to a decline in the importance of children's allowance (8.5 per cent of expenditure in 1980), the real rate of which had been allowed to decline so that it did not keep pace with the growth in GDP nor with the growth in relative prices (Maguire, 1984). Social assistance payments increased slightly to over 30 per cent of total spending. The proportion of funding from employers increased substantially from 15 per cent in 1965 to 31.5 per cent in 1980. This allowed a decrease in state funding from 68 per cent in 1965 to 56 per cent in 1980 while employee funding declined slightly to 12 per cent (table 2). As a proportion of GDP, social welfare spending increased sharply from 6.2 per cent in 1965 to 7.6 per cent in 1970 and 10.7 per cent by 1980 (Maguire, 1987, p. 464; see figure 3). There was a steady growth in the period to 1976 followed by a drop in spending as a proportion of GDP between 1977 and 1979 before a further increase in 1980.

The end of the 1970s probably marked the high point in the expansionist phase of the scheme. As we have seen, a Green Paper on earnings-related pensions was published in 1976. This was followed by a Green Paper on the expansion of social insurance to the self-employed in 1978. In 1974, a limited pay-related contribution had been introduced to finance pay-related benefit

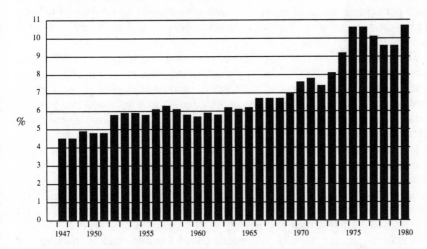

Figure 3: Income maintenance expenditure as a percentage of GDP 1947–80

SOURCE: Maguire (1987)

and, in 1979, the contribution system was altered from a flat-rate system to a pay-related system (PRSI). Thus, at the end of the 1970s, the Irish system looked as though it might develop in the same way as the UK system with an expansion of social insurance to the self-employed and a move towards earnings-related contributions and benefits. The UK system had itself been moving more towards the Continental system of earnings-related benefits in the 1970s. However, the move towards a pay related system in Ireland did not develop further, and the marked change in the UK system was already under way with the election of the Conservative government in 1979.

Crisis and consolidation (1980–94)

Growth in social welfare spending and cost containment The sustained economic boom of the 1960s and early 1970s has not been repeated in more recent years and there has been a sharp rise in unemployment over the period in question with the numbers in receipt of unemployment payments rising from 109,000 at the start of 1980 to 290,000 at the end of 1993.[8] This has been reflected in cuts introduced in some areas of social welfare. However, unlike the situation in the UK, there has been no large-scale assault on social welfare spending and in many areas the social welfare scheme has expanded. Social welfare expenditure continued to grow sharply in the early 1980s, reaching 13 per cent of GDP in 1985. It subsequently declined to 10.7 per cent in 1990 before rising again to almost 12 per cent in 1992 as unemployment increased.[9] In 1993, the state financed 56 per cent of expenditure with 29 per cent coming from employers, 13 per cent from employees and 2 per cent from the self-employed. The trend towards increased expenditure on social insurance payments has been reversed, and in 1993 only 44 per cent of expenditure was in this area with 45 per cent on social assistance, 6 per cent on child benefit and 5 per cent on administration. The shift towards assistance appears to arise largely from the sharp increase in the numbers in receipt of means-tested unemployment payments.

The Coalition government (1982–87) had found it impossible to halt the rise in the proportion of GDP spent on social welfare in the light of the continuing economic crisis and the opposition to social welfare cuts from the Labour party – the smaller coalition partner. However, the Fianna Fáil government, on its return to office in 1987, made determined efforts to control costs. These policies broadly continued under successive administrations to date and, indeed, Fianna Fáil Minister Dr Michael Woods has been in charge of the Department for most of this period. In particular, these policies centred on controlling the cost to the state of the Social Insurance Fund. This involved increasing the contribution requirements for several benefits, thereby tightening the link between benefit entitlement and participation in the paid labour force. This in turn had the effect of forcing people with inadequate contribution records to rely on means-tested benefits and increasing the importance of social assistance as a proportion of spending. The level of the state subvention to the Social Insurance Fund dropped from 31 per cent in

1986 to a mere 6 per cent by 1990 and a planned 3 per cent in 1994. The extension of social insurance to the self-employed in 1988 can also be seen as part of this trend (albeit a short-term measure) as funding from the self-employed (4 per cent of the Social Insurance Fund by 1993) will greatly exceed expenditure in the early years. The rèduction and eventual abolition of pay-related benefit (1994) formed part of this policy of making the Social Insurance Fund self-sufficient and also reduced the notional replacement ratio for short-term benefits. This shift away from social insurance payments towards social assistance echoed developments in the UK, where it was argued that means testing allowed payments to be concentrated on those most in need.

In 1992, the newly appointed Minister for Social Welfare, Charlie McCreevy, introduced a range of social welfare cuts – immortalised in the 1992 election campaign as the 'dirty dozen'. Some of these cuts were quite minor, but widespread concern about the future of the social welfare system was caused by the manner of their introduction, combined with McCreevy's claims that the cost of the social welfare system was almost out of control (at a time when spending as a percentage of GDP was significantly lower than it had been in 1986) and warnings that 'in the years to come we will not have the resources to pay those in need, for example, the old, the sick and people on pensions' (quoted in Council for Social Welfare, 1992). It is commonly believed that this had a negative impact on Fianna Fáil's performance in the subsequent election; 1993 saw the return to the Department of Michael Woods and the partial reversal of some of the cuts.

The issue of the taxation of short-term social welfare benefits was addressed with disability benefit and unemployment benefit becoming taxable in 1993

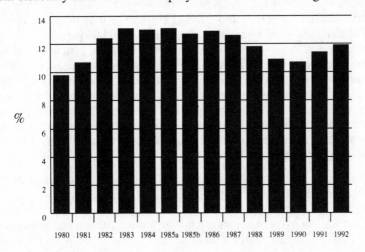

Figure 4: Social welfare expenditure as a percentage of GDP 1980–92

SOURCE: Department of Social Welfare, *Statistical Information on Social Welfare Services; Statistical Abstracts* (for Department of Health expenditure); GDP figures provided by CSO.
NOTE: The basis of calculation of GDP figures was revised in 1985.

and 1994 respectively. In 1993, following the general election, a Minister of State, Joan Burton TD, was appointed at the Department of Social Welfare, one of whose responsibilities was a consideration of the integration of the tax and social welfare systems. An Expert Group was appointed to consider this issue but had yet to report at the time of writing (although it has produced an interim report, 1993).

Commission on Social Welfare   One of the main features of this period was the report of the government-appointed Commission on Social Welfare (1986). The Commission, which had undertaken the first comprehensive review of the social welfare code since the 1949 White Paper, made a total of 65 recommendations. It generally recommended a consolidation and expansion of the existing scheme rather than any radically new approach. Its priority recommendations were for increased rates of benefits; improvements in child income support; the extension of the social insurance base and improved delivery of services. Although there has been no clear government commitment to the full implementation of the report, in practice the thrust of many of its recommendations has been followed. The Commission played an important role at a time of financial difficulties for the social welfare system both in expressing and confirming a consensus on continued support for the Irish welfare system and in setting targets for 'adequate' welfare rates. In 1991, the government and the social partners agreed to raise benefit levels to the 'priority' rates set by the Commission by 1993 (Ireland, 1991). This commitment was achieved in 1994.

Social insurance   The major initiatives in recent years were the extension of social insurance to the self-employed in 1988 and to part-time workers in 1991. The former extended social insurance to about 130,000 persons, although they were only entitled to a very limited range of benefits, primarily old age and widows pensions. This allowed an initial increase in insurance revenue through the extra contributions. It is anticipated that the benefits payable will, in many cases, replace existing means-tested payments which are being paid to elderly self-employed persons and their survivors. In 1991, social insurance was extended to all workers earning over £25 (now £30) per week; this meant that a further 25,000 workers (predominantly women) became entitled to pro-rata short term benefits.

Social assistance   Several means-tested schemes were introduced in the period 1988–90. These included a pre-retirement allowance which was largely a measure to get unemployed persons approaching retirement age who were in receipt of unemployment assistance to 'pre-retire' whereby they received the same rate of payment without having to be available for and seeking employment. As a result, the state was able to reduce the recorded unemployment figures. A lone parent's allowance was introduced in 1990 which amalgamated and extended the existing lone parent's schemes. A carer's allowance was also introduced, although take-up has been much lower than expected to date. These two payments recognised the caring responsibilities of women (96 per cent of lone parent claimants and 77 per cent of carers are women). In 1986, the responsibility for funding the supplementary welfare allowance scheme was transferred entirely to central government and local authority funding was abolished. This represented the final stage in a long process of transferring responsibility for such funding from local authorities (as under the Poor Law) to central government, a process which can also be seen in relation to health services (Barrington, 1987). The special scheme of unemployment assistance for farmers was abolished in 1983, but about 12,000 smallholders continue to claim unemployment assistance.

Child income support   Income support for children was restructured in the mid 1980s with the introduction of a means-tested family income supplement (FIS) (1984), the general abolition of child dependant allowances under the tax code and the renaming of children's allowance as 'child benefit' (1986). The original intention was that the child benefit would be increased significantly and would be taxable, eventually replacing FIS (Ireland, 1984). However, the amount of child benefit was not increased significantly when the tax allowances were abolished in 1986. Family income supplement is a payment to low income families in employment and is largely based on the similar UK payment. However, unlike the UK scheme, it does not apply to self-employed persons, and proposals to extend it to farmers have not come into effect. It has encountered similar difficulties to the UK scheme in terms of low take-up of benefit (Blackwell, 1989b). It appears that family income supplement was chosen as an alternative to the more costly option of increasing child benefit payments.

EU Equality Directive   The implementation of the EU directive on equal treatment for men and women in matters of social security (79/7/EEC) created major difficulties for the Irish scheme as it required considerable amendment of the welfare code (see chapter 7). This led to a delay in implementation of the directive between 1984 and 1986, during which period many married women continued to receive lower rates of benefits than their male counterparts (Whyte, 1988; 1995). This delay led to considerable litigation which, in turn, led to a government decision to pay arrears of benefit to over 40,000 married women amounting to over £60 million. The legislation, which came into effect in 1986, removed direct discrimination against women in those areas within its scope, and in 1994 the widow's pension scheme was extended to widowers. However, directly discriminatory provisions remain in relation to some family payments and it is arguable that the social welfare scheme as a whole remains based on various assumptions which tend to disadvantage women and, in particular, married women (chapter 7).

Over the period from 1980, there has been a number of distinct trends in the social welfare system. The rise in unemployment has led to greatly increased numbers of claimants relying on social welfare support. This, in turn, has led to a growth in the level of cost and attempts to limit spending. The level of total spending as a percentage of GDP has been at a historically high level over the entire period, fluctuating with the performance of the economy and employment levels. There has been a restriction of the social insurance scheme, with the state attempting to cut its subvention to the fund. While there has been an increased reliance on means tested payments over the period, the real value of many payments has increased. Moreover, a sustained attack on the level of social welfare payments, particularly from employer's organisations and economists, has not been reflected in government policies, and the same employer's organisations have agreed to substantial rises in social welfare rates in the three National Programmes from 1987.

CONCLUSION

In this chapter we have looked at some of the main developments in the Irish social welfare system. These are summarised in schematic form in Table 3 for ease of reference. In the next chapter we look at some of the main issues relevant to the development of the Irish social welfare system and at some of the possible theoretical explanations for this development.

Table 1: Structure of Social Welfare Spending (% of spending)

Year	Social insurance	Social assistance	Chidren's* allowance	Administration	Other
1924	33	67	–	+	–
1935	28	72	–	+	–
1945	22	55	14	+	9†
1955	28	46	20	7	0
1965	46	28	20	6	0
1975	51	32	12	4	0
1980	56	32	9	4	0
1985	53	36	8	4	0
1990	47	41	8	5	0
1993	44	45	6	5	0

* Children's allowance was introduced in 1945. From 1986, it became known as child benefit.
+ Administration costs recorded under individual headings.
† Widow's and orphan's pension the figures for which are not broken down into social insurance and social assistance components.

SOURCES: Department of Social Welfare, *Social Security* (1924–1945), *Reports* (1955–1980), *Statistical Information on Social Welfare Services* (1985–1993). NOTE: The data for the period from 1955 to 1993 do not include expenditure by local authorities on home assistance/supplementary welfare allowance nor by the Department of Health. The inclusion of these figures would increase slightly the proportion of spending on social assistance.

Table 2: Funding of Social Welfare Spending

Year	State	Employees	Employers	Self-Employed	Income from Investments and receipts	Local Authorities
1956	76	9	10	–	3	1
1965	68	14	15	–	1	1
1975	57	16	26	–	1	1
1980	56	12	32	–	0	0
1985	60	13	27	–	0	0
1990	53	13	32	2	0	–
1993	56	13	29	2	0	–

SOURCES: Department of Social Welfare, *Reports* (1955–1980), *Statistical Information on Social Welfare Services* (1985–1993). NOTE: This table relates only to spending by the Department of Social Welfare and so does not include spending by local authorities in relation to home assistance/supplementary welfare allowance nor spending by the Department of Health.

Table 3: The Development of the Social Welfare System

Year	General	Elderly	Unemployed	Disability	Family, Survivor and Lone Parents
1838	Poor Law				
1847	Outdoor Relief				
1897	Workmen's Compensation				
1908		Old age pension			
1911	National insurance		Unemployment benefit	Sickness benefit	
1924	Poor Law reform	Cut in pension			
1929	Married women excluded from insurance				
1933			Unemployment assistance		
1935	Amalgamation of insurance societies				Widows pension
1939	Public assistance				
1944					Children's allowance
1947	Establishment of Department of Social Welfare			Infectious diseases maintenance allowance	
1949	White Paper				
1952	Social Welfare Act				
1954				Disabled persons maintenance allowance	
1961		Contributory pension			
1967				Occupational injuries	
1970		Retirement pension		Invalidity pension	Deserted wife's allowance

Table 3: The Development of the Social Welfare System (contd.)

Year	General	Elderly	Unemployed	Disability	Family, Survivor and Lone Parents
1973		Pension age reduced from 70 to 66 by 1977			Deserted wife's benefit Unmarried mother's allowance
1974	Social insurance extended to higher earners Pay related benefit				
1975	Supplementary welfare allowance				
1979	PRSI system EU directive on equal treatment				
1984			Social employment scheme		
1986	Commission on Social Welfare EU directive implemented				Family income supplement Child benefit
1988	Social insurance for self-employed		Pre-retirement allowance		
1990					Lone parents allowance Carers allowance
1991	Social insurance for part-time workers				
1992				Abolition of pay related benefit	
1994			Abolition of pay related benefit		Survivors pension

Table 4: Funding of Social Insurance Fund (%)

Year	State	Employees	Employers	Self-Employed	Other
1955	26	30	34	–	10
1965	40	28	30	–	3
1975	22	29	47	–	1
1980	24	21	55	–	0
1985	28	23	49	–	0
1990	6	26	64	4	0
1993	6	28	61	4	1

SOURCES: Department of Social Welfare, *Reports* (1955–1980), *Statistical Information on Social Welfare Services* (1985–1993).

Table 5: Social Insurance Coverage ('000)

Year	Total Numbers Insured*	Numbers fully insured (% of total insured)
1923	418	241+
1935	538	400+
1945	608	410+
1955	726	639 (88%)
1965	744	671 (90%)
1975	969	832 (86%)
1980	1034	864 (84%)
1985	1174	949 (81%)
1990	1343	937 (70%)
1993	1363	881 (71%)

* Excluding Class K which does not provide cover for any social insurance benefits. Figures for 1923–1945 are for those insured under the national health insurance scheme.
+ Prior to the amalgamation of the social insurance schemes in 1952, there were three schemes (national health insurance, unemployment insurance and widow's and orphan's pensions) which operated separately. Figures for the numbers covered under all three schemes are not published. The figure shown here is for the number insured under the smallest scheme, i.e. the unemployment insurance scheme.

SOURCES: Department of Social Welfare, *Social Security* (1923–1945), *Reports* (1955–1980), *Statistical Information on Social Welfare Services* (1985–1993).

Towards an Analysis of the Irish Social Welfare System: Economy, Politics and Ideology

'. . . . it is not only by economic facts that the history of a people can be documented. It is a complex and intricate task to unravel its causes and in order to do so, a deep and widely ranging study of all spiritual and practical activities is needed.'

Antonio Gramsci, *Studi Gramsciani.*

In this chapter we look at some of the main issues relevant to the development of the Irish social welfare system and consider some of the theoretical explanations for these developments. However, there has been only limited empirical and theoretical study of the Irish system to date and, in this context, this chapter must be seen as the initial stages in the development of discussion on these issues rather than a completed theory.

THEORIES OF DEVELOPMENT

There are two broad approaches to any analysis of the growth of welfare states (including social welfare systems). The first is a system-based approach; the second emphasises the role of specific actors. Within each approach there are a wide range of divergent, and frequently contradictory, theories. For example, a systems based approach includes both functionalism – which would see the development of social welfare systems as part of the 'logic of industrialisation' (Kerr et al., 1964) – and some Marxist theories which see the welfare state 'as an inevitable product of the capitalist mode of production' (Esping Andersen, 1990, p. 14). The latter approach sees the social welfare system as having two functions, that of accumulation and legitimation or, in alternative terminology, of ensuring system integration and social integration and control (Mishra, 1977, p. 70). In other words, the social welfare system in advanced capitalist society assists both in ensuring the continuation, stability and efficient working of the economic system and in ensuring the integration of social classes and groups and the maintenance of order. Social welfare payments, such as unemployment benefits, are seen as playing a role in system integration through assisting in the stabilisation of the economic cycle. The social integration/social control aspect can involve both the incorporation of the 'welfare class' as part of an existing regime (as in Bismarck's Germany; see

Mishra, 1977) and the use of welfare provisions as a direct method of controlling that class (as, for example, the Poor Law in Ireland; see Powell, 1992). Such a Marxist account emphasises the contradictions and tensions within such a development.

Within the actor-based approaches, there are again a wide range of divergent theories. One approach would emphasise the role of the working classes (and representative bodies such as trade unions and political parties) in the development of strong welfare systems – sometimes referred to as the class formation or social democratic approach (Korpi, 1980; Väisänen, 1992). However, while this approach may provide some useful insights, it has been criticised as being inadequate to explain the development of social welfare in many countries without any strong leftist influence – Ireland being one obvious example. Baldwin (1990, p. 43) points out that not all the most advanced or stable welfare states are explicable in terms of the left's power and that Catholic parties and general corporatist tendencies have played significant roles in many countries. More recent theories have emphasised class coalitions, and, in particular, the role of the middle classes in the development of social welfare systems (Esping Andersen, 1990; Baldwin, 1990).

A further approach has seen the state as (at least potentially) an autonomous actor with its own interests to pursue (Evans et al., 1985).[1] Such theories 'explain national differences in the timing and content of welfare policies in terms of historical variation in state structures' (O'Connell and Rottman, 1992). Important variations are seen as including the state's administrative capacity and the degree to which it can act autonomously (i.e. independent of powerful organised interest groups).

THE IRISH CONTEXT

In the Irish context, O'Connell and Rottman (1992) have rejected both the systems-based and social democratic approaches and have argued for a state-centred approach while recognising economic and political constraints on state interventions. They also stress the growth of social citizenship as a 'fundamental dynamic shaping contemporary Irish society'. They argue that the growth of social citizenship was not an inevitable consequence of the growth of industrial society in Ireland. However, they conclude that 'the expansion of the welfare state, and of social citizenship, was accomplished in such a manner as to leave privilege essentially undisturbed'. In contrast, Bew et al. (1989, p. 184) argue that the welfare state in Ireland was introduced 'as part of the political strategy of the bourgeoisie', in contrast to the position in the UK where it largely came about as a result of the post–1945 compromise between labour and capital.

O'Connell and Rottman see the state as a quasi-autonomous body seeking, for its own interests, to establish social citizenship and to expand the welfare state but being constrained in its efforts by 'other powerful social actors' so that the end result has been to reinforce existing inequalities. An alternative to this approach would see the development of the welfare state as, in part, a reflection of the objectives of the dominant classes, with the state as a relatively autonomous mediator of the interests of these classes (Poulantzas, 1968; 1974). The reason, according to this analysis, that the welfare state replicates existing inequalities would be not that the state had failed but rather that it had succeeded in successfully reflecting those interests in the development of social welfare policy (and income support and taxation policy generally).

In this book, the analysis will follow a system-based approach while taking into account the specific economic, political and ideological factors in Ireland. Thus, we assume that a social welfare system would develop as a consequence of the industrialisation and modernisation of Irish society but argue that the specific shape which it took was and is influenced by the specific social class and gender construction of Irish society and by ideological factors (in particular, the role of the Catholic Church). In addition, the Irish case is particularly influenced by its history as a British colony in that a social welfare system developed in an entirely different context was largely applied to Ireland, despite the distinct economic, political and religious structure of Irish society.

In recent decades, postmodernism (exemplified by Lyotard, 1979) has argued for an incredulity with regard to grand explanatory theories. Yet Lyotard's own account of postmodern society is arguably a grand theory, albeit one characterised by uncertainty and flux. The present analysis, while retaining a belief in the explanatory powers of some master theories, also reflects uncertainty as to the supremacy of any one approach and underlines the shifting range of influences which have shaped the social welfare system.

ISSUES IN THE DEVELOPMENT OF THE SOCIAL WELFARE SYSTEM

The influence of the UK   The development of the Irish social welfare system has been greatly influenced by its colonial past as both the Poor Law and the social welfare legislation introduced around the turn of the century (workman's compensation, old age pension and national insurance) established the basic structure of the Irish system (Cook, 1986). While there have been many changes of detail in the intervening period, this basic structure is still clearly recognisable today. In addition, and leaving to one side economic factors which are considered below, the geographic and linguistic closeness to the UK have meant that policy development in that country has often been very influential in Ireland. However, the Irish system never developed to the extent to which the UK system did in the period from 1945 to the 1970s nor has it suffered from the same major cutbacks and shifts in policy which occurred in the UK since the late 1970s.

The links with the economy   The development of the social welfare system has clear links with the economic policy of successive governments. The initial Cumann na nGaedheal government adopted a *laissez faire* approach to the economy and correspondingly sought to keep social welfare spending to a minimum with, as we have seen, a 10 per cent cut in old age pensions in 1924. The failure of this policy to lead to economic development, in the context of course of the world depression in the late 1920s, was one of the reasons for the success of Fianna Fáil in the 1932 election. Fianna Fáil embarked on a policy of economic development by way of protectionism and import substitution industrialisation (Girvin, 1989). At the same time, it launched a series of social policy measures, including a large public housing programme, and made significant improvements in the social welfare system (unemployment assistance, widow's pensions and, somewhat later, children's allowances). However, while this policy did have some initial success, there was a failure to adjust to the postwar situation which led to stagnation and widespread emigration in the 1950s.

This, in turn, led to the development of a policy of export-led industrialisation, given expression in *Economic Development* (Department of Finance, 1958) and the first Programme for Economic Expansion (Ireland, 1958; see Bew and Patterson, 1982). This gave rise to a period of sustained economic growth in Ireland. The Department of Finance had argued that capital social spending should be cut in order to allow for increased economic spending and this was incorporated in the projections in the First Programme. However, Kennedy and Dowling (1975, p. 226) point out that the projected cuts in social spending were not, in fact, adhered to: social spending grew in the period 1958–63. They argue that attempts to shift the balance of investment by cutting social expenditure in 1957 and 1958 'retarded the development of the economy; and there can be little doubt that, had the attempt been maintained after 1958, it would have been impossible to achieve the rapid growth that was attained'. In addition, it is clear that as economic growth continued, significant political pressure developed to have the benefits of growth shared amongst all classes (Bew and Patterson, 1982).

The expansion of the social welfare system in the 1960s clearly facilitated the major shift in the composition of the work force in this period. The stagnation in agriculture and the policy of industrial growth required that large numbers of the existing agricultural work force should move into industry and services, and the reliance on foreign capital and the removal of protective barriers meant that many existing Irish firms could be expected to (and did) close. An expanded social welfare system helped to act as a safety net during this period of major change and provided financial support for a residual group of small holders who were unable to make the shift to new employment (Hannan and Commins, 1992).

When recession hit in the 1970s, social welfare spending expanded sharply in real terms in 1975 and again in 1979 and thereafter until the recovery in growth in 1987. In 1987, as we have seen, the government initiated a range of welfare cuts. The subsequent Programme for National Recovery (Ireland, 1987) negotiated with the social partners contained a commitment to 'maintain the overall value of social welfare benefits'. The government was thus able to increase most benefits in line with the low rise in the consumer price index, thus seeing social welfare spending as a percentage of GNP decline until 1991 as GNP growth recovered sharply over this period. Then a further 'growth pause' and an increase in unemployment again caused the level of spending to rise. In these periods of recession, social welfare spending played an important role in maintaining consumer spending and political stability.

O'Connell and Rottman (1992, p. 206) argue that the expansion of social citizenship was not 'an inevitable consequence of the development of industrial society in Ireland' and point out that 'expansion occurred despite the strong opposition of the main economic planners'. However, Walsh's (1974) econometric analysis of income maintenance spending between 1953 and 1971 found that (i) economic growth *was* a major factor in the long-run growth of income maintenance policies and (ii) the amount of money disbursed in income maintenance payments varied counter-cyclically resulting in an automatic stabilisation effect which was quite important. As shown above, social welfare spending since 1971 has clearly responded to economic crises in the mid and late 1970s, the first half of the 1980s and the early 1990s. O'Connell and Rottman correctly point out that system-based theories 'encounter difficulties in accounting for welfare state variation among countries at similar levels of development': other political and ideological factors must be taken into account in this regard. However, they arguably underestimate the links which do exist between economic development and the growth of the social welfare system and overestimate the role of the state (and its economic planners) as an autonomous actor independent of wider economic forces.

In economic terms, it is clear that Ireland's post colonial position has fundamentally affected its economic position (Mjøset, 1993; Johnston and Gallagher, 1994) and thus, indirectly, the development of its social welfare system. Ireland was initially largely dependant on trade with the UK; its export-led growth in the late 1950s and 1960s was largely dependant on foreign capital, in particular from the USA; and its current economic position is very dependent on membership of the EU and the economic position of the EU as a whole (O'Hearn, 1994). Thus, when we go on to discuss the role of national classes in the formation of the social welfare system, the international constraints within which those classes were and are operating should be borne in mind.

Social class interests   We have already argued that there are close links between the development of the social welfare system and the performance of the economy. In this section we examine how different social classes have been affected by the Irish social welfare system. The specific interests of sections of the bourgeoisie can be seen in the fact that the social welfare system has always aimed merely to provide a basic level of social welfare provision with additional support being left to the market. This can be seen in the successful opposition by sections of the medical profession to the extension of medical benefit to Ireland in 1911 and in the continued support for the insurance and pensions industry in the provision of occupational and personal pensions. The 1949 White Paper on social security, in opting for flat-rate benefits, specifically recognised the role of private insurance. More recently, the National Pension Board, chaired by a representative of the insurance industry, opted again for flat-rate pensions and recommended that the coverage of occupational schemes and personal pension arrangements should continue to be encouraged and the existing tax treatment should be maintained.

The self-employed havè, until recently, been excluded from the scope of the social insurance scheme. They have however benefited to a considerable degree from tax-funded social assistance payments, in particular widow's and old age pensions and unemployment assistance, while at the same time making little contribution to the costs of such payments in that the level of tax paid by farmers has always been extremely low. The Department of Social Welfare estimated that, prior to the extension of social insurance to the self-employed, two thirds of means-tested old age pensions and 80 per cent of widow's pensions were payable to self-employed persons and their families (Luckhaus and Dickens, 1991). In addition much financial support for farmers has not come directly through the social welfare system but through agricultural supports both at EU and national level. Breen et al. (1990, p. 91 *et seq.*) show that in 1973 and 1980 farmers benefited significantly from direct transfers from the state (which do not include indirect transfers by way of price support mechanisms) and that because of the low level of direct taxes which they paid 'regardless of their income levels, all farm categories received substantially more in cash transfers than their households paid in taxation'. In contrast, all categories of employees, except unskilled manual workers,[2] were worse off after direct transfers and taxes were taken into account. This pattern of redistribution to farmers arose mainly in relation to taxation because whereas cash transfers were allocated on a broadly progressive basis that was not the case with regard to direct taxes, which were only weakly progressive. Thus large sectors of the self-employed have received significant cash transfers without having to pay direct taxes corresponding to their income levels. This contrast between the broadly progressive nature of social welfare payments and the weakly progressive nature of taxation emphasises the importance of considering both spending *and* funding in any consideration of income redistribution through the social welfare system.

It is unlikely that the extension of social insurance to the self-employed will significantly affect this position (see National Pension Board, 1988). In terms of administrative logic, once the income taxation system had been extended to the farming sector, it was difficult to argue against the extension of the social insurance system to the self-employed. In the long term, it would seem likely that the self-employed will broadly retain their previous position in that the cost of the existing provision of social assistance payments was disregarded by the National Pensions Board in estimating the cost of social insurance to the self-employed and the level of contribution finally imposed by the government was less than that calculated by the Pensions Board. It has been estimated that the state will subsidise over 70 per cent of the cost of social insurance for the self-employed, over twice the then level of subsidy to employees' schemes (Luckhaus and Dickens, 1991, p. 51). The timing of the extension is best seen as a short-term measure to raise funds for the social insurance system in that contributions received in the initial ten years or so will significantly exceed the additional cost of benefits as most self-employed persons will not become entitled to contributory old age pensions until at least 1998.

We have seen how the expanded social welfare system acted as a safety net for many farmers and members of farm families who transferred from agricultural to service and industrial work in the period since the late 1950s and the role played by the social welfare system in the recessions of the 1970s, 1980s and 1990s. Hannan and Commins (1992) show that, with the exception of a residual class of smallholders unable to make the adjustment who are now largely dependant on state transfers, many small holders successfully transferred to employment (aided by policies such as the dispersal of new industries thought the country), with the result that those most badly hit by the recessions and now most dependant on social welfare transfers are the old working class.

In the absence of any effective working class mobilisation, either by way of political parties or through the trade union movement, the working classes have not been in a position to influence the development of the social welfare system significantly in their favour. Insofar as the trade unions have been able to achieve gains in relation to social welfare (through national agreements), these have largely related to the rates of payment rather than to structural or redistributional issues (Hardiman, 1988). Thus, while all sections of the working class do receive significant direct transfers from the state, they also pay disproportionately high direct taxes to fund those benefits so that in both 1973 and 1980 only unskilled manual workers received more than they paid (Breen et al., 1990).

It should be noted that the rates of most social welfare payment have increased in real terms over the last decade (NESC, 1993), although the rate of unemployment benefit has dropped as pay related benefit was cut during the 1980s and eventually abolished in 1994 (IPA, 1994, p. 405). The increase in the real rates is particularly marked in the case of long-term unemployment assistance which is, *inter alia*, payable to unskilled manual workers and to marginal small holders. While agreements on welfare rates have been included in the three recent Programmes agreed by the social partners (including the trade unions), the fact that welfare rates for the long-term unemployed have increased sharply over a period when the actual amounts of short-term benefits paid to people with a closer connection with the work force (and more likely to be trade union members) have been cut (through the abolition of pay-related benefit, taxation of disability and unemployment benefit and tighter claim control) suggests that the increase in rates owes as much, if not more, to the need of the dominant classes to legitimate the existing political structure in the face of an unemployment crisis as it does to the negotiating strength of the trade union movement (Habermas, 1976; 1987).[3]

The middle classes generally do quite poorly out of the social welfare system (Breen et al., 1990) although this is perhaps not surprising, given that they are not greatly affected by the contingencies likely to trigger social welfare payments, such as unemployment and poverty (Whelan et al., 1992). However, the two-tier Irish welfare system (what O'Connell and Rottman refer to as the 'pay related welfare state') means that the middle classes benefit from the largely unseen aids of tax expenditures, such as relief for mortgage interest and occupational and private pensions (on occupational pensions see Hughes, 1994). Unfortunately there is limited information available on the cost and distribution of tax expenditures (see McCashin, 1986; NESC, 1986, p. 92; Revenue Commissioners, 1993, table 49). However, it is interesting to note that in 1990–91 the costs of tax allowances in respect of broadly 'social welfare' functions (and ignoring the costs of general exemptions) amounted to over £560 million (Revenue Commissioners, 1993), i.e. about 20 per cent of social welfare spending, with the major proportion of that involving relief on pensions and mortgages which goes disproportionately to persons on higher incomes. The expansion of the social insurance system to all employees in 1974 (which affected many persons categorised as middle class), the introduction of pay-related contributions between 1973 and 1979, and the proposed extension of social insurance to new civil servants from 1996 can be seen as measures to raise funds for the system rather than arising from any class pressure for their inclusion (although the introduction of pay-related contributions was cushioned by the simultaneous introduction of the – subsequently abolished – pay-related benefit). However, the existence and retention (despite many proposals to remove it) of an upper limit on pay-related social insurance contributions means that the burden of social insurance contributions falls more heavily on the lower than the upper middle classes (Hughes, 1985; McCashin, 1986).

Thus the social welfare system, in conjunction with the tax system, provides a real increase in disposable income to all farm categories (regardless of income level), while all employees, with the exception of unskilled manual workers, are worse off after the allocation of direct transfers and direct transfers.[4] The question then arises as to the theoretical explanation for this pattern. It obviously does not support the social democratic approach which sees the working class as the main driving force in the development of the social welfare system. In contrast, it would seem to support a class-coalition approach to the development of the system which takes into account the interests of a wider range of social classes. However, in contrast to the situation in other countries (Baldwin, 1990), the social welfare system in Ireland has not been expanded to benefit groups such as the middle class or farmers but rather has been restricted so that many farmers benefited through not having to pay social insurance contributions whereas less well-off farmers had the benefits of means-tested, tax-funded payments to which farmers as a whole contributed little, while the middle classes and public servants benefited through occupational pensions and favourable tax treatment rather than primarily through the social welfare system itself. The extension of the social insurance system to the middle classes and the self-employed did not (unlike the countries studied by Baldwin – UK, France, Germany, Denmark and Sweden) reflect pressure from those social classes for their inclusion but rather reflected the interests of other social classes or of the state (depending on whether one subscribes to a neo-Marxist or state-centred approach) in securing additional funding for the system.

As in other small peripheral countries, the state has played an important role in the development of economic and social policies, and this is no less true of the development of the social welfare system. As we have seen above, O'Connell and Rottman assign a predominant role to the autonomous state in the development of the system, although recognising the importance of economic and political constraints and of 'other powerful social actors'. In contrast a neo-Marxist approach would see the state, while operating with relative autonomy from class interests, as ultimately reflecting the interests of the dominant classes. In the Irish context, I would suggest that, as yet, insufficient empirical research has been carried out on the development of the social welfare system to support a definite choice between either option. In addition, it is clear that other factors besides the immediate interests of social classes have been instrumental in the development of the system.

The role of the Catholic Church The ideology of the Catholic Church in Ireland during much of the twentieth century has supported the general tendencies in the social welfare system outlined above, i.e. the provision of a basic level of social welfare support and the opposition to extensive state intervention in such areas, with a reliance on the principles of subsidiarity and supplementation (Kavanagh, 1954, p. 54). However, the Church has, since the 1960s, been much more supportive of state intervention in this area and of increased levels of social welfare support. This has again coincided with the state's own policies and the Church, in general, has shown little sustained concern for the redistributive consequences of existing state policies.[5]

While the general approach taken by the state up to the 1950s may well have been guided by Catholic principles, we have seen in the case of Bishop Dignan that the relationship between the Church and state was far more complex than is sometimes suggested in the light of the Mother and Child scheme (on this see Barrington, 1987; McKee, 1986–7; Whyte, 1980). It is clear that the state did not directly follow the dictates of individual members of the hierarchy and the social welfare system which emerged in the Social Welfare Act 1952 was considerably different to the proposals which had been put forward by leading churchmen, owing considerably more to economic and bureaucratic considerations than to Catholic social teaching. Korpi (1992), in a comparative study of the Irish social welfare system, notes the absence in Ireland of the type of corporatist social welfare system (with different insurance programmes for different groups and tripartite participation by employers, employees and the state in the administration of the system) which is common in other European countries with a strong Catholic presence.[6]

Given the extent of Catholic involvement and control in other areas of social policy, such as education and health (Fahey, 1992a), and the involvement of Catholic groups in working against poverty, the absence of the Church from the management of the social welfare system is surprising. Although representatives of the Church have, from time to time, been involved in the administration of social welfare there appears to have been no sustained effort to consolidate the role of the Church in this area (in marked contrast to the position in relation to health and education).

Patriarchy Social welfare policy over the period has tended to support and sustain the patriarchal nuclear family whereby women have been treated as dependants of men (Daly, 1989). This is so despite that fact that women appear to have made up a majority of persons in receipt of assistance payments both in the early days of the Poor Law (Burke, 1987) and today (Daly, 1989).[7] However, there are a range of conflicting policy trends within this general tendency. While there has been a shift over time towards a recognition of the individuality of women, this has not been a linear development and there was a regression in the position of women after Independence (see chapter 7). Despite the support for the nuclear family, there has been little support for women in the home or for women during pregnancy and maternity (except for women at work). Indeed there has been only limited support provided directly to families (e.g. by way of child benefit) with a preference for support being provided directly to the breadwinner (by way of dependency allowances). This can be seen as reflecting the patriarchal approach of policy with its reluctance to intervene directly in the family.

In relation to lone parents, however, while the current payments are still linked to policies of dependency, there has been a developing acceptance of lone parenthood as a legitimate way of life (see chapter 6).

The role of the state, political parties and the administration We have already emphasised the importance of the role of the state and of the administrators of the social welfare system in the development of that system. The state has played an influential role in mediating the economic, political and ideological interests of the various interests in society. In the Irish context, the state has tended to take the initiative in developing proposals for social welfare policy. The importance of this role has been heightened by the fact that, with some important exceptions (such as the insurance industry and the farmers organisations), few clearly defined interest groups are directly affected by detailed changes in the social welfare system and it is only in recent years that effective claimant organisations have begun to develop. This has meant that the state's role in planning the social welfare system and balancing the interests of broader social classes is of greater importance than in those areas where interest groups are more directly represented – such as in relation to the education, health and tax systems.[8]

In relation to the role of political parties, it is clear that the lack of development of the social welfare system up to 1932 and the subsequent growth in the 1930s were linked to the differing political ideologies of the Cumann na nGaedheal and Fianna Fáil parties. However, in the period after the Second World War it is more difficult to identify any major differences of approach between the different parties in their actual activities in government. Mair

(1987) states that a commitment to building the welfare state was shared by Fianna Fáil, Fine Gael and Labour from the 1960s. He distinguishes between Fine Gael and Labour who saw welfare as 'a matter of right, an essential component of what had been defined as "social citizenship"' and Fianna Fáil whose 'commitment to welfare was much more contingent, tending to be viewed as a function of munificence or Christian charity, rather than a matter of right *per se*.' It is not so clear how this distinction carried though to governmental action. Many of the reforms introduced by the Fine Gael-Labour coalition in the 1970s had already been signalled in the Third Programme for Economic and Social Development published in 1967 under Fianna Fáil rule and Hughes (1985), in an analysis of the growth of welfare rates, found that 'the level of social welfare payments during the period 1952–81 were not affected by the political party or parties in government'. While the past decade has seen differences of emphasis between the various parties in government, it is different to identify any clear and consistent approach to social welfare spending by the major parties.[9]

The role and development of the administration of the social welfare system requires a detailed study which has yet to be carried out. However, some trends can already be discerned. One important tendency is the centralisation of the administration and the abolition or neutralisation of quasi-democratic bodies such as the Boards of Guardians (and its successor bodies) and the old age pension committees (chapter 9). This can be seen as reflecting Weber's (1968) views of bureaucracy as the most effective method of administration in a mass democracy. However, Habermas (1987, p. 350) argues that, given a general trend towards the neutralisation of the role of citizens in mass democracy, the welfare state plays a part in this neutralisation by transforming citizens into 'clients' of the welfare state: clients as 'customers who enjoy the rewards of the welfare state', thereby making acceptable 'political participation that has been evaporated into an abstraction and robbed of its effectiveness'. One could argue that the transfer of power from quasi-democratic institutions to bureaucratic structures not only reflects the perceived superiority of this type of structure in administering mass claims but also forms part of the neutralisation of the political role of the citizen.

The way in which power of the administration is exercised has altered significantly over the years from the close and direct control of the Poor Law workhouses, to the supervision of health visitors and investigating officers through most of the twentieth century to the development of the unseen control of information technology (symbolised by the introduction of 'personal social service numbers' intended ultimately for all persons in 1993).

In his work on prison reform in the eighteenth century Jeremy Bentham developed the idea of the Panopticon: a building whereby all the inmates could be observed from a central control tower (Foucault, 1977; 1980). The expansion of the social welfare system so that more and more of the population come within its remit and the development of information technology so that greater and greater amounts of information about claimants and contributors can be stored and accessed on demand means that, in effect, the social welfare system is developing its own Panopticon whereby the 'inmates' can be observed from a central computer. So, in terms of the supervision of the social welfare population by the administrators, we have moved from the discipline of the workhouse to a postmodern Panopticon.

CONCLUSION

In this chapter, we have attempted to set out and analyse some of the main trends in the development of the Irish social welfare system. In the following chapters we will consider the development of specific aspects of the system. As one might expect, the story of these developments is not a simple one nor are there any monocausal explanations. No development is just a welcome reform nor simply a 'project of the bourgeoisie', an expression of patriarchy nor a reflection of the views of the Catholic Church or the bureaucracy. All these elements and more are combined in any development, and it is the task of this book, not to provide a conclusive explanation, but to outline some possible explanations and theories as to how the system has developed

CHAPTER THREE

Atypical Workers and the Social Welfare Code

Atypical working patterns are increasingly in evidence in most European countries as a consequence of the generally rising levels of unemployment, the growing number of women with children in the paid labour force and the demand for greater labour force flexibility on the part of employers. This trend towards a situation in which the paid labour force is composed of a core of permanent, relatively well paid, 'typical' workers and a fluctuating number of 'atypical' workers who are often lower paid and have fewer employment and social welfare rights has been well documented elsewhere.[1]

Ireland has been no exception to this general increase in atypical working, and the social welfare authorities have taken important initiatives to ensure that some categories of atypical workers, particularly part-time workers, receive comprehensive social welfare cover. However, other categories are excluded from entitlement to benefits and receive little or no social welfare protection. This chapter looks at the extent of social welfare provision for atypical working in Ireland and highlights both the main positive initiatives and the areas in which much remains to be done.

ATYPICAL WORKING PATTERNS IN IRELAND

In this section we look briefly at the extent of atypical working patterns in the paid labour force and at the definition (if any) of such working patterns under the social welfare code (Blackwell, 1986a, 1989a, 1990; Dineen, 1992; Luckhaus and Dickens, 1990, 1991).

Part-time workers In 1991 there were over 90,000 persons working fewer than 30 hours per week, i.e. 8 per cent of the active population (Central Statistics Office, 1993). There is no definition of part-time workers as such in the social welfare code, but persons who work below a certain earnings limit – £30 per week for employees and £2,500 per year for self-employed workers – are excluded from social insurance.

Temporary workers This category includes all workers not in reasonably permanent employment, such as casual, seasonal, fixed-term and agency workers. It has been estimated that there are about 70,000 workers in temporary employment, i.e. 6 per cent of those at work (Luckhaus and Dickens, 1990, p. 9)

Again, there is no general definition of temporary worker in the social welfare code. This has given rise to anomalies. Thus it has been held by the High Court in an employment law case that agency workers, who are provided to the 'employer' by an employment agency and whose contractual relationship is with that agency, are not employed under a contract of service.[2] Logically such workers should not then be insured under the social welfare code as employees, but it appears that in practice they are.

Self-employed workers This category includes a wide variety of workers, as some self-employed workers are well paid and may be covered by private insurance arrangements while others, e.g. homeworkers, are very badly paid and have very little (if any) social welfare cover. The Labour Force Survey for 1991 shows 184,000 persons categorised as self-employed, in addition to 59,000 employers, a total of 243,000 or 22 per cent of those at work. The social welfare code provides that 'every person who, being over the age of 16 years and under pensionable age . . . , has reckonable income or reckonable emoluments [other than from employment] shall be a self-employed contributor for the purposes of this Act, regardless of whether he is also an employed contributor'. However, as already noted, self-employed workers earning less than £2,500 a year are statutorily excluded from the social insurance scheme, as are self-employed persons in receipt of unemployment assistance.

Scheme workers Under Irish social welfare law, and indeed under labour law, the legal position of scheme workers (persons employed on work experience, employment training or job creation schemes) is extremely unclear (Cousins, 1994b). There are many different types of scheme work, ranging from part-time work experience with an economic or socioeconomic goal to placement of previously unemployed persons in a normal full-time job with the state subsidising part of the employee's wages. In 1994, there were more than 30,000 participants in work experience schemes. These schemes have recently been restructured as Community Employment which is intended to involve 40,000 persons per year. Unfortunately, these schemes are almost entirely non-statutory, so in many cases there is no statutory ruling as to whether scheme workers are in insurable employment or not. It is not clear if administrative decisions as to eligibility are based on whether such workers are employed under a contract of service or on some other criterion.

Some scheme workers – those on the Social Employment Scheme – were specifically excluded from the definition of employed contributors and were therefore outside the scope of insurable employment; such workers were covered only for occupational injury benefits. In the case of other work experience schemes, e.g. the Teamwork Scheme, the workers were considered to be fully insurable. This may constitute an implicit acceptance that such work is done under a contract of service.

Assisting spouses and relatives The 1991 Labour Force Survey gives a figure of 17,900 assisting spouses and relatives, 10,700 of whom were male and 7,200 female. Blackwell states that the Labour Force Surveys probably underestimate the contribution of assisting relatives, as many cases where women work part time on the farm are not likely to be picked up (Blackwell, 1986a, p. 27). In support of this contention he cites a survey of farm structures conducted by the EU which showed that in 1979/80 the work time of female family workers amounted to a quarter of the work time of the family farm labour force, a far higher proportion than the proportion of women to all persons engaged in agriculture (Eurostat, 1985).

It is likely that many assisting relatives do not work under a contract of service (i.e. as employees). Even where such a contract exists, employment in the service of the husband or wife is excluded from the categories of insurable employment under the social welfare code. Similarly, employment – other than under a written contract – by close relatives in cases where the employed person is a member of the employer's household and the employment is related to a private dwelling or farm in or on which both reside is also excluded. In relation to self-employment, a spouse or other close relative who is not a partner but who participates in the business of the self-employed person and performs the same tasks or ancillary tasks is excluded from insurance. It also seems likely that the majority of assisting spouses thus excluded from insurance are women, and these provisions may therefore be in breach of the EU directive on equal treatment for men and women in matters of social security (79/7). In addition, the EU directive on equal treatment in self-employment (86/613) provides that, where a contributory social security system for the self-employed exists, spouses of self-employed persons (who are not employees or partners but who habitually participate in the activities of the self-employed worker and perform the same or ancillary tasks) must be allowed to join a contributory scheme voluntarily. No such facility exists under the Irish system, which may therefore breach this EU provision too.

Persons on 'home duties'   A further, and, in fact, the largest, category of people who are not covered by social insurance are persons working in the home who are categorised as being on 'home duties', e.g. caring for family members. This group of people are not officially categorised as being in the paid labour force at all (although see Fahey, 1992b) and indeed would not generally be seen as falling within the category of atypical workers. This group are not covered by social insurance because they are nether 'employed' nor 'self-employed', i.e. in receipt of 'reckonable income or reckonable emoluments'. The National Pensions Board (1993, p. 114) estimated that there were 460,00 such persons between the ages of 16 and 65.

THE SOCIAL WELFARE SYSTEM

As we have seen, there are three main types of social welfare payments: *social insurance*, which is largely restricted to those who have paid regular contributions into the scheme; *social assistance*, which is broadly payable to those who have no other source of income and which includes a residual payment known as supplementary welfare allowance (SWA); and *child benefit*. The rules governing the first two, and their impact on atypical workers, are complex and will be examined in the following two sections. Child benefit, by contrast, is a universal payment made to all persons who have a dependent child residing with them. It is not related to previous contributions, to employment or to income. This means that it avoids the possible disincentive effects of poverty and employment traps which can arise in relation to social insurance and social assistance benefits, and is neutral as between working patterns.

SOCIAL INSURANCE

Access to social insurance benefits is conditional on being insured under the scheme and (except in the case of occupational injury benefits) on past payment of contributions and the establishment of a satisfactory ongoing contribution record. Entitlement to benefits is also dependent on the occurrence of certain contingencies related to loss of employment, e.g. unemployment, disability, old age and retirement. Separate provision is made within the social insurance scheme for occupational injuries. Payments are normally made at a flat-rate, with additional allowances for adult and child dependants. Payments vary only to a limited extent according to the contribution record once the minimum requirements are satisfied. The occupational nature of this scheme has obvious implications for its interaction with atypical working patterns, and these are considered in greater detail below.

Insurance   To be insured under the social insurance scheme, a worker must be in insurable employment or insurable self-employment. Insurable employment is defined in the social welfare code as employment 'under a contract of service or apprenticeship, written or oral, whether express or implied'. Persons in such employment are covered for all risks but, as we have seen, employees earning below £30 per week are excluded from insurability as are persons in 'subsidiary employment'.

Up to 1991 most employees working 18 hours per week or less where excluded from the social welfare code. The Department of Social Welfare estimated that over 30,000 persons were affected by this exclusion each year. Since 78 per cent of them were women, the validity of this exclusion under the EU directive on equal treatment in social security seems questionable (although several Appeals Officers have held that the exclusions were not in breach of EU law; see Cousins, 1993b). However, in 1991 the Minister of Social Welfare extended social insurance cover to include most part-time workers. The concept of part-time worker is not defined under the Social Welfare Acts but it is laid down that 'employment in any contribution week . . . in one or more employment (other than systematic short-time employment) where the total amount of reckonable earnings . . . is less than £30 in or in respect of that week' is not insurable employment. Persons working in a limited number of occupations deemed to be 'ordinarily adopted as a subsidiary employment only and not as a principal means of livelihood' are also excluded. The National Pensions Board (1993, p. 108) has estimated that about 12,000 part-time workers are now excluded from insurance by these provisions. In addition, as we have seen, some scheme workers are also excluded from full insurance.

Persons with earnings which are not obtained from employment as an employee are eligible for self-employed insurance. However, those who earn less than £2,500 annually are excluded from such insurance, as are self-employed persons in receipt of unemployment assistance, and assisting relatives. It has been estimated that 3,500 self-employed persons are excluded by this limit (National Pensions Board, 1993, p. 107), in addition to 12,000 farmers and 4,000 other self-employed persons whose incomes are so low that they are in receipt of unemployment assistance, and 18,000 assisting spouses and relatives. Persons eligible for self-employed insurance are covered for a very limited range of benefits (old-age, widows' and orphans' pensions only).

The occupational injuries scheme is part of the general social insurance scheme but different rules apply as to insurability. All employees are insured under the scheme regardless of earnings or age, as are almost all scheme workers, but self-employed persons and assisting spouses and relatives are excluded.

Once a person enters insurable employment or self-employment under the Social Welfare Acts that person becomes insured under the Acts and remains so insured throughout his or her life. However, this does not mean that such a person will at all times be liable to pay employment contributions or entitled to benefit. To establish entitlement to benefit one must have paid a certain number of contributions; membership of the scheme is not in itself sufficient to establish entitlement. However, in the case of occupational injury benefits, no contributions are paid by the employee and membership of the scheme at the time of the occurrence of the contingency is sufficient to entitle a claimant to benefit.

Employed and self-employed persons are liable to pay social insurance contributions (subject to the exceptions set out above) up to an earnings limit of £20,900 (1994–95) per year. Where an employed person liable to contribute earns £60 or less per week, he or she does not have to pay the relevant contribution, but a contribution will be recorded as though it had been paid. Where a contribution is payable by the employee, the employer is also liable for a Pay-Related Social Insurance contribution, again as a percentage of earnings up to an earnings limit of £25,800. Self-employed persons who are not liable to tax pay a minimum flat-rate contribution.

Where a self-employed contributor pays the full contribution in respect of periods effectively worked during a contribution year, he or she is regarded as having paid contributions for each contribution week in that year. If the full contribution is not paid, the contributor is regarded as not having paid any contribution at all. Thus, unlike employed contributors, self-employed contributors are granted either a full year's contributions or none at all. This provision works to the advantage of self-employed contributors since they obtain 52 full contributions once the relevant contribution is paid even if it is only in respect of a short period of self-employment in that year (assuming of course that the income limit has been reached).

A system of credited contributions 'is designed to help those who are already established in the insurance scheme but who, for reasons beyond their control, are unable to continue paying contributions to maintain their insurance record. A credited contribution is given, for example, for each complete week of unemployment or incapacity for work. Credits may also be granted to persons in receipt of maternity, retirement and carer's benefits and to persons on various work experience and training schemes. Credits are only granted in respect of a full week: someone who is unemployed for only part of a week does not qualify for a credit. Credits are generally granted only where the person has a previous paid contribution record: persons who have never been employed contributors cannot qualify for credits.[3] In addition, where a period of two consecutive contribution years passes without a paid or credited contribution being obtained, the claimant is not entitled to credits until a further 26 contributions have been paid.

Qualification for benefit For most benefit payments, two sets of contribution requirements must be satisfied in order to establish entitlement. First, a certain number of contributions must have been paid at some time during the claimant's entire working life; second, a certain number of contributions must have been paid or credited either within a recent period or over a period of years prior to the claim. The rationale for this is both to establish a certain minimum involvement in the social insurance scheme (by way of paid contributions) before benefits become payable and also to establish a continuing involvement by way of either paid or credited contributions. Generally the contribution requirements fall into two categories. Short-term payments such as unemployment and disability benefit require 39 contributions to have been paid at any stage in the claimant's working life and 39 paid or credited in the previous year. Long-term payments, e.g. retirement, old-age and widow's pensions, on the other hand, require a greater number of contributions to have been paid and a certain average of paid or credited contributions over the person's period in insurable employment or over a period prior to the occurrence of the contingency. Over the past few years, the contribution requirements for various payments have been markedly increased with the result, for example, that at least 13 contributions must now have been paid in a recent year in order to qualify for certain payments, including disability benefit.

People engaged in atypical work may have difficulty in acquiring the required number of paid or credited contributions in each year in order to remain entitled to short-term benefits. This difficulty may also arise in the case of long-term benefits where the atypical worker may have problems establishing an average number of paid or credited contributions over the relevant periods.

We will now look at the qualifying conditions for unemployment benefit which have a particular relevance for atypical working patterns. In order to qualify for unemployment benefit a claimant must be (a) unemployed, and (b) capable of, available for and genuinely seeking work, and (c) under 66 years old. Entitlement to unemployment benefit is established on a daily basis. However, in order to establish initial entitlement to benefit, a claimant must be unemployed for at least three days in a period of six consecutive days. Subject to these rules, claimants are paid in respect of each day of unemployment at one sixth of the weekly rate. Therefore a claimant may work for several days in a week and still claim unemployment benefit, but benefit is not payable in respect of the first three days of any interruption of employment.

These provisions allow persons to work part-time and in some cases to claim benefit. However the waiting period is likely to disadvantage some atypical workers because casual or temporary workers who work intermittently are more likely to be affected by the three-day disqualification.

In claiming benefit, a day is not treated as a day of unemployment if the claimant does any paid or remunerative work on that day unless that work could have been done by the claimant in addition to his or her usual employment and outside the ordinary working hours of that employment and provided that either the payment or profit does not exceed £10 per day or the claimant has at least 117 paid contributions in the previous three years. Therefore it is possible to do some part-time work and still claim unemployment benefit for that day.

Claimants must be available for work (i.e. in a position to take up suitable employment immediately) and must be genuinely seeking employment (i.e. making real efforts to find employment, for example by applying for jobs, or being registered with FÁS, the state training and employment agency). The condition requiring a claimant to be available for and genuinely seeking work is interpreted by the Department as referring to full-time work. Persons who wish to work part time may be refused unemployment benefit because they do not satisfy this condition.

Following the extension of social insurance to part-time workers, a new rule has been introduced in relation to entitlement to unemployment benefit. This states that in order to qualify for unemployment benefit, a claimant must have 'sustained a substantial loss of employment in any period of six consecutive days'. The regulations which bring this rule into effect specify that, to have sustained a substantial loss of employment, a claimant must have lost one day's employment and the claimant's earnings must be reduced as a consequence. This means that workers whose normal working week is less than four days will not be able to claim unemployment benefit for the full week unless they lose an additional day's work. This is similar to the unemployment legislation in the UK which has proved extremely difficult to operate in practice and has led to much litigation (Ogus and Barendt, 1988). For example, how does one decide what is a 'normal week' in the case of a worker with a varying work pattern? Reflecting these difficulties 'casual workers' have been excluded from this requirement in 1994.

Self-employed workers are not covered for unemployment benefit although they may be entitled to the means-tested unemployment payment (see below).

Rates of benefit   Generally speaking, the rate of benefit is not proportional to a claimant's previous income, the main exception being maternity benefit. A pay-related benefit scheme, introduced in 1973, was initially payable with disability, injury and unemployment benefit but was abolished in the case of disability and injury benefit in 1992 and unemployment benefit in 1994. With the extension of social insurance to part-time workers, low-paid workers now receive reduced short-term benefits proportional to their previous wages (see below). Rates of payment in respect of dependants can vary according to the income of the claimant's spouse (or cohabitee), and other benefit rates can be affected to some extent by a claimant's contribution record.

Under the maternity benefit scheme for employed women, the rate of payment is 70 per cent of weekly earnings in the relevant tax year, subject to a maximum payment of £158.90 per week and a minimum payment of £74.20 per week. Because of the minimum payment, low earners are protected from inadequate income during maternity leave and the maternity benefit rules concerning the calculation of benefit amounts do not disadvantage those on low pay.

Following the extension of insurance to part-time workers, the conditions of entitlement to unemployment benefit and some disability payments have been modified so that now full benefit is only payable where the previous earnings are above a specified amount. Where previous earnings are below that amount (£70 per week), benefit is paid at a reduced rate.

Additional allowances are paid to claimants in respect of adult and child dependants. Child dependants are normally aged under 18 or, for some benefits, 21 where the child is in full-time education. The definition of adult dependant has significant implications for atypical workers. Since the implementation of the EU directive (79/7) on equal treatment for men and women in matters of social security in November 1986, the payment of an adult dependant allowance to a claimant on social welfare payments is subject to the income of the adult dependant. Where the dependant is in receipt of a social welfare payment or is employed or self-employed and earning £60 gross per week or more, no adult dependant allowance is payable. Similarly, where the spouse is in receipt of such a social welfare payment or such earnings, only one-half of the relevant child dependant allowances (if any) is payable. While this rule does allow spouses to do some low-paid part-time work without affecting the social welfare income of the family, in effect the limit acts as a disincentive to such workers seeking to increase their earnings (NESC, 1992).

To a small extent, benefit rates vary according to the contribution record of the claimant, e.g. a claimant with the minimum annual average number of contributions required to qualify for an old-age pension will receive about 92 per cent of the pension paid to a person with the highest possible annual average. The National Pensions Board (1993) has recently proposed that the amount of old age and other long term pensions should bear a much more direct relationship to the claimant's contribution record.

SOCIAL ASSISTANCE

Social assistance payments-are designed to ensure a minimum subsistence income for claimants with no or inadequate incomes (although the amounts are not calculated according to any independently determined standard of adequacy). The full rate is paid where there is no assessable income (subject to rules concerning disregarded income) and assistance is reduced according to any income received. Benefits are paid according to the category into which a claimant falls, generally for the standard contingencies related to loss of employment – unemployment, old age, long-term disability, etc. In recent years, several further types of payment have been introduced to support persons who are likely to find it difficult to take up work owing to caring responsibilities, e.g. lone parents and those caring for an incapacitated person (see chapters 5 and 6). As with the social insurance benefits, payments are made at a flat rate with allowances for dependants. In addition, there is a residual subsistence benefit, known as supplementary welfare allowance (SWA), payable to any person whose means are insufficient to meet his or her needs (excluding those in full-time work, those involved in an industrial dispute and students). Besides the normal weekly payments, lump sums can be paid on a once-off basis to meet exceptional needs. As with social insurance, the assistance scheme has important implications for atypical working patterns, and these are also considered in detail below.

The means test   In order to qualify for a social assistance payment, one must satisfy a means test of which there are four main varieties under the social welfare code: one for unemployment assistance (UA), one for family income supplement (a payment to low-income families in employment), one for the residual SWA and one for most remaining social assistance payments (including payments to lone parents).

These tests generally take into account any income earned or otherwise available to the claimant and (except in the case of family income supplement) the yearly value to the claimant of any capital assets. The earnings and assets of any spouse, cohabitee and, in some cases, the claimant's parents are also taken into account. In the case of the unemployment assistance test, however, the calculation of income available to the claimant was recently modified. Entitlement to UA is calculated on a daily basis and if a claimant worked at all during any day, he or she is not entitled to UA in respect of that day. However, any earnings under a contract of service on any other day of a week were previously not taken into account in assessing a claimant's entitlement to assistance. This rule was changed in 1992 and further revised in 1993 so that now all earned income is taken into account (although claimants are allowed to earn £15 per day above the level of assistance to which they are entitled). This is clearly a retrograde step for many atypical workers.

Atypical workers are more likely to need to rely on means-tested payments than typical workers because, as we have seen, they generally find it more difficult to qualify for social insurance benefits. To aggravate matters, the fact that the test takes into account earnings within the claimant's family unit reduces atypical workers' chances of qualifying for social assistance payments.

Disregards of some earned income are allowed under some of the means tests. Although they are formally neutral as between working patterns, in practice earnings disregards are aimed at low-income workers and therefore do benefit atypical workers. The intention is to allow claimants to take up (atypical) work both to supplement their social welfare income and to prepare them for reinsertion in the paid labour force, possibly by progressing to typical work. However, as we have seen in the case of unemployment assistance, the disregards currently available are often set at such a low level that they are of very limited advantage to such workers. In 1994, the disregards for the lone parent's allowance were increased significantly to a level of £30 per week with only 50 per cent of earnings over that amount being taken into account as means.

Other qualifying conditions   Claimants must also satisfy other conditions in order to qualify for most means-tested payments, e.g. as regards unemployment status, long-term incapacity for work and old age. These requirements affect atypical working patterns in several ways.

Unemployment assistance (UA)   The qualifying conditions are similar to those for unemployment benefit set out above. As with unemployment benefit, entitlement is established on a daily basis but the claimant must be unemployed for a period of three days within a week in order to establish initial entitlement. Two such periods not separated by more than 52 weeks (rather than 13 weeks in the case of unemployment benefit) are to be treated as one continuous period of unemployment.

A person is not deemed to be unemployed for the purposes of UA if on any day he or she works for wages or other remuneration in whatever form. The definition of unemployment is thus stricter than in the case of unemployment benefit where a person is allowed to do some work. So, workers who undertake almost any sort of work will not be considered to be unemployed on that day. As with unemployment benefit, a claimant must be available for and genuinely seeking work and again this is interpreted by the Department as referring to full-time work.

In the case of self-employed workers whose yearly income is below the level giving entitlement to UA, the Department allows such persons to claim even in respect of periods in which they are fully self-employed, and the appropriate amount of assistance (i.e. the difference between the full rate for the claimant and the claimant's yearly means divided by 52) is paid each week. Presumably this is because of the impossibility of monitoring a self-employed person's employment status in any particular period. It must also be assumed that the Department considers the self-employed person's efforts to obtain work satisfy the requirements regarding availability and genuine search for work. In practice, though, these conditions do not appear to be enforced in the case of the self-employed, that is, no pressure is put on such persons to obtain more work or to increase their income from self-employment. The result of this interpretation does at least mean that self-employed persons on low incomes can receive some social welfare income. However, these rules are extremely unclear in practice and are not publicised, so the whole question of unemployment entitlements for the self-employed is a very grey area.

Family income supplement (FIS)   This is a weekly cash allowance to provide financial assistance to working parents on low incomes. In order to qualify, the claimant must normally be engaged in remunerative employment and he or she or the claimant's spouse must be so engaged for an aggregate of not less than 20 hours per week. Thus part-time workers on low hours are excluded. Some scheme workers are specifically excluded from entitlement to FIS. The self-employed are also excluded by reason of the requirement that a claimant must be 'engaged in full-time remunerative employment *as an employee*'. Workers must be expected to continue in employment for a period of at least six months in order to be entitled to FIS. Thus many temporary and casual workers are also excluded from entitlement.

Supplementary welfare allowance (SWA)   As noted earlier, this is a residual benefit payable to persons with no or insufficient means to meet their needs or those of any dependants. Under this scheme, weekly supplements (e.g. for rent) and once-off exceptional needs payments are made to recipients of the basic social welfare payments. However, full-time workers are excluded from entitlement: there is no statutory definition of what constitutes full-time work, but the Department of Social Welfare Guidelines for the Health Boards administering the scheme state that employment of 30 hours or more per week is to be regarded as full time. SWA is payable to such workers only in urgent cases or when their earning capacity is reduced owing to disability.

CONCLUSION

As we have seen, there have been several positive developments in the social protection of atypical workers in recent years, such as the extension of social insurance to the self-employed and to part-time workers. However, significant numbers of workers remain excluded from cover: in particular, about 20,000 low-paid self-employed workers, over 30,000 'scheme' workers, at least 18,000 assisting spouses and relatives, and about 12,000 employees earning below the earnings threshold – which makes a total of over 80,000 atypical workers (7 per cent of all those at work) excluded from social insurance. In some cases these exclusions may be in breach of EU law. In addition the social insurance cover for self-employed persons is very limited. Despite the positive moves to extend social insurance to atypical workers, there remain many barriers to their qualification for social insurance benefits, and the more stringent contribution conditions introduced in recent years have increased these difficulties. One result of this is that many such workers must rely on social assistance for support. However, the fact that the means test frequently takes into account earnings by other members of the family unit makes it difficult for atypical workers to qualify for such benefits, while the structure of the social assistance scheme – with its limited disregards for earnings and the rules concerning payment of adult dependant allowances – means that many atypical workers are trapped in low-paid employment (NESC, 1992). A major review of the operation of the scheme needs to be undertaken to ensure that atypical workers are not discriminated against and to facilitate their integration into the social welfare scheme as recommended by the OECD (1991). Some possible measures are outlined below.

Extending social insurance   It would appear comparatively easy to include several (relatively small) groups in the insurance scheme. For example, it would appear more logical, given the emphasis on the 'employment' nature of the Community Employment scheme, to devote government resources to funding full social insurance cover for such workers, rather than, as at present, allowing such workers to keep 'secondary benefits' which inevitably create barriers to such persons moving into mainstream employment. Equally, it would not seem impossible to extend social insurance to the declining number of assisting relatives, possibly by charging a flat-rate contribution in respect of such persons (although a majority of the National Pensions Board (1993, p. 114) recommended against this on the basis of the declining numbers involved, their irregular income and the fact that many would become self-employed contributors in their own right). In relation to part time workers, some earnings threshold in probably inevitable. However, it is not clear why the self-employed threshold of £2,500 per annum should be so much higher than that which applies to employees (£1,560).

The expansion of social insurance cover for the self-employed raises more difficult issues. Any such expansion would obviously require an increase in contributions either generally or from self-employed contributors. Given the evidence, set out in chapter 2, as to the manner in which self-employed farmers benefit from the redistribution of income through the tax and welfare systems, the latter would appear more appropriate. While some areas of cover, such as disability and invalidity, may raise definitional problems (National Pension Board, 1988), these appear to have been resolved in other EU countries where the self-employed are more fully insured and other areas (such as maternity and treatment benefit) create no conceptual difficulties at all. However, such an expansion would require a shift in policy toward increased public provision and away from encouraging private provision by way of tax incentives.

In relation to people on home duties, an extension of social insurance would mark a significant shift in the structure of the Irish system. This raises a series of broader questions·which are considered in chapter 11.

General measures   There are a series of general social welfare measures which would have the effect of improving the position of atypical workers. These are considered in more detail in chapter 11 and might include:

• a shift towards child benefit (possibly taxable) which, as we have seen, is neutral as between working patterns and away from the contingent child dependency increases and family income supplement which discriminate against atypical working patterns;

• further improvements in the provision of employment schemes;

• more generous disregards for earned income, targeted at groups who are likely to be sensitive to such measures, and increased disregards for spousal income.

A combination of such measures could significantly improve the position of this growing sector of workers.

CHAPTER FOUR

The Treatment of Households

The treatment of households under the social welfare code has been under re-examination in Ireland in the light of the change in the composition of households, the increase in the number of married women in the paid labour force and EU legislation on equal treatment. The implementation of the EU directive on equal treatment in social security led to a change in the rules governing the treatment of married couples claiming several welfare payments. However, one aspect of the legislation which implemented the directive in Ireland was subsequently found to be in breach of the provisions of the Irish Constitution which protect the institution of marriage because it permitted more favourable treatment of cohabiting couples. Subsequently a Review Group was established by the Minister for Social Welfare to consider the issues involved (Review Group, 1991). Recent reports from the National Economic and Social Council (NESC, 1992) and the OECD (1991) have also considered some of the principles and practices which affect the treatment of households.

This chapter looks, first, at the number and composition of households in Ireland and, in particular, in the social welfare population. The development of social welfare provision for households under the social welfare code is examined. We go on to examine the issues which have arisen in relation to the present treatment of households in the context of the reports referred to above.

HOUSEHOLD COMPOSITION AND FAMILY UNITS

The census figures show that in 1986 there were almost one million households in Ireland (Central Statistics Office, 1991). Of these 616,000 (63 per cent) were husband and wife (or an unmarried couple) living either alone or with children or other persons. There were 181,000 (18 per cent) persons living alone, 98,000 (10 per cent) were lone parents (with children of any age),[1] in 69,000 (seven per cent) cases two or more unrelated persons shared accommodation, and in only 13,000 (one per cent) cases were two or more families living in the same household. The general trend has been for the number of households comprising single family units, including lone parents, to increase, while multi-family households and households comprising family units living with other persons have decreased. For example, one-person households have increased from 14 per cent in 1971 to 18 per cent in 1986, lone-parent households from 6.5 per cent in 1971 to 10 per cent in 1986. The average size of households has also declined from 3.9 in 1971 to 3.5 in 1986.

FAMILIES AND HOUSEHOLDS IN THE SOCIAL WELFARE CODE

As we have seen, the social welfare system consists of contingency-based social insurance (or contributory) payments and a range of contingency-based social assistance (or means-tested) payments. There is also a residual means-tested scheme (known as supplementary welfare allowance) and a universal child benefit. The concept of 'family' is only defined in relation to family income supplement. In this case family means husband and wife (or cohabiting couple), or lone parent and any dependent children. Thus this concept excludes the more extended family and the income of, for example, a brother or sister or parent of the claimants will not be taken into account for the purposes of FIS even if they are living in the same household.

There is no definition of the concept of household in the social welfare code and the extent to which this concept is relevant in practice varies from one social welfare scheme to another. In some cases, entitlement to payment is entirely unrelated to whether or not the claimant is living alone or as part of any particular type of household: in other cases the income of any spouse or partner may be taken into account; in other cases again the income of not only the spouse or partner but also parental and other income may be assessed.

In 1985, 32 per cent of households contained one person on social welfare, with 9 per cent containing two recipients and 2 per cent with three or more recipients (Commission on Social Welfare, 1986). Adult dependant payments were payable in 160,000 cases in 1993, a decline from over 180,000 in 1986. The majority of adult dependants are women. Family income supplement is payable to over 9,600 families, the vast majority of whom are married couples. A high percentage of persons living alone and lone parents are in receipt of social welfare payments. There were over 53,000 persons receiving a lone parents payment (97 per cent of whom were women) and it is estimated that in 1987 about two thirds of all people living alone were in receipt of social welfare.

THE SUPPORT FOR FAMILIES AND HOUSEHOLDS UNDER THE
SOCIAL WELFARE CODE

Legal obligation to maintain The family law provisions of the legal system imposes an obligation on parents to support their children up to the age of 16 (or older in certain circumstances) – Family Law (Maintenance of Spouses and Children) Act, 1976. Spouses are also obliged to support each other. Under social welfare law, the liability to maintain members of one's family and the obligation to contribute to social welfare payments made to them, derived from the Poor Law, has recently been updated and extended in the area of lone parents payments. A spouse is obliged to contribute to payments made to the other spouse and a parent is obliged to contribute to payments made in respect of his or her children to the age of 18 (or 21 if in full-time education). There is no maintenance obligation on cohabiting couples nor on the more extended family. However, under the operation of the 'benefit and privilege' rule, the social welfare code imposes a maintenance obligation in practice where none exists in law whereby, in the case of claimants of unemployment assistance and supplementary welfare allowance who are living with their parents or with a partner of the opposite sex, payments are reduced on the basis of the income of the parents or partner.

This rule provides that any 'benefit and privilege' enjoyed by a claimant is assessed as means. There is no further statutory definition of this concept but it is interpreted by the Department of Social Welfare as requiring the income of other persons in the household to be taken into account in assessing the means of the claimant. The extent to which this rule is applied is somewhat unclear but the income of parents and cohabiting partners is assessed as means, whereas the income of siblings is not. A personal or family allowance is deducted from the net earnings of the person involved and the remaining income is then allocated amongst the nonearning members of the household including the claimant. The amount allocated to the claimant is treated as his or her means. This administrative rule of thumb is applied in the vast majority of cases and the factual allocation of resources within the household is not normally taken into account by the authorities. Thus, the current Irish practice appears to be similar to the prewar operation in the United Kingdom of the stringent household means test (Fulbrook, 1978, p. 168–71) and is more onerous on the claimant than the means test currently applying to the UK income support scheme (see Ogus and Barendt, 1988, p. 441 and *R. v. West London S.B.A.T., ex p. Clarke* [1975] All ER 513). Under the current UK legislation, only the income of the claimant and of any partner (married or unmarried) is taken into account.

Development of social welfare support   The earliest social welfare payment, the Poor Law, was intended to provide a minimum means of support to persons unable to support themselves through work. This payment was means-tested and, with a view to enforcing the subsidiary nature of the support and to keeping the cost to a minimum, members of the immediate and extended family were liable to repay to the administrators any support paid to a claimant.[2] The great dissatisfaction felt with this system led to the introduction of more structured payments, as we saw in chapter 1, including the first social insurance payments.

Social insurance payments were paid without means testing and regardless of the income of other members of the family. This was based on the assumption that the occurrence of one of the contingencies was a very good indicator of lack of income, an assumption which has been shown to hold true today in Ireland (Callan et al., 1989). However this assumption was not applied to all persons. At the time of the introduction of these schemes, the typical family was assumed to consist of a breadwinner husband and dependent wife and children. Therefore payments were targeted at the husband. Few married women, at that time, were active in the paid labour force. The social welfare system assumed that those married woman who were active in the paid labour force were not doing so to provide the basic income of the family, which was provided by the husband, but to top up this income; so married women generally had lesser entitlements to payments on the assumption that they did not really need them or did not need them to the same extent as a married man.

Payments for dependants   It followed from the assumption that the breadwinner husband would support the family, that his social welfare payments had to be sufficient to support not only himself but also any dependants. Two different approaches were taken by social welfare schemes in order to achieve this:

(i) Payment of an earnings related benefit. The aim was to pay the claimant a large proportion of his previous wage on the assumption that this would be sufficient to support him and any dependants. This system applied under the workmen's compensation scheme and was continued up to the 1960s.

(ii) Payment of flat rate adult dependant allowances. This is the approach which now applies in relation to most Irish social welfare payments.

Prior to 1986, adult dependant allowances were automatically paid to married men in respect of their wives even if their wives were working or in receipt of a social welfare payment themselves. On the other hand, increases were only paid to married women if their husbands were incapable of self-support by reason of physical or mental illness. The assumptions behind these rules had become considerably outdated by the 1980s and 1990s with up to 27 per cent of married women now active in the paid labour force (or almost one third if one uses ILO data (Fahey, 1993)).[3] In addition, the EU equality directive required that these discriminatory rules be removed. The current system requires that financial dependency be shown in order to qualify for an adult dependant allowance. Thus adult dependant allowances are only paid in respect of people who have an income of less than £60 per week and who are not in receipt of a social welfare payment themselves.

Payments to 'assumed dependants'   The other side of this question is the extent to which the social welfare income of a claimant is reduced because of the fact that he or she is a member of a family or household. The social insurance system implicitly adopted the concept of the immediate family. Thus the only persons taken into account are the husband and wife (or cohabitee) and any children. Social insurance income is not reduced because the claimant lives as part of an extended household. However the fact that the claimant was part of the immediate household was formerly taken into account, though not by way of means testing. So, for example, married women were paid lower rates of benefit for shorter periods and young claimants were treated less favourably on the assumption that they would be receiving some support from their parents or had lower needs due to living at home. The fact that the extended household was disregarded may have been due to administrative convenience but also to the widespread dissatisfaction with the Poor Law system which had adopted the extended family concept.

Following the implementation of the equal treatment directive, full personal social insurance benefits are paid to all adult persons regardless of sex or of gender based assumptions of dependency. Thus, in this area at least, the concept of 'assumed dependency' was removed.

In relation to social assistance payments, a very varied approach is taken, largely dependent on the origin of the scheme. So, for example, in relation to supplementary welfare allowance and unemployment assistance, both of which derived directly or indirectly from the Poor Law, the concept of the extended family was retained by way of the benefit and privilege rule. The income of the immediate family was also taken into account in that the income of the spouse (or partner) was considered in assessing the means of the claimant. In relation to lone parent's allowance, however, only the claimant's own income is taken into account and the income of any extended family is entirely disregarded. In the case of this payment, maintenance from a spouse is a relevant factor in deciding entitlement and cohabitation is an absolute bar.

ISSUES IN RELATION TO TREATMENT OF HOUSEHOLDS

The implementation of the Equal Treatment directive   The EU directive on Equal Treatment for Men and Women in matters of Social Security (79/7/ EEC), which came into force on 23 December 1984, necessitated changes in the treatment of households. This directive prohibited any discrimination on grounds of sex, either directly or indirectly, as from that date. As we have seen, the implementation of the directive resulted in a change in the definition of adult dependant and, under the social insurance scheme, an end to inferior benefits for married women. Another area of the social welfare code where change was required was that of unemployment assistance. Prior to 1984, a married woman was not able to claim unemployment assistance unless her husband was incapable of self-support. On the other hand, a married man was, in all situations, entitled to claim unemployment assistance and received an additional payment in respect of his wife who was deemed to be dependent on him even if she was herself working or in receipt of a social welfare payment.

The EU directive necessitated the removal of this rule. The Irish government aimed to achieve equal treatment by removing the general prohibition on access to unemployment assistance for a married woman through abolishing the requirement that she could only claim where her husband was incapable of self-support. This created the possibility that many married women would apply for unemployment assistance in their own right with, from the government's point of view, the danger of increased social welfare costs. Accordingly, the Irish legislation implementing the directive contained a capping provision concerning claims for unemployment assistance (section 12 of the Social Welfare (No. 2) Act 1985). The result of this was to ensure that, even if married women claimed unemployment assistance as a result of the change in the law, the married couple would not be any better off financially. Luckhaus's (1990) criticism of the implementation of the directive in the UK, i.e. that there had been 'a reformulation and reshuffling of legal rules ingeniously reproducing the effect existing prior to the rule change' could equally apply to this aspect of the Irish implementation.

However, the Social Welfare Act did not apply to cohabiting couples and, even at the time of the passing of the Act several commentators (Kelly, 1987, p. 180; Casey, 1987, p. 484) doubted the constitutionality of this provision in the light of a previous case in which tax provisions which discriminated against a married couple as against a cohabiting couple were held to be unconstitutional (*Murphy v. Attorney General* [1982] IR 241).

Indeed, it was not long before these provisions were challenged in *Hyland v. Minister for Social Welfare* ([1989] IR 640). The Supreme Court found these provisions to be unconstitutional in so far as they limited the income of a married couple in circumstances where the income of a cohabiting couple in the same situation would not have been limited. In response to this decision, the government, presumably with a view to the cost involved and the potential increase in the number of persons registered as unemployed, extended the capping provision to cohabiting couples. At the same time, the Minister for Social Welfare established a Review Group on the Treatment of Households in the Social Welfare Code.

The Review Group on the Treatment of Households The Minister announced that the Group would have the task of examining the social welfare code as it affects households (in the context of the decision in the *Hyland* case) with particular regard to the equal treatment provisions. The Group consisted of seven members, including independent experts in the areas of social policy, economics and law and members nominated by the Department of Social Welfare and the Department of Finance. The Group decided on the following terms of reference (Review Group, 1991, p. 2):

(i) to examine the treatment of different household types under the existing rules for determining entitlements to social welfare payments;

(ii) to examine the practice in other countries in this regard, and

(iii) in the light of (i) and (ii) to identify ways in which the social assistance schemes could be adapted so as to ensure that different households which could be said to have similar needs are treated in a consistent and equitable way having regard to: (a) the requirements in relation to the treatment of married couples arising from the Constitution; (b) the requirement of equal treatment for men and women under EEC directives; (c) the means of households and the economies arising from the sharing of expenses within households; (d) the need to contain Exchequer costs; (e) the provisions of the Social Welfare (No. 2) Act 1985 as amended; and

(iv) to outline the financial implications of any alternative approaches which are considered.

The Group considered that, while the extension of the limitation to cohabiting couples had remedied the constitutional defect identified by the Court in the *Hyland* case, that action did not address the question of possible discrimination against married couples *vis-à-vis* other household situations. The Group considered that the possibility of a further challenge would be 'at least arguable'. Accordingly the Group based its consideration on the assumption that the existing payment structure (referred to as Option 1) could not be retained. The Group went on to consider three further options:

Option 2 – Abolition of the limitation. This involved the payment of the full personal rate of social assistance to each party of a married or co-habiting couple regardless of whether the other party was in receipt of a social welfare payment or not. This is in line with the proposals which had been made by the Commission on Social Welfare (1986).

Option 3 – Extending the Limitation:

(a) The extension of the limitation to claimants living in a common or joint household which includes at least one other claimant (estimated to affect about 50,000 people). This would mean that claimants would be paid 0.8 of the personal rate (on the assumption that the appropriate rate for a couple is 1.6 times the personal rate). Presumably recognising the administrative difficulties inherent in deciding what constituted a 'joint household', the report suggests that married or cohabiting households might be deemed to constitute '*a priori*' joint households in that it would not be open to them to claim otherwise. Members of other types of households would be able to argue that they were not part of such a joint household and this issue would be decided on through the normal Departmental adjudication system.

(b) Predetermined rates of payment. This would introduce a radical restructuring of the current system of payments whereby the rate of payment would be explicitly determined by the household situation of the claimant and would attempt to reflect the (assumed) economies which occur in different types of households. However, the Group considered that this option involved fundamental changes and was not a system which could be introduced in the short term.

Option 4 – Household Supplements. Under this proposal, a uniform rate of payment would be made to all claimants regardless of household status, designed to meet personal needs such as food and clothing. This would be accompanied by a household supplement to meet household expenses (e.g. rent, heating, etc.) Only one such payment would be made to each household. Again the Group felt that this option could not be introduced in the short term.

Having rejected the option of leaving things as they were and the options of predetermined rates of payment and household supplements as involving fundamental changes in the social welfare code, the Group was left with two options, either abolishing the limitation or extending it. The Group evaluated these two options against the criteria which it felt to be relevant:

(i) The Group felt that both approaches were compatible with the Irish Constitution and with the principle of equality of treatment of men and women.

(ii) There were felt to be arguments for and against both options in terms of equitable treatment of different types of households.

(iii) Both systems were felt to introduce greater consistency into the system but neither was seen to be more advantageous than the other.

(iv) In the area of behavioural implications, abolition could create a significant financial incentive for both of a couple to make themselves available for employment. The Group also felt that the spouses of persons on unemployment assistance in low paid employment would have an increased incentive to quit employment because of the increased replacement ratio. On the other hand, extension could have implications in relation to living arrangements, e.g. by discouraging an elderly parent from living with a son or daughter.

(v) Abolition would simplify the system whereas extension would inevitably introduce an extra degree of complexity into the system.

(vi) The costs of abolition of the limitation could be significant. First, about 8,000 people were affected by the limitation and its abolition would cost approximately £7.6 million in a full year. Secondly, it was felt that many additional persons, in respect of whom an adult dependant allowance is currently paid, would claim a full payment in their own right with consequent extra costs. The Group estimated that between 28,500 and 50,000 extra claims would be made with costs of between £28 million and £50 million in a full year. Finally, the Group felt that additional costs would arise to the extent that persons currently in employment might be induced by the higher household social welfare payment to quit employment voluntarily and claim social welfare. Extension of the limit would have no cost implications and would, in fact, result in some savings.

The Group split in two between those who favoured abolishing the limitation and those who favoured extending it. Those in favour of abolition argued, as did the Commission on Social Welfare, that the social welfare system is a contingency based one and that all persons experiencing a specific contingency should be treated in the same way. They recommended phasing out the limitation over a period not exceeding five years. Those in favour of extending the limitation argued that the underlying criterion of entitlement is need and that the extension of the limitation would ensure that households with similar needs were treated in a consistent and equitable way. The Group also considered several other areas where it identified discrimination between the treatment of married and cohabiting couples. It recommended that the treatment of cohabiting couples should generally be brought into line with the treatment of married couples. The Group also recommended that adult dependants should be entitled to a share of the overall payment in their own right and that the term 'adult dependant' be replaced by an alternative such as 'qualified partner'.

Issues concerning work disincentives and households   In addition to the issues raised by the Review Group, the issue of the disincentive effects of the existing treatment of households in the social welfare code has been raised in recent reports from the National Economic and Social Council (NESC, 1992) and from the OECD (1991). The NESC report showed that the current treatment of households acted as a disincentive to the participation of married women in the paid labour force and encouraged participation in very low paid jobs. Similar trends have been found in the United Kingdom (Millar and Glendinning, 1989). The NESC referred to the report of the Review Group and stated that in further discussion of the report, regard should be had to:

> the desirability of convergence between units of benefit for social welfare and units of taxation; the preference for a unit of payment for social welfare payments which corresponds with generally accepted norms of mutual financial obligation; the need to ensure equity in the social welfare treatment of households in similar financial circumstances; the importance of maintaining the incentive to take up employment; the constraints in public expenditure which require that any additional costs are phased in such a way that there is no real increase in aggregate public expenditure. Additionally the impact of proposed changes in the unit of social welfare payments on the live register measure of unemployment [i.e. the number of persons registered as unemployed] and on replacement ratios should be assessed. (1992, p. 8)

The NESC also recommended that 'a strategic perspective on equality issues in the social welfare system and a plan for their implementation on a systematic and long term basis' should be adopted.

The disincentive effects were also recognised in a recent report to the OECD which stated that:

> Policies based on the sole breadwinner two-adult family – such as joint income testing for social security benefits and dependent spouse allowances – have disincentive effects on women's employment and men's ability to play a greater role in family care. (1991, p. 10)

The report recommends that the sole breadwinner two-adult family should be eliminated as the primary norm for social welfare policies.

COMMENTS ON THE REPORT OF THE REVIEW GROUP AND
ON THE CURRENT TREATMENT OF HOUSEHOLDS

The remit of the Review Group   The area of welfare payments to households is one which clearly needs to be examined. It is, therefore, disappointing that the remit of the Group was so narrow. It is not clear whether this narrow approach was chosen by the Group itself or whether it was imposed (explicitly or implicitly through restrictions of time and resources) by the Minister for Social Welfare. First, the Group concentrated on a limited number of social assistance (or means-tested) schemes only, with the consequence that the treatment of many other types of household in receipt of social welfare were ignored, e.g. the difficulties which affect the operation of the cohabitation rule in relation to lone parents' payments.

Secondly, the Group were examining the 'needs' of different household types against a background where existing social welfare payments are not related in any empirical way to the 'needs' of individuals or households (Commission on Social Welfare, 1986, p. 128). In addition, the Group did not carry out any research to establish the extent to which social welfare claimants live in households, the different household types which exist, the respective costs of households nor the extent to which social welfare payments already take into account the fact that people do live in households of various types. The Group apparently had no remit to undertake research into any of these issues and its examination of social welfare practices in other countries was cursory to say the least.

The equality issue The Group considered that 'neither option would conflict with this objective since in both instances, the same provisions would apply to both men and women' (1991, p. 49). This is an overly simplistic approach to the principle of equal treatment and fails to take into account the issue of indirect discrimination, i.e. a provision which is neutral on its face but which, in fact, acts to the disadvantage of one sex to a disproportionate extent. It is clear from the report itself that the majority of those affected by the existing limitation are women (mainly married women). Therefore the existing limitation may be in breach of the EU directive unless it can be objectively justified on grounds unrelated to sex (Whyte, 1992).

It is not clear whether or not a majority of those affected by the putative extension of the limitation would be men or women and, therefore, it is not possible to assess whether this proposal might create any difficulties in terms of compatibility with the directive. However, it is clear that the option of abolishing the limitation would be compatible with both the spirit and the wording of the EU directive and would be a step towards the principle of individual entitlement proposed by the EU Commission (and apparently by a number of those who made submissions to the Group).

The Review Group also make no reference to the issue of intra-household resource sharing. Research in the United Kingdom has indicated that households' resources are not shared equally amongst all members of the household. frequently to the disadvantage of women (see, for example, Pahl, 1988). Recent work has highlighted the importance of expanding this research further so that policy responses can be developed to the problems indicated by the initial studies (Jenkins, 1991; Borooah and McKee, 1992). Nor did the Group refer to the problems of a social welfare system based on derived entitlements in the light of the increase in cohabitation outside marriage and in marital breakdown (Brocas et al., 1990).

Equity and work disincentives   One of the purposes of the social welfare system should be to provide an adequate income to all persons and to do so in a way which does not act as a disincentive to taking up employment. A system should also be consistent (in so far as possible) and equitable. However, it is arguable that the Review Group entirely misconstrued the concept of equity. The approach of the Group seems to be to level down all payments to the lowest common level in so far as is possible. For example, its recommendation on adult dependant allowances would involve the reduction of the maximum earnings which a person can receive from the then £55 per week (now £60) to a level of £31 with a tapered allowance where the means of the dependant exceed this limit. The Group says that one of the effects of the current provision is

> . . . that it results in the same level of support being provided to households with different needs, i.e. a household which has income from part-time employment receives the same level of support as a household totally dependent on social welfare. This approach is in conflict with the objective of treating households with similar needs in a consistent and equitable fashion since this implies that households with different needs should be treated differently. (1991, p. 59)

The approach recommended by the Group would appear to imply an even greater disincentive for married women to take up employment and is contrary to the recommendations in the NESC and OECD reports. In the long term it is to the advantage of the social welfare authorities and the economy generally that the maximum number of people should be in employment since this generates tax and social insurance revenues and ultimately reduces social welfare costs (NESC, 1992; Gillion, 1991). Therefore the social welfare system should aim to encourage people to take up employment. This will obviously mean that people should be allowed some financial incentive if they do so and that, therefore, a person in part-time employment should be allowed to achieve a higher net income than he or she would have achieved without working. If one accepts the principle that the social welfare system should not act as a disincentive to work, then it is neither inequitable nor inconsistent to allow such a financial incentive.

The argument in relation to incentives to take up work is not to be confused with the 'disincentive' argument advanced by the Group in relation to the replacement ratio. The Group argues that, in the context of the abolition of the restriction leading to an increase in household social welfare payments, persons in low paid work would be likely to give up work and claim unemployment payments because of the increased replacement ratios (1991, p. 35). Leaving aside the fact that the Department of Social Welfare already has control measures to prevent such behaviour, the available research suggests that this view is not backed by empirical evidence. Studies suggest that 'there is little evidence that increases in unemployment benefits lead to a marked increase in voluntary quitting of jobs' (Blackwell, 1986b, p. 35) and that the incidence of the unemployment trap is 'extremely low' and that its 'impact upon the labour market appears marginal.' (Arthur Andersen, 1991, Chapter 6).

Research in the United Kingdom has shown that 'disincentive effects' and labour market flexibility involve a complex range of issues which vary according to sex, age, qualifications and other factors. The social welfare replacement ratio is only one of the issues considered by unemployed persons in deciding whether to take up a particular employment (see, for example, McLaughlin et al., 1989; McLaughlin, 1991). Careful research is necessary to identify the relevant factors in different situations and broad generalisation such as those adopted by the Review Group appear to be unlikely to predict accurately labour force behaviour.

Household economies The Group's terms of reference indicate that it was to attempt to 'ensure that different households which could be said to have similar needs are treated in a consistent and equitable way.' However, as we have seen, the Group has undertaken no research to establish which type of households can be said to have similar needs nor as to what might be considered a consistent and equitable manner in which to treat such households. The report is based on various assumptions by the Group, in particular, first 'that the needs of married (and cohabiting) couples are less than those of two single people living apart and maintaining separate households because they benefit from economies arising from their living together' and, secondly, that 'the appropriate rate of payment for a married couple is around 1.6 times that payable to a single person.' The Group cites no statistical evidence for the first assumption and indeed it appears that no such research evidence exists in Ireland.

The Group notes that 'research in other countries supports the contention that the appropriate rate of payment for a married couple living together is 1.6 times that of a person living alone' but points out that it is important to stress that no research has been undertaken in Ireland. In fact, Whiteford's (1985) extensive study of the research in this area shows that there is a very wide divergence amongst the theoretical approaches to equivalence scales as well as a very wide divergence between the various proposed scales. Given the wide divergence which exists in the research and the total lack of research in Ireland it cannot be assumed that 1.6 is the appropriate rate. In order to calculate such a figure, one would first have to work out how much a two-adult household, for example, should be paid in relation to a single person and then to find out to what extent the social welfare system already pays benefits on a household basis. The Household Budget Survey for 1987 (Central Statistics Office, 1989) provides some interesting, although inconclusive, information in this area. The Survey allows the expenditure of *inter alia*, one, two, three and four adult households to be compared in urban, rural and rural farm situations. The information provided in the survey does not allow an estimate of appropriate ratios (even if there was an agreed approach to how such ratios should be calculated, which there is not). However, a straightforward comparison of the spending of the one and two adult households would give a ratio of 1.98 in urban areas, 1.92 in rural areas and 1.78 on rural farms. The figures do show trends in relation to possible household economies, i.e. that overall these economics are concentrated in specific areas, in particular, in the area of fuel and light and, in urban areas, in relation to housing expenses. Therefore it would appear that household economies are concentrated in areas where social welfare provision is already paid on a household basis, e.g. the National Fuel Scheme, free electricity, gas, etc. All these schemes operate on the basis that only one payment (or credit) is made to each household. Rent allowance under the supplementary welfare allowance scheme and differential rents, where applicable, are also calculated on a household basis.

Therefore, to summarise, the 1.6 rate cannot, in the absence of much further research, be said to be appropriate. Furthermore, the available evidence suggests that household economies are concentrated mainly in those areas which are already taken into account by social welfare provision.

CONCLUSIONS

It is obvious that this is a very complex area with vital implications for the future development of the social welfare code. Should the concept of the immediate family as the relevant unit in the social welfare code be retained and reinforced? Should we move towards a recognition of the importance of equal treatment of men and women and of the increased participation of married women in the paid labour force, or should we, in reaction to the growth in social welfare expenditure, move back to the concept of extended family solidarity? The Review Group took a very short term approach to this question without considering the broader issues involved and, as a result, its (split) recommendations are not based on any coherent approach. The government had already amended the social welfare legislation to ensure that cohabiting couples were treated in the same way as married couples in other areas of the social welfare code even before the Group reported. However, there has been no official response to the main recommendations beyond a request for submissions on the report from interested parties. Reforms in this area need to be part of a long-term strategy on the treatment of individuals and households. However, no adequate assessment has been made of possible strategies and further research is necessary to allow meaningful decisions to be arrived at. Research needs to be commissioned into the numbers and trends in social welfare households, their respective costs and the extent to which these are taken into account under the social welfare code. One encouraging sign is that the Combat Poverty Agency, whose functions include advising the Minister for Social Welfare on social welfare policy, have commissioned research into income distribution within families (Rottman, 1994) and into support for lone parents. (Millar et al., 1992). This may lead to a more considered and better informed debate about the treatment of households in the social welfare code.

CHAPTER FIVE

Social Welfare Support for Informal Caring

This chapter looks at the policies of social welfare support for informal carers in Ireland. The demographic context and the overall policy context are outlined, including a brief summary of the institutional and community care services available. The development of social welfare policies is then examined, in particular the recent establishment of a means-tested carer's allowance in 1990. Finally, some of the issues surrounding social welfare and informal carers are discussed.

Unlike many other European countries, the Irish system provides support directly to the carer (Glendinning and McLaughlin, 1993). However, the main payment involved – the carer's allowance – is very restrictive and is strictly means-tested. This payment is criticised on the basis that, rather than providing adequate support to carers in their own right, it tends to reinforce the existing gendered division of labour by providing a small financial incentive for carers (mainly women) to provide long hours of demanding unpaid work. It is argued that research needs to be undertaken as to how a broader range of support can be provided for informal caring (such as day care, respite care, etc.) rather than relying mainly on cash payments and that social welfare provision needs to be more flexible and better integrated with other forms of support.

THE DEMOGRAPHIC CONTEXT

The 1991 census reported 402,900 persons aged 65 years or over – 11 per cent of the total population (Central Statistics Office, 1994b). There were 162,823 persons aged 75 or over (5 per cent of the population). The number of elderly persons is predicted to rise both in total and as a percentage of the total population but not dramatically in the short-term. It is estimated that 11.6 per cent of the total population will be 65 or over by 2006 (Central Statistics Office, 1988). The government appointed National Council for the Elderly has estimated that 66,300 elderly persons in the community require care of whom about 50,000 are cared for by members of the same household (O'Connor et al., 1988). Unfortunately there is relatively little information about the number of non-elderly persons who requiring care. The 1981 Census of Mental Handicap reported that there were a total of 12,304 persons suffering from medium or more severe mental handicap. There is no comprehensive survey of persons suffering from physical disability. In 1992 there were about 85,000 persons in receipt of the long-term invalidity payments,[1] but it is not possible to say how many of these require care and attention. There is also no accurate estimate of the number of young persons who require such care.

THE OVERALL POLICY CONTEXT

Government policy in regard to care of the elderly and of people affected by disabilities has, over the past 25 years, emphasised the importance of community care (Blackwell, 1992 p. 8 *et seq.*). However, there remains a considerable provision of institutional care. The main services available – both institutional and in the community – can be summarised briefly as follows:

Institutional care   Blackwell (1992) reports that in December 1988, there were over 19,000 long-stay beds for elderly persons. Public geriatric hospitals and homes provide 7,000 beds. Seventy per cent of patients are 75 and over and 60 per cent are chronically sick. Public welfare homes provide 1,600 beds for ambulant patients who are not in need of extended nursing care. General hospitals also provide an estimated 1,500 long-stay geriatric beds. In addition there are over 9,000 beds provided by nursing homes which are run either by charitable and voluntary bodies or on a commercial basis. These figures are in addition to an unknown number of elderly persons occupying acute hospital beds and an estimated 3,600 persons in psychiatric institutions. Blackwell reports that about one third of those in long-stay geriatric beds have been admitted for social rather than medical reasons. On the one hand it appears that institutional care is being provided for persons who could be cared for in the community if adequate support was available. On the other hand, there is considerable confusion as to the legal entitlements of those requiring nursing home care so that many low income persons are either unable to obtain access to institutional care or are forced to rely on financial support from family members in order to pay the fees (Cousins, 1992, 1994a).

Community care services   A range of community care services are provided by the eight regional health boards which administer health services, by local authorities and voluntary organisations, but the information available as to the detailed provision of services is often very limited. These services include public health nursing which combines both preventive health care and domiciliary nursing. Home help services, which provide assistance with everyday living, are also provided by the health boards either directly or through the provision of funding to voluntary organisations. There are currently 12,000 recipients of home help services, of whom 9,500 are elderly. There is a considerable degree of regional variation in the provision of this service (see Dramin, 1986; NESC, 1987). Some health boards provide day centre care (involving non medical care) and in 1988 there were 6 day hospitals providing investigation, treatment and rehabilitation services. Again regional variations are considerable with four of the six day hospitals being in Dublin. Sheltered housing is provided by both local authorities and voluntary bodies and in 1989 there were 3,500 such units.

Informal caring   A national survey undertaken by O'Connor et al. (1988) estimated that there are over 66,000 elderly persons in Ireland who require some degree of care. It was estimated that 24,000 (36 per cent) require 'a lot of care' with a further 25,000 (38 per cent) requiring some care and 17,000 (26 per cent) needing occasional care. About 50,800 persons receive care from other members of their household. Of these 92 per cent are cared for by a relative, most often a daughter or daughter-in-law (44 per cent), spouse (24 per cent) or son (16 per cent).

Seventy eight per cent of carers were women and 38 per cent were 55 or over. About 15,500 elderly persons were cared for by persons from outside the household and again the majority of carers (71 per cent) were women. There have been three in-depth studies of carers (O'Connor and Ruddle, 1988; Blackwell et al. 1992; Ruddle and O'Connor, 1993; see also Noonan, 1983; and Winslow, 1993). These studies did not focus on the role of social welfare in supporting informal caring, but the information which they did provide in this regard is outlined below.

Taxation policy   There is one tax allowance which is specifically targeted at persons who require care and attention. This provides an allowance of up to £5,000 towards the employment of a person to provide care and attention (section 3 of the Finance Act, 1969). The numbers availing of this allowance are not published but the estimates of the tax expenditure costs of the allowance which are produced by the Revenue Commissioners (1993) would suggest that the numbers claiming the allowance are quite low – the estimated cost of the allowance in the year 1990–91 being £200,000. In addition some personal medical expenditure is allowed against tax under the income tax code and the cost of private nursing home care may, in some cases, be allowed under this category. There are also general tax allowances in respect of incapacitated children and of dependant adult relatives but these are not specifically linked to caring costs and the levels of the allowance are quite low.

THE DEVELOPMENT OF SOCIAL WELFARE POLICY

Prescribed relative's allowance   The main social welfare provision for informal carers dates from 1968 when increases in pensions for the elderly (then over 70 years of age) were introduced for claimants who were so incapacitated as to require full-time care and attention where a 'prescribed female relative' lived with the claimant to provide such care. The only female relatives initially prescribed by regulation were a daughter and stepdaughter. The increase was only payable where the prescribed relative had left insurable employment in order to to provide full-time care and attention and where she had paid 156 weeks employment contributions within the five years before leaving employment. The payment was paid to the pensioner. The weekly rate represented 69 per cent of the then non-contributory old age pension and 62 per cent of the higher contributory pension.

The payment, which became known as the prescribed relative's allowance (PRA), was thus very restrictive. First it was only paid to persons over 70 in receipt of a pension, thus ruling out younger persons who required care and persons over 70 who were not entitled to a social welfare pension. Second, the categories of prescribed female relative were extremely restrictive and initially only applied to daughters (or stepdaughters) of the claimant who had been regularly employed and who gave up work to care for him or her. The restrictions meant that few persons qualified for PRA (240 *Dáil Debates* 411) and, in the following year, the contribution rule was abolished and the definition of prescribed relative was extended to include a wider range of female relatives. The then Minister for Local Government explained that by this extension of the scheme 'an inducement is being given to people to keep their aged relatives at home rather than have them go into institutions' (241 *Dáil Debates* 1146).

In 1972, the scheme was extended to the corresponding male relatives and in following years it was extended to a wider range of relatives. The government-appointed Commission on the Status of Women (1972) recommended that credited contributions be granted to a person who gave up employment to provide care and attention and this was implemented in December 1972. The scheme was subsequently extended to persons in receipt of an invalidity pension below retirement age in 1982.

However, PRA remained quite restrictive in that the prescribed relative could not be engaged in employment outside the home of the person for whom full-time care and attention was being provided. In addition if the prescribed relative was in receipt of a social welfare payment him or herself, no PRA was payable. Finally, the prescribed relative could not be a married person who was being wholly or mainly maintained by his or her spouse. This effectively disqualified most married women from qualifying as a prescribed relative – a group which made up a large percentage of actual carers. The rational given for this exclusion was that the scheme was intended to compensate for a situation which does not normally arise and therefore situations in which a wife cared for her husband (or for other relatives in the matrimonial home) were excluded (248 *Dáil Debates* 1699). From 1986, this rule was arguably in breach of the EU directive on equal treatment for men and women (see *Drake v. Chief Adjudication Officer* [1986] ECR 581 and Whyte, 1986, p. 149).

The limited and unsatisfactory nature of PRA led to several proposals for the introduction of a less restrictive payment for carers. The government-appointed Commission on Social Welfare (1986) recommended that prescribed relatives should have entitlement in their own right to a means-tested payment. This recommendation was supported by the National Council for the Elderly, which also recommended that this payment should be extended to cover carers who were married and other persons not already covered by the existing scheme (O'Connor and Ruddle, 1988). As a first step in this direction, the Social Welfare Act 1989 provided that PRA was to be paid directly to the carer. The following year saw the introduction of a fully fledged carer's allowance.

As might be expected, given the very restrictive eligibility conditions, the numbers in receipt of PRA were always quite low. In the 1970s, over 3,000 persons received the allowance but this subsequently declined to only 1,850 in December 1989 just before the introduction of the carer's allowance. The vast majority of the persons in receipt of care were elderly although precise figures are not available. Following the introduction of the carer's allowance in November 1990, PRA is no longer payable in respect of new claims, but, it remains payable to any persons who were in receipt of the allowance at that time and who did not qualify for carer's allowance. At 31 December 1993, 420 people were still in receipt of PRA. Over the years the value of PRA relative to other social welfare payments was allowed to decline so that by 1990 it represented only 55 per cent of the non-contributory old age pension or 48 per cent of the contributory pension.

Constant attendance allowance   Under the occupational injuries scheme, introduced in 1967, a constant attendance allowance is payable to a person who, as a result of an occupational accident or disease, is suffering from 100 per cent disablement and who, as a result, requires 'constant attendance'. This scheme is largely based on the UK industrial injuries code and this payment is derived from the constant attendance allowance under the UK scheme (Ogus and Barendt, 1988, p. 307). A weekly payment (currently £33.90) is made to a person who 'is to a substantial extent dependent on [constant] attendance for the necessities of life and is likely to remain so dependant for a period of not less than 6 months' where such attendance is required 'whole-time'. Benefit is paid at a reduced rate where constant attendance is required on a part-time basis while an increased rate is paid where greater attendance is required because of 'exceptionally severe disablement'. Finally, twice the standard rate is paid where the person is 'so exceptionally severely disabled as to be entirely or almost entirely dependent on such attendance for the necessities of life' where this condition is likely to last for at least six months and where attendance is required whole time. Figures for the numbers in receipt of this payment are not published but given that only around 200 people suffer from 100 per cent disablement, the numbers in receipt of the constant attendance allowance are obviously quite low.

Carer's allowance   The Social Welfare Act 1990 introduced a means-tested carer's allowance. This is payable to a person who resides with and provides full-time care and attention to a person in receipt of a range of social welfare payments who is so incapacitated as to require full-time care and attention.[2] The qualifying persons are those in receipt of an Irish pension who are over the age of 66 or those under that age in receipt of a long term invalidity or blind payment. The Social Welfare Act 1991 extended this to apply to corresponding social insurance payments from other EU countries or countries with which Ireland has a reciprocal agreement.

The Minister for Social Welfare, introducing the new legislation, said that despite changes in society such as the greater mobility of young people and the increased participation by married women in the paid labour force

> the family continues to be the strongest and most reliable source of care for elderly incapacitated people. (397 *Dáil Debates* 755).

The aims of the legislation, as expressed by the Minister, are to give 'official recognition to the role of carer' and to provide 'a secure and independent source of income' while ensuring that resources are directed at those who need them most (397 *Dáil Debates* 755, 757 and 1042). Accordingly, the allowance is subject to a strict means-test and the disregard for income is minimal (although an increased disregard for spousal income was introduced in 1994). In addition, the means of the claimant are to include such amount as the person cared for 'could reasonably be expected to contribute'.[3] The carer, who must be 18 years of over, must not 'be engaged in employment or self-employment outside his [or her] home'. A person who is in receipt of another social welfare payment or in respect of whom an adult dependant increase is being paid is not entitled to carer's allowance. However, all married persons are now eligible to claim the allowance. It had been estimated by the Department of Social Welfare that over 8,000 persons would be entitled to carer's allowance (397 *Dáil Debates* 756), but by December 1993 only 4,328 were in receipt of the payment. In 1991, almost 6,000 claims were received but 53 per cent of claims adjudicated on were rejected – a very high refusal rate compared to other social welfare payments. In addition, 458 cases were appealed to the Social Welfare Appeals Office. Again this is a comparatively high figure which may suggest confusion and dissatisfaction on the part of claimants. Indeed the Chief Appeals Officer (1992) in his annual report commented on the large number of appeals brought by persons who clearly could not satisfy the statutory requirements, in particular because their means, often derived from the means of the spouse, were considerably over the limit or because they were receiving a social welfare payment in their own right (or an increase was being paid in respect of them) and they were therefore disqualified for allowance.

The majority of recipients are women (77 per cent) which broadly corresponds to general estimates of the sexual division of caring responsibilities. However, the carer's allowance is heavily concentrated on carers in the 40–64 age group (75 per cent). Only 5 per cent of payments go to people of 65 and over compared to an estimated 25 per cent of carers of the elderly in this age bracket. This suggests that elderly carers are themselves likely to be in receipt of an old age pension (or persons in respect of whom an adult dependant increase is in payment) and therefore ineligible for carer's allowance. Unfortunately no indication is given of the age of the persons requiring care and attention but it seems likely that, like the PRA scheme, the carers allowance is largely concentrated on the elderly who require care.

Domiciliary care allowance   In 1973, a scheme of allowances for domiciliary care of severely handicapped children was introduced by the Department of Health. The scheme was aimed at severely mentally or physically handicapped children who were living at home and who required constant care. It was 'designed to alleviate, in some measure, the additional burdens created by the retention of such children in the home' (Circular 24/73). The scheme was operated under section 61 of the Health Act 1970 which enabled arrangements to assist in the maintenance at home of sick or infirm persons or a person who would otherwise require maintenance otherwise than at home. No statutory instrument was made in relation to the scheme and it is operated on the basis of an unpublished circular.

The scheme applies to children between the ages of two (children below the age of two are assumed to require constant care and attention in any event) and 16 who 'require from another person constant care or supervision, i.e. continual or continuous care or supervision substantially greater than that which would normally be required by a child of the same age and sex'. The scheme is intended to apply to long term disabilities only, i.e. which are likely to continue for at least one year, and is not intended to apply to disabilities which only intermittently or infrequently give rise to a need for 'constant care'.

The care may be provided by the parent(s) or by another person or persons. The allowance is normally to be paid to the mother of the child but may be paid to the father or to the person who is caring for the child. Only the means of the child are taken into account in determining eligibility. In this context, means includes payments of compensation for injuries or disabilities. The payment was originally set at a rate of £25 per month and is currently payable at £95.30 per month. In 1992, there were 7,660 allowances in payment (figures provided by the Department of Health). This shows a steady increase from 4,044 in 1976 and 6,365 in 1986 (Hensey 1979; 1988). It appears that the design of the scheme was influenced by the UK Attendance Allowance but the Irish payment is significantly different in that, first, it is confined to children and, second, unlike Attendance Allowance, the purpose of the payment is explicitly to compensate for the 'additional burden' of caring for a child.

The impact of social welfare on informal caring   Unfortunately the in-depth studies of carers of elderly persons have not concentrated in much detail on the effect of social welfare policies and, as we have seen, there is little information available on the situation of carers of children or other adults. However, O'Connor and Ruddle's (1988) study of 200 carers reported that only 8 (4 per cent) were in receipt of the prescribed relative's allowance. The lack of coverage was attributed to the limited eligibility requirements, in particular, the fact that married women were generally ruled out and, in farm families, the fact that a son or daughter who was working on the farm to even a limited extent was considered not be be providing 'full-time' care and attention.

This study examined the factors which influenced persons to become a carer but the possible social welfare benefits available were not referred to by respondents in this context. However, 35 per cent of carers did report experiencing financial strain. Only 16 per cent of carers were in paid employment and almost 20 per cent of the elderly persons cared for were not financially independent. Sixty-four households (31 per cent) were totally dependent on social welfare payments.

A study of 207 households by Blackwell et al. (1992) again provides little information about either the financial position of carers or social welfare support available to them. While it does report that only 22.5 per cent of carers were employed or self-employed, the majority of carers are recorded as being on 'home duties' (i.e. housewives) and it is not possible to estimate the financial circumstances of this group (1992, p. 145). However, the study does report that 37 per cent of carers experienced financial strain and that 77 per cent agreed that direct payment of the carer would help their situation.

Both studies indicated that carers were spending a considerable number of hours per week in caring for the elderly person. O'Connor and Ruddle (1988) found that 50 per cent of carers spent 4–7 hours per day (i.e. 28 to 49 hours per week) on caring with 35 per cent spending more than this. Blackwell et al. (1992) found that carers spent an average of 47 hours per week in caring activities; but, Blackwell (1992, p. 213) found that less than a quarter of carers would prefer to have the services they provided replaced by outside paid care.

Ruddle and O'Connor's (1993) study of 100 carers of dementia sufferers found that only five were in receipt of carer's allowance and Winslow's (1993) in-depth study of eight carers found that none were working outside the home, only one was in receipt of carer's allowance and all the other carers were in receipt of other social welfare payments and either could not take up the carer's allowance or would be no better off if they did.

POLICY ISSUES

Social welfare policy for informal carers must be seen in the context of overall policy for providing care. Thus if overall policy concentrates on providing institutional care then the need for social welfare support is much reduced. Conversely, as has increasingly been the case in many European countries, if the concentration of policy has been on providing care in (or by) the community, then social welfare policy is of much greater importance (on the increasing emphasis on home care, see European Observatory on Family Policies, 1991; 1992).

One of the main reasons given for supporting care in the community is that it is significantly cheaper than institutional care. However, this argument normally refers solely to savings in *state expenditure*. Blackwell (1992) costed both institutional care in four hospitals and care in the community. The cost of care in the community included the cost to the carer of the time spent in providing care. The time of the carer was costed at a low value (£1.21 per hour) which took account of the age and lack of educational and occupational skills on the part of many carers. At this level of labour cost and at low levels of dependency, informal care in the home was generally about the same level of cost as in 3 of the 4 hospitals surveyed. This picture changed as the level of dependency increased and at the highest level of dependency, hospital care was more expensive in all cases. These findings are very dependent on the cost placed on the labour of the carer. Blackwell used an alternative level of value by costing the carer's time at the level of pay of home helps (£2.40 per hour). At this level of cost, care in the home was generally more costly than institutional care and even at the highest level of dependency, it was of the same order of cost as 3 of the 4 hospitals surveyed.

Subsequent to the publication of Blackwell's report, an Equality Officer decided, in a case involving home helps in one health board area, that the predominantly female home helps are being underpaid contrary to the legislation implementing EU law on equal pay for men and women (*Irish Times*, 6 January 1993). The Equality Officer held that the women involved were entitled to be paid at a rate of £4.52 per hour. If one uses this rate in costing the care at home then home care is significantly more expensive than institutional care in most cases. Thus care in the home is only less expensive than institutional care if one assumes a low value for the labour of the carer. While the economic analysis is only one factor to be considered and the research was able to measure only the costs and not the outcomes of the different types of care, this research does suggest that (largely unsupported) informal caring in the community may not be the most effective method of providing care and that further research needs to be undertaken into ways of providing more cost-effective care possibly by providing support for informal carers such as home help services, respite services, hospital day care, support groups, etc. Indeed it is hardly surprising that overworked, often elderly carers (who are frequently in poor health themselves) may not provide the most cost-effective provision of care.

Strategies for social welfare support   The financial costs arising from informal caring may be categorised under two main headings:
  a) the costs to the carer of the loss of employment opportunities;
  b) the extra costs arising from the caring needs of the person cared for. This is separate from the general costs associated with disability and would include items such as extra transport and phone costs, substitute care, etc.

A range of other costs may also be incurred including the stress involved in caring and the opportunity costs of lost leisure time but it is likely that compensation through the social welfare system will focus mainly on the more explicitly financial costs involved.

There are a number of different approaches which social welfare policy can take in meeting these costs through providing support for caring and carers. These can be summarised as follows:
  i) Caring as an individual risk – The possibility of needing care can be seen as a risk for an individual. A payment would then be made to the person who

required care on the occurrence of the risk. This approach is taken in Germany whereby an insurance-based payment is paid to a severely handicapped person in need of domestic care (Bieback, 1992). This amounts to about £160 per month which would appear to be unlikely to meet actual caring costs. As we have seen, this is also the approach taken under the Irish occupational injuries scheme. There is no clear statement of the type of costs intended to be met by this scheme.

ii) Compensation for the carer/family – Alternatively having to provide care can be seen as a risk to the family of the person involved or to the individual carer. A payment would then be made to the carer to compensate for the financial costs incurred. This can be seen in the Irish domiciliary care allowance whereby a payment is made to the family of the child who needs care to compensate for the additional costs involved. It would appear that domiciliary care allowance is intended to meet primarily the extra costs related to the needs of the child and is not linked to the costs arising from loss of employment. This scheme involves a transfer of resources from households without persons requiring care to households which include such persons.

iii) A minimum income for carers – A further alternative is to provide a means-tested benefit. In this case the principal aim is not to compensate generally for the costs of caring but rather to provide a minimum income so as to prevent poverty or to provide a (small) financial incentive (above the official poverty line) to a potential carer. This type of payment may also compensate (partially) for income loss. It is into this latter category that the Irish carer's allowance falls.

iv) Caring as paid work – Under this approach caring would be seen as work and would be remunerated in the same way as 'ordinary' employment, but despite the debates about recognising the value of (predominantly) women's work in the home, no EU country seems to have introduced a payment intended to pay a wage to a carer. However, some countries have at least provided social insurance cover for persons with caring responsibilities. For example, the French system provides insurance cover for persons (whose means do not exceed a set limit) caring for a handicapped child or adult who are not themselves insured under an occupational social insurance scheme. The insurance contribution is payable by the social welfare authorities and gives rise to entitlement to an old age pension (Dupeyroux and Prétot, 1989).

The development of the Irish model The prescribed relative's allowance (PRA) initially developed as a payment for daughters who gave up work to care for their elderly parents and who would not otherwise be entitled to any benefit. It was structured as an adult dependant addition to the parent's payment although it is not clear why this option, rather than that of a payment direct to the carer, was chosen. Thus it was intended to provide an (indirect) minimum income for the carer rather than to compensate the person requiring care. No means test applied to such dependency additions because adult dependency payments were in the vast majority of cases made in respect of wives who were assumed not to be in work (this assumption was reasonably well supported by the facts as in 1966 only 5.3 per cent of married women were active in the paid labour force (Blackwell, 1986a)). However, as it became obvious that there were many persons other than daughters who were caring for elderly persons and as PRA was extended to further categories of relatives, the structure of the payment made less and less sense and pressure increased to have it paid directly to the carer. Under the logic of the original payment a married woman, who was dependant on her husband, should not be paid PRA which was also an adult dependency payment. From this point of view, a married woman, if she was being supported by her husband, had no need for additional support from the person being cared for. In addition, it was assumed that for a married woman to care for an elderly or disabled person was a normal eventuality, requiring no financial support. However, pressure increased to have a payment made to married women who made up a large proportion of carers but were excluded from PRA.

Not surprisingly, the Department of Social Welfare accepted that the structure of PRA was no longer sustainable and introduced the carer's allowance. This is a further categorical payment which follows the tradition of the Irish scheme of introducing categorical payments for 'deserving' categories of claimant; yet, because of its stringent means test, the carer's allowance appears to have benefited few persons except the previously excluded married women. The primary aim of the carer's allowance was to provide a minimum income for carers but also to do so in a way which provided an independent income for (some) carers. For some carers, the allowance replaced the PRA or the residual supplementary welfare allowance payable to any person whose 'means were insufficient to meet his [or her] needs'. For others it provided a direct income replacing an adult dependant allowance payable to the carer's spouse. At the same time the rate of allowance was increased from the PRA rate of £28 in 1989 to £45 in 1990. Thus it provides a minimum income and can be seen as compensating in a limited manner for any loss of earnings and providing a (small) financial incentive to carers to provide such services; but, it is obviously quite limited, and it is likely that any carers who were in receipt of unemployment or invalidity payments continued to claim these payments since they were paid at a higher rate than the carer's allowance. As from July 1993, the rate of carer's allowance has been increased to the same level as most means-tested benefits, including the old age pension and unemployment assistance.

A criticism of existing social welfare support for carers   In many ways the development of the Irish payments has paralleled that of the UK invalid care allowance. The ICA is a non-contributory benefit but subject to income limits. It is payable only to those of working age who provide care for at least 35 hours per week. It is payable at a low rate (60 per cent of standard pension rate). From 1986 to 1990 earnings of only £12 per week were allowed but the income limit was raised to £20 in 1990 and and has since been raised incrementally to £50 per week. ICA was also introduced to (partially) compensate caring relatives who gave up work to provide full-time care (Brown, 1984 p. 256 et seq.). Married women were excluded since they might well be at home in any case. As in the Irish case, the pressures to extend it to a wider group of carers proved impossible to resist: first to extended relatives, non-relatives and common law husbands in 1982 and after much resistance to married women in 1986, the latter leading to a six fold increase in the numbers receiving the benefit. Again it applies to only a small proportion of carers (McLaughlin 1992; Glendinning 1990, 1992).

While highly critical of the rate at which ICA is paid McLaughlin (1992, p. 11) argues that

> The two main ideas behind ICA – that carers, as adults and citizens, have a right to independent income ('money of their own') and that working age carers providing high levels of care need protection from loss of earnings – are good ones.

She points out that the UK and Ireland are the only countries in the EU to acknowledge these needs and rights. However, it is arguable that the structure of the carer's allowance (and ICA) does not treat carers as 'adults and citizens' at all but rather than it reinforces the existing gender based division of labour within the household with the (female) carer receiving a small financial incentive to go on providing long hours of demanding unpaid work. Both schemes are structured in such a way that the carer is obliged to become a full-time carer and is, at best, able to engage in limited part-time work (which is likely to be low paid). Thus both schemes i) require that the carer him or herself provide full-time care and attention (specified as being at least 35 hours in the UK case), and ii) prohibit the carer from well paid employment – in the Irish case by prohibiting employment or self-employment outside the home and strictly means-testing any earnings and in the UK case by allowing an earnings disregard of only £50 (and remember that the carer has already to have worked for 35 hours *as a carer*).

In Ireland there is a total lack of information as to how receipt of carer's allowance impacts on intra-household resource transfers and, equally importantly, on the distribution of intra-household expenditure responsibilities. We have no clear picture as to whether carers are in fact any better off financially as a result of receipt of carer's allowance or whether receipt of the allowance results in the termination or reduction of resource transfers from the persons cared for or other family members. Thus while carers have a (limited) right to 'money of their own' we do not know how this affects their incomes. This is an issue of some importance which deserves further study.

The carer's allowance can be seen as an attempt to legitimise the state's reliance on women's informal care and as a case study of the way in which a patriarchal state will tend to reproduce patriarchal structures in its welfare system. While even a patriarchal, capitalist state is likely to be more effective than the market in redistributing income, one might question the extent to which reliance is put on the state in intervening within families and households. There is perhaps more possibility of flexibility and of change within families (even the patriarchal family) than within the patriarchal state (Humphries, 1977). Thus the maximum flexibility in the provision of payments or services to the individual (or family/household) would be preferable to tightly structured payments such as the carer's allowance.

In contrast to the rigid approach of the carer's allowance, the type of scheme provided by the Irish domiciliary care allowance simply requires that the child needs constant care and attention and that such care is provided by one or both parents or by another person or persons. Any parental earnings are not taken into account. Thus the structure of the benefit allows some freedom for the parent(s) to organise their lives as they wish and to provide care themselves or to get another person or organisation to provide some or all of the care. The family is allowed to decide on resource allocation in relation to the care of family members with minimal interference from the state as to how this is done. In practice, the level of the payment is quite low (at current home help rates it would allow the purchase of 9 hours assistance per week) but this is a problem which, at least conceptually, is easier to deal with. The National Council of the Elderly have argued that a constant care allowance should be paid in respect of persons who require full-time care (O'Connor and Ruddle, 1988). This payment would be made regardless of the carer's means subject to medical certification of the person's dependency on constant care. (See Baldwin et al., 1988 for a consideration of some issues concerning this approach.)

In terms of administration, carer's allowance is administered by the Department of Social Welfare in one centralised office. Those administering the benefit have no responsibility for the co-ordination of care services nor for providing advice on the other support services which may be available. Thus there is little incentive for the planners or administrators to consider the most effective integration of the allowance with other support services. In contrast, domiciliary care allowance is administered by the regional health boards who are responsible for the provision of the other support services and who should be, at least in theory, better placed to provide support and information for carers.

CONCLUSION

In summary then, we have argued that a policy based on maximising the involvement of informal carers with a social welfare policy based largely on providing them with a minimum income, while it may be cheap in terms of state expenditure, is not likely to be the most cost-effective method of providing care. Such an approach is only cost-effective if the labour costs are discounted. Informal caring is likely to continue to play a major role in any strategy since this type of care appears to be preferred by both carers and the persons requiring care. If policy is not based on reliance of cheap, (predominantly) female labour, then research is needed as to the most effective ways of supporting informal caring, including social welfare support which compensates for some of the costs of care.

The carer's allowance, which requires full-time caring by one person (who will in the majority of cases by a woman), has the effect of reinforcing the existing gendered division of caring duties and thus makes any alteration in that division more difficult to achieve. It would be ironic if, in arguing for individual payments for carers, one reinforces the gendered division of labour. It would, of course, be naive to suggest that the structure of support for carers will in itself have a major impact on the gendered division of labour. However, one could at least hope that social welfare provision in this area would not reinforce the existing position.

Support through the social welfare system should compensate the needs of those requiring care and of carers in a more flexible manner than does the current carer's allowance, for example, by a development of (almost) universal payments such as the domiciliary care allowance. Such a payment should be integrated both structurally and administratively with the other support systems available. This approach does not assume that carers will generally require a minimum income support. However, where it is required, it should be provided in a flexible manner rather than in the rigid way in which the carer's allowance operates.

Some immediate measures which could be taken in relation to the carer's allowance include the extension of the payment to all persons who require care (and not just social welfare claimants), the abolition of the prohibition on work outside the home by the carer and an increase in the earnings disregard. As we have seen, some countries acknowledge the value of the work done by the carer and establish an element of compensation by providing them with social insurance cover. While the Irish system provides limited assistance towards preserving one's social insurance record by granting credited contributions, this is of much less value to carers, both symbolically and practically, than a scheme whereby a contribution is paid for them by the social welfare authorities.[4]

CHAPTER SIX

Lone Parent's Allowance: A Reform of the Social Welfare Code?

This chapter looks at the financial support provided for lone parents by the state and, in particular, at the lone parent's allowance (LPA) introduced in 1990. Much criticism had been directed at the provisions for lone parents which has existed prior to 1990 (Commission on Social Welfare, 1986) and several organisations had made detailed proposals on the need for a lone parent's payment. The fact that the lone parent's allowance provided for payment to lone parents on the basis of need rather than on the basis of the particular status of the claimant was generally seen as a welcome development. However, several specific aspects of the allowance give rise to concern, in particular the provisions relating to the involvement of lone parents in the paid labour force; the cohabitation disqualification; and the provisions concerning spousal maintenance and the liability of persons to contribute to any social welfare payments made to a lone parent. These are discussed in detail below.

INTRODUCTION

The financial needs of lone parents have not been provided for in any comprehensive way under the social welfare system until recently. Originally, lone parents would have been dependent on the general Poor Law (subsequently home assistance: Commission on the Relief of the Sick and Destitute, 1927; Brown, 1989). Subsequently, payments were introduced on an *ad hoc* basis to cover specific categories of people based on their status. Thus the widow's pension was introduced in 1935, deserted wife's allowance in 1970, deserted wife's benefit and unmarried mother's allowance in 1973 and prisoner's wife's allowance in 1974. The Social Welfare Act 1989 introduced a deserted husband's allowance and a widower's (non-contributory) pension.

Many lone parents – in particular separated persons and unmarried fathers – were excluded from the scope of these payments and had to rely on the lowest social welfare payments. The provision of payments on the basis of categories of claimant rather than on that of financial need was criticised by many organisations including the Commission of Social Welfare which recommended that payments should be made on the basis of the 'income needs of claimants rather than on the categorical basis which exists at present' (1986, p. 360).

The Social Welfare Act 1990 provided for the introduction of a lone parent's allowance which was brought into effect in November 1990. This is a means-tested payment and is payable to a lone parent of either sex who has at least one qualified child residing with him or her. Thus the categorical basis which had existed up to 1990 has largely been ended and, as a result, lone parents in receipt of existing payments were automatically transferred to the lone parent's allowance. In 1993, there were over 36,000 parents in receipt of LPA of whom 96 per cent were women.

Two social insurance (or contributory) payments which applied only to women – the widow's (contributory) pension and the deserted wife's benefit – had been retained and thus there continued to be discrimination against widowers and deserted husbands. In 1993, there were 7,200 claimants of the widow's (contributory) pension with children (out of a total of 86,000) and 9,600 claimants of deserted wife's benefit with children (out of a total of 13,000).

The High Court has twice held that discrimination against deserted husbands in this way is not unconstitutional.[1] The EU directive on equal treatment in matters of social security (see chapter 7) provides that the directive does not apply to survivor's benefits nor to family benefits and thus is not relevant in relation to these areas.[2] However, the EU Commission's proposed Directive on completing the implementation of the principle of equal treatment in social security (COM (87) 494 final) provides for the extension of the principle of equal treatment to both survivors and family benefits. The implementation of this proposed directive would require the abolition of all discrimination between men and women as regards these payments. Although the proposal has been blocked by the Council of Ministers of the EU since 1987, it is likely that it had some effect on the decisions by the Minister for Social Welfare to reduce the extent of unequal treatment in relation to these areas. In 1992, an upper income limit of £14,000 was imposed on the deserted wife's benefit. This would mean that the number of men able to claim the payment would be substantially reduced should it ever be applied to married men. The Social Welfare Act 1994 transformed the existing widow's (contributory) pension into a survivor's pension for both sexes.

PARTICIPATION IN THE LABOUR FORCE

The Combat Poverty Agency report *Poverty and the Social Welfare System in Ireland* (1988) showed that lone parents are particularly likely to be affected by poverty. In that study almost 70 per cent of lone parents surveyed were found to be living below the poverty line corresponding to an income equivalent to 60 per cent of average income. A comparative study of policies in relation to lone parents found that 'in most countries it seems that employment secures a higher income for lone parents than relying on state support' (Millar et al., 1992). Yet, in Ireland lone parents, the majority of whom are women, find it particularly difficult to become involved in or return to the paid labour force and the number of lone parents in employment is the lowest in the EU (ibid).

Following the findings of several reports (Millar et al., 1992; McCashin, 1993) and the interim report of the Expert Working Group on the Integration of the Tax and Social Welfare Systems (1993), the income from employment disregarded in assessing the means of a lone parent was increased to £30 per week with a 50 per cent reduction of all income over that amount. In addition, lone parents are allowed actual travel and childminding expenses. The increase in disregards is a welcome improvement on the previous position and should help to encourage lone parents to take up employment. In 1993, the Department also established a small grant fund (currently £200,000) to support initiatives assisting lone parents to return to the work force or to take up second chance education.

However, the interaction of the social welfare and tax systems remains quite complicated and, because of this and because of the general lack of comprehensive information, many lone parents are not aware of the way in which the systems operate nor of their full entitlements. It can be extremely difficult for claimants who wish to take up work to find out if they will be better or worse off by doing so. Claimants who take up employment may also be entitled in some cases to family income supplement; their take home pay will depend on the relevant tax payments and on the PRSI rate which will vary according to the average weekly income; entitlement to a medical card may also be affected by earned income. The tax system also provides some support to lone parents by way of an additional tax allowance for a lone parent (estimated to cost around £11.4 million in 1990–91). Again there is no co-ordination of the operation of this tax incentive with the operation of the various social welfare payments.

While the overall 'disincentive' effects of the social welfare system have been greatly overestimated (see NESC, 1993), specific groups can be particularly affected by a badly structured interaction of the various systems. At present the various social welfare payments, health care, the tax code and the PRSI system all operate independently of each other and there is no coherent system which would provide an incentive for claimants to return to the paid labour force. In addition, many lone parents find it impossible to take up employment because of the inadequacy of child care facilities (Ireland has one of the lowest levels of public child care in the EU) and because their employment training and work experience is either insufficient or outdated.

These difficulties can only be tackled by a variety of measures. The increase in the means disregard on its own, though welcome, will not be a sufficient response to this problem. It is necessary to provide a more coherent approach throughout the social welfare system in co-ordination with the tax and PRSI codes, and the provisions for health care, so that there are not sudden disincentives and poverty traps for lone parents who take up employment (Blackwell, 1989b). Adequate child care provisions are essential if lone parents are to be given a real opportunity to enter the paid labour market. Finally, if lone parents who take up work are not simply to become low paid, low status workers, adequate access to vocational training and work experience is essential. A coordinated approach from all the relevant departments will be necessary if a solution to this problem is to be found. It should be noted that all research indicates that the number of lone parents in Ireland has increased over the last decade and is likely to continue to increase. A failure to deal with the present disincentives to return to work may have significant future cost implications for the Exchequer and, in particular, the Department of Social Welfare and it is perhaps for this reason that this Department has been to the fore in encouraging an employment strategy as an alternative to long-term dependence on welfare payments.

THE COHABITATION DISQUALIFICATION

The cohabitation disqualification applies to the various payments which can be loosely described as lone parent's or survivor's payments. Where a person is cohabiting he or she is thereby disqualified from receiving any of these payments. Cohabitation, in this context, is thus an absolute bar to payment and not merely a factor which is taken into account in deciding the level of payment to be made. The concept of cohabitation is defined in the Social Welfare Acts as involving 'living with another person as man and wife'. There has been no attempt to provide a more detailed statutory definition[3] but the Department of Social Welfare considers three factors of the relationship in deciding if cohabitation exists, i.e. social, sexual and financial. The Department looks at the social aspects of the couple's relationship: do they go out together? It investigates whether there is a sexual relationship between the two and it looks at the financial arrangements between them, i.e. is the claimant being financially supported by the other person or is there any sharing of their financial costs? It appears that, provided one or more of these criteria are satisfied, the Department may decide that cohabitation exists. Thus it is not necessary that there be any financial support of the claimant by the 'cohabitee' in order that cohabitation should exist. The Department's interpretation of the law on this point has been upheld by the High Court in a case in which the Court rejected the argument that the cohabitation rule should be interpreted in a purposive manner so as only to apply where actual financial support was being provided.[4]

The disqualification has existed in more or less the same form in Ireland for many years (although when originally introduced in relation to widow's pensions in 1935 it acted in some cases as only a partial disqualification for payment). Originally the cohabitation rule applied only to payments to women. It appears that the rationale being the rule was that support should only be provided to a woman when she was not being supported by a man. Thus, once a woman was married it was assumed that her husband would support her. It was only where the man was no longer supporting her – because he was dead or where he had deserted her and refused to provide support or where he was in prison – or where the woman had never been married, that the state would provide financial support.

Given that the original rationale behind these payments was that women heads of one parent households were not capable of self-support, it appears that the legislators felt that, if and when, such women subsequently obtained the support of a man – because of (re)marriage, where a husband ended his desertion or was released from prison – the justification for state support was ended and therefore the payments terminated. The legislators apparently felt that a woman who cohabited with a man was in an analogous situation and therefore also provided that cohabitation should result in disqualification for payment. Thus it appears that there was a legislative assumption that a woman cohabiting with a man was being supported by him and therefore did not require state support.[5]

Whatever the original justification for the cohabitation rule, these arguments are not supported in practice in many cases. As we have seen, claimants can be disqualified on the grounds of cohabitation even where it is accepted by the Department that there is no financial support of the claimant and in circumstances where the 'cohabitee' is in receipt of a basic social welfare payment and could not possibly be providing any support to the claimant. There is no legal obligation on a person to provide support for a cohabitee and thus a woman would be unable to take the cohabitee to court for maintenance for herself (although there is a legal obligation to support one's children). The rule thus operates to reinforce women's dependence on men even in situations where there is no legal right to support.

The operation of the rule can also infringe on a claimant's privacy. The Department of Social Welfare, while its principal aim is to provide financial support to those in need though the various schemes which it administers, must also ensure that assistance is granted only to those who fulfil the qualification conditions. In order to do so, some level of intrusion into the privacy is inevitable. However, the privacy of claimants should be respected to the greatest extent possible consonant with the efficient administration of the social welfare system. This is particularly so in view of the importance of an individual's privacy under Irish law where a Constitutional right to privacy has been recognised by the Courts.[6] In practice the privacy of claimants is often seriously infringed in the course of investigations concerning cohabitation. Even if stricter guidelines were applied to the practices of social welfare officers, any investigation in regard to cohabitation is automatically going to involve extremely personal questions as to one's private life. The intrusive nature of cohabitation enquiries now fits uneasily into the routine administrative nature of the (post) modern bureaucratic apparatus.

In practical terms, however, it is difficult to envisage a simple solution to the cohabitation issue within the structure of the existing social welfare system. Any relaxation of the existing rule would inevitably lead to suggestions that married couples were being discriminated against, possibly in an unconstitutional manner.[7] In the long term, the best solution may be to move towards an individualisation of payments and to shift the emphasis of financial support towards the child by way of increased child benefit. As child benefit is payable in all circumstances, no issue in relation to a cohabitation rule will arise. An emphasis on integration into employment by way of the provision of childcare and training facilities will also tend to lessen the importance of this rule. However, only a movement to an individualised payment will finally remove the need for a cohabitation rule (see chapter 11).

SUPPORT FROM THE SPOUSE/PARENT

The obligation to seek maintenance   Under the deserted wife's and deserted husband's schemes, there was, until November 1990, a requirement that in order to qualify for a payment the claimant must have made 'reasonable efforts' to trace and obtain maintenance from his or her spouse. In practice, this requirement was interpreted by the Department of Social Welfare in a very strict manner. Claimants were often required to make an application to court for maintenance even in circumstances where it was clear that there was no realistic possibility of obtaining support from the spouse. If a court order was made but was not paid, the claimant would then be expected to go back to court – possibly on several occasions – in an attempt to have the order enforced.

It is, in practice, extremely difficult in many cases for claimants to bring their cases to court. There may be a history of violence or other personal reasons why the claimant does not wish to approach the spouse for financial support. The vast majority of claimants will be unfamiliar with the procedure and the rules to be applied by the courts but generally they will not be able to afford a private solicitor and the state scheme of legal aid and advice (although expanded in 1994) remains quite limited. The end result is that many claimants have to appear in court unrepresented. If and when they do get to court, the awards made are very low. Ward (1989) reports that in 80 per cent of orders in the District Court, the total order was less than £60 per week with over half the awards being for £40 or less. He also shows that 60 per cent of all current orders were below the level of supplementary welfare allowance and that no less than 81 per cent of such orders were less than the rate of deserted wife's benefit. Ward shows that even where a maintenance order is made, such orders are not paid regularly in 87 per cent of all cases. In the cases studied in the survey, there as no record that the order had ever been paid in 28 per cent of cases and 49 per cent were in arrears for 6 months or more. It is clear that the enforcement procedures in regard to maintenance orders simply do not work and there has been little change in the legal position since the publication of that report. Indeed these difficulties have been shown to apply in international studies (OECD, 1990).

Therefore, in practice, some claimants were being required by the Department of Social Welfare to make totally unreasonable efforts to obtain maintenance with little prospect of being financially better off as a result of these efforts. Ward indicates that, of deserted wife's claims surveyed, 34 per cent of all claims refused were refused on the grounds that reasonable efforts to obtain maintenance had not been made. Clearly, therefore, a high number of claimants were refused because they had failed to satisfy a requirement which was in any case unlikely to improve their financial position.

The reform of the lone parents payment in 1990 changed the requirement of having to make 'reasonable efforts' to one requiring the claimant to 'make and continue to make appropriate efforts' to obtain maintenance. However, this small change in wording masks a more fundamental change in approach. From 1990 on, the practice of the Department has been to interpret this provision in a much more flexible way than the previous rules and it is only in situations where the Department feels that the claimant should be able to obtain maintenance at such a level that no social welfare benefit will be payable that the Department will insist on the institution of court proceedings. In other circumstances, the Department may grant the payment to the claimant and then pursue the spouse under the liable relative provisions set out below. Such a policy is a significant improvement of the previous situation. Unfortunately, there has been no published research on the position post–1990 so it is difficult to gauge how this has affected the operation of the schemes in practice.

The liability to maintain The Social Welfare Acts of 1989 and 1990 introduced the provisions concerning the liability of family members to maintain persons and to repay payments to the Department of Social Welfare. A person is now liable to maintain his or her spouse and children. The Department can require any liable relative to repay some or all of the amount of a payment made to a claimant. If the liable relative does not contribute, the Department can apply to the District Court for an order directing the person to make the repayments.

While such liable relative provisions have existed for many years in relation to the Poor Law, home assistance and supplementary welfare allowance, these provisions do not seem to have been applied to any great extent in recent years. These provisions now apply to lone parent's allowance and also to deserted wife's benefit. There are several major difficulties in regard to the practical operation of these proposals.

Firstly, there is no legislative guidance as to what factors the Department, and ultimately the courts, are to take into account in deciding how much, if any, of a payment will be recouped from the liable relative. The Department have adopted internal guidelines as to how the liable relative's income, expenses, family circumstances and so on are to be taken into account (Cousins, 1992b) but there is no reason to suppose that the courts will follow these guidelines in cases coming before them. Secondly there are various technical difficulties in the operation of the legislation, arising from a Supreme Court decision,[8] which mean that, in the enforcement of the liable relative provisions, the question as to the claimant's initial entitlement to the payment may be reopened in the District Court. Thirdly, it is unclear if the liable relative will be allowed to rely on defences such as the fact that circumstances of the case (including the conduct of the claimant) would make it repugnant to justice to order the liable relative to contribute. In the area of family law, such a defence would mean that the relative would not be liable for maintenance but it is not clear if the same rules will apply in the social welfare area. Thus the legal rules concerning the recovery of contributions from the liable relative through the courts are not properly integrated either with the operation of the social welfare system itself or with the family law provisions applied by the courts.

At the time of writing, few cases have yet reached the courts. However, the difficulties in enforcing the liable relative provisions are already apparent.

Out of 11,153 parents investigated by the Department of Social Welfare, 47 per cent were living on social welfare payments and so not liable to contribute, a further 30 per cent were untraceable, with the majority thought to be living abroad. Only 23 per cent were found to be in a position to make payments and, of these, only one in eight is already paying some maintenance. Up to 1994, the Department had only recovered £221,000 from 342 fathers.[9]

CONCLUSION

The lone parent's allowance is a marked improvement on the previous provisions for lone parents and, as such, is to be welcomed. It has improved the financial position of several thousand claimants and has removed labels such as 'unmarried mother' from the social welfare code. In the long run, it marks a significant validation of the role and status of lone parents compared to the approach taken by the Commission on the Relief of the Sick and Destitute in 1927 (Powell, 1992, p. 179). However, it is arguable that the allowance cannot be seen as a fundamental reform of the social welfare code but rather as an incremental improvement in the existing provisions (although more recent developments may lead to a more fundamental shift in approach). As set out above the new allowance has carried over many of the failings of the previous schemes. In particular, although it is now formally sex-neutral, the allowance still retains the notion of women's dependency on men and there is a lack of vision as to how lone parents are to be allowed to obtain paid employment.

As McCashin (1993) has pointed out, social welfare policy for lone parents in Ireland has been implicitly based on an assumption of long term dependence on social welfare as the primary means of support. This has now slowly started to change. However, while the recent improvement in the disregards for the purposes of the means test and the establishment of a 'return to work' fund are to be welcomed, there remains a lack of positive action in regard to other important issues in this area, i.e. child care, access to training and tax reform. The Department of Social Welfare has taken the initiative in facilitating lone parents who wish to take up employment, obviously seeing this as an alternative to a long term dependence on welfare. However, other government departments and the social partners have shown less enthusiasm for removing the existing barriers which keep women with children out of the paid work force (NESC, 1992).

The lone parent's allowance reinforces policies of women's dependency on men through the cohabitation rule and the liability to maintain provisions. The cohabitation rule has the effect of deeming cohabiting claimants (normally women) to be dependent on the cohabitee even where there is no actual financial support thereby treating women as dependants of men even though, in the case of cohabitees, there is no legal obligation to provide support. In the case of married women, the notion of dependency is applied through the application of the liable relative provisions to all such payments.

One of the main reasons for these difficulties is the lack of any clear policy in relation to the support of lone parents and their families. Support for children in lone parent families should be seen as part of an overall programme for child support, but no such overall policy exists and the social welfare payment paid in respect of children, i.e. child benefit, is minimal. Therefore, financial support in such families is very dependant on the contingent payments paid to the lone parent, the earned income of that parent and support from the absent parent. Yet again there is no coherent policy to integrate these means of support with the result that the lone parent family is inadequately provided for both in terms of child support and as a lone parent family.

The number of lone parents in Ireland has risen over the past decade or more and shows every sign of continuing to rise (McCashin, 1993). It this context, it will be essential to develop coherent policies to cater for the financial and social needs of lone parent and their children. The development of such policies must be placed in the context of a clear policy on child support generally (Nolan and Farrell, 1990).

The Implementation of the EU Equality Directive: Individualisation or Dependency?

This chapter looks at the implementation of the EU directive on equal treatment for men and women in social security (79/7) in the Irish social welfare code. It considers this issue in the light of the overall development of the place of women in the social welfare code and in the context of women's role in Irish society. It examines the extent to which the outcome of the implementation to date has resulted in a move towards individualisation of benefits and the extent to which the reforms have simply replicated existing structures of inequality and dependency in new forms.

Social welfare benefits have traditionally been granted on the basis of the claimant's status within a family or household rather than on a purely individual basis. There has been a tendency over time to move away from taking into account the circumstances of the extended family (although this can still be found in many social assistance schemes) towards a greater emphasis on the immediate family (spouse or partner) or on the individual. At the present time, there is a tension in social welfare policy between the move towards individualisation (i.e. granting benefits without taking account of the family circumstances) and a contrary tendency towards greater emphasis on intra-family solidarity. The tendency towards individualisation is encouraged by the increase in the number of married women participating in the paid labour force, by the emphasis on equal treatment for men and women in social security in EU policy and by the increasing number of people living in non-traditional family units (e.g. the increase in the number of people living alone, in the number of lone parents and in the level of marital breakdown). The reliance on family solidarity has largely arisen from concerns about the costs of social welfare and the desire to limit costs by transferring responsibility for support of individuals from the state to the family. This involves a move from a broader community or national solidarity to a narrower concept of solidarity and an increased emphasis on subsidiarity (in one of its many guises). The issue of individualisation can involve intergenerational as well as gender aspects, but in this chapter we concentrate on the latter.

WOMEN IN THE SOCIAL WELFARE CODE (1911–79)

The Irish social welfare system, as we saw in chapter 4, has traditionally seen married women as part of the immediate family. Thus married women were assumed to be dependent on their husbands and, under the National Insurance Act, 1911, paid lower rates of social insurance contribution in return for lower rates of benefit. Indeed, reflecting the lower rates of pay received by women generally, under the 1911 Act, all women paid lower rates of contributions and received lower rates of benefit. As we saw in chapter 1, this construction of women as dependants was reinforced by the Cumann na nGaedheal government in 1929 which provided that women's membership of the national insurance scheme terminated on marriage with women receiving a once off marriage benefit.[1] This change had been recommended by the (all male) Committee of Inquiry into Health Insurance and Medical Services (1925) and was not opposed by Fianna Fáil. The result of this was that married women were not generally entitled to national insurance benefits (including sickness benefit and maternity benefit payable on their own insurance) and women who continued working after marriage were treated as new entrants to insurance.

The Social Welfare Act 1952 abolished some aspects of direct discrimination in relation to single women who, in future, received the same level of benefit, although paying a lower contribution rate. However, differential treatment for married women proved more enduring. The 1952 Act provided that a married woman was disqualified for unemployment, disability and treatment benefit, maternity allowance and maternity grant (on her own insurance) after marriage unless she worked in insurable employment for at least six months after marriage. In return for the termination of her insurance in this way, she received a lump sum marriage grant of between £3 and £10. If she did re-enter insurance and qualify for unemployment or disability benefit, she received a lower rate of benefit as she was deemed to be dependent on her husband (unless her husband was incapable of self support) although she paid the full contribution rate for a woman. The husband, however, when entitled to a social welfare payment, was automatically entitled to an increase in respect of his wife who was deemed to be dependent on him, even if she was in fact in receipt of benefit herself or in employment (although in 1961 only 5 per cent of women over the age of 15 were active in the paid labour force (Blackwell, 1986a)).[2]

The Commission on the Status of Women   The above remained the position at the time of the report of the Commission on the Status of Women (1972, chapter 5). The Commission pointed out that 'it is becoming increasingly common for women to continue in employment after marriage and it seems to us to be unfair and discriminatory that they should be debarred from benefit for a period of time solely due to the fact of their marriage' (para. 339). The Commission recommended that women should retain their rights to benefit and that the marriage grant should be abolished: this change was implemented in 1973. In relation to the lower rates of benefit however, while 'in sympathy with the ultimate objective that a woman, should not, because she is married, suffer any reduction relative to other persons in the rate of social welfare benefit payable to her' (para. 343), the Commission felt unable to make any short term detailed recommendations but recommended that the Department of Social Welfare should have as an objective the abolition of the lower rate for married women and its replacement by the single person's rate.

In relation to the amount of (then flat rate) contribution, the Commission felt that the differentiation between men and women was reasonable in view of the fact that women received lower rates of pay. The Commission felt that the best way to resolve this issue was to introduce a pay related contribution scheme. As we have seen, such a scheme was introduced in the period 1973–79.

Among the other areas of discrimination, one of the most important was the treatment of women claimants of unemployment assistance. In order to qualify for assistance, a widow or a single woman was required to have at least one dependant or to have been insured for at least one year in the four years preceding the claim. A married woman was completely debarred from claiming unemployment assistance unless her husband was incapable of self-support or, if neither was a dependant of the other, she had one or more child dependants. The Commission of the Status of Women explained that the limitations on single women arose from the fact that when the scheme was introduced in 1933 it was feared that 'large numbers of single women, especially in rural areas, not really in the labour market' would claim assistance with consequent costs to the scheme and without any real possibility that such women would find work. The Commission recommended the abolition of this limitation and this was implemented in 1978.

The exclusion of most married women was motivated by the view that such women did not form part of the labour force. Surprisingly, the Commission made no recommendation of the position of married women and no action was taken by the government until the constitutionality of part of this limitation was legally challenged in 1981 (*Conroy v. Minister for Social Welfare*). That case had questioned the constitutionality of the rule requiring married women to have child dependants in order to claim assistance (Clark, 1985) and was settled after the rule had been abolished in the Social Welfare Act, 1982. However, no alteration was made in the general rule whereby most women were deemed to be dependent on their husbands until the implementation of the equality directive (see below).

Amongst the other recommendations of the Commission were that children's allowance should normally be paid to the mother rather than the father (implemented in 1974), and that payments for unmarried mothers and prisoners' wives should be introduced (1973 and 1974).

The Commission also considered the extent to which changes in the social welfare system were necessitated by the proposed introduction of equal pay in order to comply with EU law. In order to ensure that certain families – those in which the mother was unable, due to the age or number of her children, to take up employment and benefit from equal pay and families in which the mother would have to pay for childcare if she did enter employment – did not have their relative standards of living affected by the introduction of equal pay, the Commission recommended that an allowance be paid to families with at least one child under the age of five or, where there are two or more children, where the youngest was under the age of seven. This was to be in addition to any other social welfare entitlements. Thus the allowance was intended to compensate for the woman's inability to enter employment and to assist with the cost of child care. This proposal was, however, never implemented.

So, we can see the notion of equal treatment in social welfare is one which predates the EU directive on equality and significant developments had taken place in Ireland prior to the implementation of that directive. One can also see that the development of equality has not been a progressive movement from inequality in 1911 to a greater degree of equality in the 1970s. Indeed the relative position of women clearly worsened after independence in the 1920s and 1930s with the exclusion of married women from national insurance in 1929 and the exclusion of most women from entitlement to unemployment assistance in 1933. These developments reflect the economic difficulties of the time, the conservative views of the Cumann na nGaedheal government, the equally conservative views of Fianna Fáil in relation to the role of women, and the ideology of the Catholic Church. Indeed similar developments can be seen in relation to many other employment related issues, including the marriage bar for married women in the civil service and women teachers and the restrictions on women's work imposed by the Conditions of Employment Act 1936. This tendency can also seen in relation to a range of 'social' issues, including divorce and contraception (Whyte, 1980). The position improved somewhat after the 1952 reforms, with single woman becoming entitled to equal rates of benefit and the introduction of a maternity allowance. However, few further changes occurred until the 1970s when significant changes were made, including the ending of the exclusion of married women from entitlement to many social insurance benefits on marriage, the introduction of equal pay related contributions, the establishment of a number of payments for lone mothers and the payment of children's allowance to mothers. However, there remained significant instances of direct discrimination against married women in addition to the fact that the whole social welfare code was based on discriminatory assumptions about the roles of men and women. While the changes which were achieved in this period predated the adoption of the directive on equal treatment in social security, they must be seen in the context of Ireland's obligations under EU law which led to the abolition of the ban on married women's employment in the public service (1973) and the legislation on equal pay (1974) and equality in access to employment (1977) which had consequences for the structure of the social welfare system.

EU EQUALITY LAW AND THE DIRECTIVE ON SOCIAL SECURITY

Article 119 of the Treaty of Rome provides that men and women are to receive equal pay for equal work (see generally Curtin, 1989; Prechal and Burrows, 1990; Watson, 1980). The inclusion of this article in the Treaty was motivated by economic as well as social reasons in that member states, in particular France, wished to ensure that no member state could improve its economic competitiveness by relying on cheap female labour. The Court of Justice of the EU held that this provision had direct legal effect in the national legal systems in the second *Defrenne* case [1976] ECR 455 (i.e. it creates enforceable rights which can be relied on by an individual before the national courts).

While the Court of Justice held that social welfare payments did not fall within the meaning of 'pay' within the terms of Article 119 (first *Defrenne* case [1971] ECR 445), it was clear that the employment and social welfare systems were so closely bound up that it would be impossible to achieve equality in employment without also introducing legislation in the area of social welfare. In 1975 the EU Council of Ministers adopted a directive in relation to equal pay and in 1976 a second equality directive on equal treatment in relation to access to employment, vocational training and working conditions. The latter was originally intended to apply to social security as well but due to the difficulties involved it was decided to adopt a third directive specifically in relation to statutory social security schemes. A proposal was published by the Commission in 1977 and was adopted with relatively minor amendments (at least so far as the Irish system was concerned) on 19 December 1978. An unusually long implementation period was allowed of six years and the directive did not come into force in Ireland until 23 December 1984. As can be seen from its ancestry in the second directive, the purpose of the social security directive was largely to achieve equality in work related areas. It applies only to work related social welfare schemes and to members of the working population.

The directive does not apply to all social welfare schemes nor to all social welfare claimants. Family and survivors benefits are excluded from the scope of the directive and the effect of subsequent decisions of the Court of Justice has been that general means tested payments (such as supplementary welfare allowance) are also excluded. Only persons at work and persons who were looking for work or whose work has been interrupted by one of the risks referred to in the directive (sickness, invalidity, old age, occupational accidents and diseases and unemployment) are covered by the directive. The directive rules out all discrimination, direct and indirect, on grounds of sex in relation to all aspects of social welfare within its scope, including the calculations of contributions and of benefits.[3] However, the directive itself, with its close links to the paid labour force, is based on differentiated assumptions as to the role of men and women. Thus people who give up employment in order to care for children (the vast majority of whom are women) are not covered by the directive.

The Council of Ministers adopted a fourth directive on equal treatment in occupational pension schemes and a further directive on equal treatment in self employment in 1986 (Prechal and Burrows, 1990). The latter has only very limited relevance in the area of social welfare and, in any case, it appears that no efforts have been made to implement it in Ireland (see pages 47 and 112).

The EU Commission published a further proposed directive to 'complete' the implementation of the principle of equal treatment in social security in 1985 (COM (87) 494 final). This proposal has not been adopted by the Council of Ministers to date and there appears to be little prospect of its adoption in the near future. This proposal would have the effect of implementing the principle of equality in relation to areas excluded from the scope of the third directive including family and survivors benefits. However, the proposal does not go so far as to require individualisation of benefits nor does it require that protection be provided in areas of particular relevance to women such as lone parents payments. Thus, while the proposal, if and when it is adopted, may achieve formal equality between men and women in most areas of the social welfare code, it will not necessarily ensure improved provision for women who remain excluded from or marginal to the paid labour force nor will it necessarily make it easier for such women to gain access to improved social protection. To a large extent, the EU directives only provide for equality for women insofar as women behave like men and participate in the paid labour force like men. Although the EU Commission has proposed specific directives in relation to issues such as maternity, atypical work and parental leave, the response of the Council of Ministers has been unenthusiastic to say the least and such proposals have either not been adopted or have been significantly watered down.

THE IMPLEMENTATION OF THE EQUAL TREATMENT DIRECTIVE IN IRELAND (1979–94)

As we saw in the first part of this chapter, while the government had taken several steps to remove discrimination against women in the 1970s, at the time of the adoption of the directive in 1979 there remained several important areas where direct and indirect discrimination still continued.

Remaining areas of direct and indirect discrimination The main areas of direct discrimination were:

1) Married women in receipt of various benefits (such as unemployment and disability benefit) received lower rates of pay than married men and single persons.

2) Married women received unemployment benefit for only 12 months as opposed to the normal 15 months (this had been increased from 6 months in 1979).

3) Married women were generally not allowed to claim unemployment assistance unless their husband was incapable of self support.

4) Married women were deemed to be dependent on their husbands (again unless the husband was incapable of self support) with the result that the husband generally received dependent increases for his wife and children while the wife generally did not receive such increases (see Whyte, 1988 for other areas of discrimination).

The first two areas did not raise any great conceptual problems and indeed were ultimately resolved simply by raising the level and period of payment for married women to those applying to other claimants. However, as we will discuss in more detail below, the issues around dependency and access to unemployment assistance raised much more important issues of principle.

The main area of indirect discrimination related to the exclusion of part time workers (generally speaking, at that time people working less than 18 hours per week), the vast majority of whom were women, from social insurance.

The implementation process   Despite the six-year implementation period, the government took little action to remove the existing areas of discrimination. It was not until late 1984 that a Bill was published to make the necessary changes to the social welfare scheme in relation to the directly discriminatory aspects. This was eventually passed by the Oireachtas in 1985 (Social Welfare (No. 2) Act 1985) but was not brought into effect until May and November 1986. The delay in implementation led to increased costs for the government and, despite the time taken to introduce the new structures, to transitional provisions which continued to discriminate against married women until their abolition in 1992.

The Social Welfare (No. 2) Act 1985 provided that the rates of social welfare payable to married women were to increase to the same level as that payable to other adults and unemployment benefit was to be payable for the normal 15 months. Thus, in this area, the reformed social welfare system treated married women as individuals for the first time with no assumption that their personal needs were less because of an assumed dependency of their husbands. The Irish legislation did not, for example, follow the Belgian approach of introducing separate (higher) rates for 'heads of household' (predominantly men) and lower rates for 'single persons' and 'cohabitees' (a person living with another person with an occupational or welfare income) both made up predominantly of women. While these groups are formally neutral as to the sex of the claimant, they reinforce existing gender constructions (although the Court of Justice held that the Belgian legislation was not in breach of the directive – *Commission v. Belgium* [1991] I–2205).

The other areas of direct discrimination created more difficult conceptual problems. In relation to the notion of dependency, the Department was faced with the option of extending the existing system, whereby a married man received a dependent increase for his wife and children even if she was not, in fact, dependent on him, to married women (Callender, 1988). This would have led to a massive increase in the number of payments as, while the majority of married women were, in fact, still dependent on their husbands, this was not true of the majority of married men. Such an approach would have led to 'dependency' increases being paid to households which already had adequate incomes in many cases. A second approach would have been to abolish dependency increases altogether. However, this would have led to severe cuts in payments to many poor households which could have only been overcome by a major increase in the level of payment made to all claimants or the introduction of a system of individualised payments. Faced with these alternatives, the decision was made to retain the existing concept of dependency but to require factual proof of dependency in all cases. In practice this meant that dependency increases were payable only where the spouse was in receipt of earned income of less than £50 (now £60) per week and was not in receipt of a welfare payment in her or his own right. Where a spouse was not dependent, any child dependency increases due were paid at half the full rate. This was implemented in November 1986 but also led to income losses in many low income households as the husbands of wives in receipt of low work incomes (but over £50 per week) lost the dependency increases. Transitional payments were introduced to compensate such families. However, as these were paid to married men and not to married women, they continued to discriminate contrary to the terms of the equality directive (as the Court of Justice held in the second *Cotter and McDermott* case [1991] ECR I–1155). Thus in this area the social welfare system arguably retained the notion of women's dependency, replacing the concept of notional dependency with a more factual approach. While one might argue that this is only a reflection of the factual situation, recent research has shown that the structure of dependency in the social welfare system makes it difficult for women to take up anything other than low-paid employment and, in reflecting women's existing dependency, thereby also reinforces it (NESC, 1992, OECD, 1991).

Difficulties also arose in relation to the entitlement of married women to unemployment assistance. A simple removal of the exclusion would have led to an increased number of women claiming assistance (with little opportunity of obtaining employment) leading to an increase in the level of recorded unemployment and extra costs for the system. It is interesting to note that these are almost precisely the same reasons why women were granted only restricted access to unemployment assistance in the 1930s. As a result, while married women were allowed to claim assistance, a cap was placed on the amount of social welfare payable to a family so that families where the wife claimed assistance would be no better off than families where the wife remained as an adult dependant (see chapter 4). As there was no financial benefit in claiming (and, in some cases, financial disadvantages) not surprisingly many married women chose not to exercise their new found right to claim assistance. Although these provisions obviously had the effect of continuing the existing exclusion of married women from the labour force, it would seem from recent decisions of the Court of Justice that such measures may not be in breach of the directive (*Commission v. Belgium* [1991] I–2205). However, in this area the implementing strategy chosen clearly reinforces the notion of women's dependency rather than creating an individual right to benefits. As we have seen in chapter 4, a successful constitutional challenge to these provisions led to the establishment of a Review Group on the Treatment of Households in the Social Welfare Code (1991) but in practice this challenge simply resulted in the extension of the cap on payments to cohabiting as well as married couples (Whyte, 1992).

The delay in implementing the directive was condemned in several cases brought before the Court of Justice (the first and second *Cotter and McDermott* cases [1987] ECR 1453; [1990] ECR I–1155; *Emmot v. Minister for Social Welfare* [1991] ECR I–4269). Ultimately, after a campaign involving a range of Irish groups including the Free Legal Advice Centres (FLAC) and faced with a threat of legal action by the European Commission, the government agreed to pay arrears of about £60 million to Irish women who were entitled to equal treatment in the period from 1984 to the dates of implementation of the directive in 1986. However, it is arguable that even then the government did not acknowledge all the arrears due: no account was taken, for example, of transitional payments made from 1986 to 1992. Several thousand Irish women pursued their claims through the courts. Settlements (involving payment of arrears and, in some cases, interest) have been made by the Minister for Social Welfare in many of these cases and, at the time of writing, many other cases are still before the courts.[4]

The 1985 legislation dealt only with areas of direct discrimination. However, it has been suggested that the exclusion of part time workers from the social insurance scheme might also be in breach of the directive (Whyte, 1988) and several cases were taken before Appeals Officers of the Social Welfare Appeals Office on these grounds, albeit unsuccessfully (Cousins, 1993b). Following shortly after the extension of employment rights to part time workers in 1990, however, social insurance was extended to part time workers in 1991 (although the social welfare entitlements of such workers was modified in this process: see chapter 3). It would seem that the EU developments in relation to equal treatment and proposed EU directives on atypical workers may have been influential in the timing of this extension. (Indeed the House of Lords in the UK has recently held that the UK employment legislation which similarly excludes part time workers is in breach of EU law: *R. v. Secretary of State for Employment ex parte EOC* [1994] 2 WLR 409.) It was originally intended to include all workers earning more than £40 per week which would still have excluded a significant number of part-time workers but, at the behest of the unions and employers who feared that this would encourage fly-by-night employers, particularly in areas such as contract cleaning, the threshold was eventually lowered to £25 (now £30) per week, thereby including the vast majority of such workers.

The issue of disproportionate impact on women may also have arisen in relation to the increase in contribution requirements in 1987 and the closer links with the work force. Although it is difficult to disaggregate the overall influences on claimant numbers, it is likely that many women, with their looser attachment to the paid labour force and poorer contribution record were adversely affected by these policies.

The issue of equality was raised in the reports of several government appointed Commissions. However, the Commission on Social Welfare did not consider issues around gender in much detail and the limitations of the Review Group on the Treatment of Households have been outlined in chapter 4. The Second Commission on the Status of Women in its recent report (1993) also considered the position of women in the social welfare code. However, the level of analysis must be considered disappointing. While the Commission called vaguely for the establishment by 1997 of 'a system of individual rights and payments in the social insurance and social welfare systems' (para. 2.5.3) some of its own recommendations would in fact have increased the extent of dependency in the system (para. 2.5.6). In relation to dependency payments, the Commission adopted the proposal of the Review Group that adult dependants be renamed as 'qualified partners', recommended the direct payment of dependency payments to such persons and proposed that there should be a more tapered approach to the level of income involved in the definition of dependency.

The National Pensions Board (1993) also averted only briefly to the general issues of the application of equal treatment (its specific proposal on survivors pensions are referred to in the next section of this chapter). In relation to the definition of dependency, it recommended that the earnings limit for dependency increases should be increased in line with increases in payments and should be tapered (and see Expert Working Group, 1993).

FAMILY AND SURVIVORS BENEFITS

Although the proposed EU directive in this area has not been agreed to date, several changes in Irish payments in this area have been influenced by the trend towards equality (Whyte, 1995). As we saw in chapter 6, a lone parent's allowance was introduced in 1990, ending discrimination against men. The deserted wife's benefit became subject to an income limit in 1992. While this affected relatively few women, it reduced the potential costs if this payment ever has to be extended to men while, at the same time, it allowed a move towards phasing out this payment which is seen by the Department of Social Welfare (and other commentators including McCashin (1993)) as being anomalous.

In relation to widow's (contributory) pension, the question arose as to whether the pension should be extended to widowers or abolished altogether to be replaced by an alternative system of personal entitlements. The original purpose of the pension had been to provide an income on the death of the husband who was assumed (accurately so in the vast majority of cases in 1935) to be the main breadwinner. This rationale was threatened to some extent by the rising number of married women in the paid labour force. However, an extension to all married men made little sense since the majority would not be financially dependent on their wives (nor would payment of benefit be targeted at child care needs or similar costs). Accordingly, the National Pension Board proposed that the widow's pension should be extended to all survivors but with an earnings limit, similar to that applying to deserted wife's benefit, being applied to all claimants under 66 after 12 months payment. This would have maintained the original rationale of supporting the surviving spouse on the death of the main breadwinner. Existing claimants of the widow's pension would not be affected by this rule. The cost of the extension would have been more than offset by the savings achieved by introducing the earnings limit (National Pension Board, 1993, p. 187). In the 1994 Budget, it was announced that such a pension would be introduced in the next Social Welfare Bill, but after some public criticism (particularly from widows' organisations), the Minister for Social Welfare, Dr Woods, announced that the income limit would be dropped and a survivors benefit introduced from October 1994. More than 9,000 widowers are expected to benefit at a cost of £27 million in a full year. Thus a spouse will now receive a pension (possibly for life) on the death of the other spouse regardless of whether that spouse was a dependant or not (and, for the first time, a significant number of the beneficiaries will not have been dependent on the deceased spouse). It is difficult to find a major reform of the social welfare code which is more difficult to justify on any rational basis (other than short term political popularity).

In the area of family and survivors benefits, the move towards equality has at least recognised that men may also take on parenting roles. However, we have seen that the lone parent's allowance retains many aspects of dependency. The introduction of a widower's pension will improve the position of many men (often those not in most need) but has not affected the position of women nor changed the approach of the dependency based widow's pension in the direction of more individualised entitlements.

AN ASSESSMENT

One can see in the measures adopted to implement the equal treatment directive in Ireland a strange mixture of contrasting, and sometimes contradictory, approaches. On the one hand, the extension of social insurance to part time workers can be seen as a move towards individualisation and a positive measure to encourage the participation of women in the paid labour force, as can the payment of full benefits to married women (although the fact that reduced benefits are paid to part time workers in some cases means that such workers are still assumed to be dependent on other income sources – presumably support from a husband in many cases). On the other, the way in which the notion of assumed dependency was replaced by a test of factual dependency acts as a barrier to women's participation in the work force at other than very low rates of pay while the way in which the unemployment assistance legislation was amended is a straightforward disincentive to married women (and now cohabitees) making themselves available for work.

The overall thrust of policy can be seen from the numbers affected by these individual measures. The extension of social insurance to part time workers is estimated to affect over 25,000 workers while the number of married women entitled to increased rates of benefit was estimated at 40,000. In contrast the number of persons in respect of whom adult dependency payments are paid was over 180,000 in 1986 (the vast majority of whom were women) and the Review Group (1990) estimated that between 28,500 and 50,000 additional claims would be made if the cap on unemployment assistance was abolished, costing up to £58 million (in 1990 terms) in a full year.

While some aspects of the implementation of the directive has been positive and will have facilitated women's participation in the labour force, the effect of the retention of the concept of dependency and the continued disincentive to married women claiming unemployment assistance means that the system has, to a large extent, retained a dependency based approach rather than representing a major move towards individualisation of benefits. This approach seems to be dominated by the view that, given the already very high levels of unemployment, there is little point in facilitating the entry of married women into the labour force in significant numbers combined with the (albeit weakened) Catholic ethos that woman's place is in the home. Indeed the government and social partners seem generally reluctant to take significant measures to include women in the labour force. While Callan and Farrell's report to the NESC (NESC, 1992) pointed to the necessity of significant action in the area of childcare, taxation and social welfare, the Council itself, while rejecting the view that the removal of obstacles to married women's partici-pation in the paid labour force was 'inappropriate in the context of Ireland's persistently high unemployment levels', was dubious about the proposed tax reforms (Cook and McCashin, 1992) and vague on the social welfare and child care issues. Nor have these issues been addressed in much greater detail in its subsequent report (1993) nor in the Programme for Competitiveness and Work (Ireland, 1994).

However, the implementation of the equal treatment directive does represent a further (albeit gradual) step away from the concept of dependency. The participation of married women in the labour force continues to grow despite the lack of governmental enthusiasm referred to above, rising from 7.5 per cent in 1971 to 15.2 per cent in 1979 and 27 per cent in 1992. This must be seen in the context of an overall rise in female participation in the labour force from 29 per cent in 1979 to 34 per cent in 1993 (Central Statistics Office, 1994a) involving a long run drop in the participation rates of younger (15–19) and older women (60 and over). Thus it seems likely that the pressures on the social welfare system to move more towards a system of individual-isation may continue to increase.

The delay in implementing the directive has been attributed to the particular structure of the Irish social welfare system and the fact that the implementation period in Ireland coincided with 'a period of particular economic difficulties and political instability' (Mangan, 1993 and see Comptroller and Auditor General, 1993). Nor indeed were such difficulties confined to Ireland with the Netherlands also failing to implement the directive in time. However, Cook and McCashin (1992) have pointed out that, in the period in question, social welfare expenditure grew rapidly and not simply because of rising numbers of claimants as real levels of payment also increased. They argue that a more strategic approach at administrative and political levels would have allowed the phasing in of 'what was bound to be a problematic structural change'. The failure to take this opportunity is attributed to institutional failings in the policy making process (referring to Lee's critique (1989)). While this is no doubt correct, it perhaps underestimates the institutional paralysis created by the political and administrative systems' inability to cope with the economic reverses of the 1970s and 1980s after a long period of economic growth.

While Callan and Farrell (NESC, 1992) have pointed out the difficulties created by the current social welfare system, as we have seen there has been little detailed consideration of how these issues can be resolved. There is clearly a need for a more comprehensive consideration of the possible options for the future treatment of women in the social welfare code. Many groups have called for 'individualisation' of benefits but there is a lack of clarity as to exactly what is involved. For example, Esam and Berthoud (1991) show that the provision of individuals benefits, in the context of a system heavily dependent on means tested payments, will result in a massive increase in the amount of means testing, a major increase in costs and may lead to an increase in employment disincentives for non working women. A comprehensive examination of the options would need to consider the unit of assessment, the basis of entitlement (insurance, assistance, basic income), the links with employment, the interaction with taxation, training and child care policy and the needs of women who are likely to remain outside the paid labour force.

The meaning and usefulness of the concept of equality itself must also be considered. Does the notion of equality, in the sense of treating like alike and unlike unalike, assist in advancing the position of women in a male dominated society? One can argue that, rather than advancing the position of women, it serves to disguise the fact that in order to improve their position women have to become like men. Simone de Beauvoir in *The Second Sex* (1972), first published in 1949, asks, What is a woman? and answers that

> humanity is male and man defines woman not in herself but as relative to him; she is not regarded as an autonomous being . . . She is determined and differentiated with reference to man and not he with reference to her; she is the inessential as opposed to the essential. He is the Subject, he is the Absolute: she is the Other.

Those implementing the principle of equal treatment in Ireland (and indeed other EU countries) have applied this notion in their interpretation of this principle by seeing women as Other to man and by then attempting to find abstract differences and similarities with men in order to apply (or refuse to apply) the principle of equal treatment.

Thus one can suggest that the principle of 'equal treatment' deserves the incredulity which Lyotard (1979) argues for with regard to grand theories. Improvements in the position of women require that the specificity of women be emphasised rather than simply their differences and similarities with men (while recognising that this specificity is a social construction rather than a biological given). Such an approach would recognise that 'the diversity of women's needs and experiences means that no single solution, on issues like childcare, social security and housing, can be adequate for all' (Fraser and Nicholson, 1988). Indeed, as we have seen, the EU Commission has, to a limited extent, already made proposals along these lines in relation to the draft directives on parental and family leave, atypical workers and pregnancy and maternity. However, the response of the members states to this approach has been generally negative emphasising the need for a change in political priorities if the position of women is to be improved.

CHAPTER EIGHT

Pregnancy and Maternity Benefits

The issue of social welfare provision for women during pregnancy and maternity is one of considerable importance in the overall context of the Irish social welfare system. There are around 50,000 births per year (although this has declined sharply from a peak of over 74,000 in 1980). However, this area has received little detailed examination, for example, the Commission on Social Welfare (1986) only mentions the issue very briefly (although see Joint Committee on Women's Rights, 1985) and social welfare provisions for pregnancy and maternity have developed (or, in some cases, disappeared) without any great discussion and without any indication of an underlying policy. This chapter looks at the development of social welfare provision in this area since the beginning of the century. It considers the provisions which currently exist and looks at possible future development in this area.

Social welfare provisions can be broadly divided into two:

• Cash grants either at or around the time of the child's birth (hereafter maternity grants). These grants are intended in some way to reflect the additional costs arising from childbirth but generally without any clear indication as to which costs are being met or as to the extent to which the grant is intended to meet these costs (i.e. wholly or in part).

• Payments during maternity leave from work (hereafter maternity allowance). These payments are in recognition of the fact that women cannot, and should not be obliged to, work for a period around childbirth. They are intended to provide a wage replacement so that working women can give up work for a reasonable period at this time.

DEVELOPMENT OF MATERNITY PROTECTION (1900–81)

Maternity grant   Many of the friendly societies, with which workers were insured in the early 1900s, had provided a cash grant to insured women, or in respect of the spouses of insured men, on childbirth. This grant was carried over as part of the national insurance system established by the National Insurance Act 1911 and was known as maternity benefit (section 8(e)). It was then set at a rate of £1.50 and was increased to £2 in 1920. This grant was renamed as maternity grant under the major reorganisation of the social welfare code implemented by the Social Welfare Act 1952 and was increased to £4 in 1965. The grant was payable either on the husband's or wife's insurance record and the contribution requirements were relatively easy to satisfy. Where the woman and her husband were both insured, two grants were paid. The grant reached a relatively high proportion of mothers when one considers that social insurance did not apply to the self-employed, then a large proportion of the Irish work force. For example, in the 1930s and 40s, maternity benefit was paid in respect of over 40 per cent of all births. The vast majority of payments at this time were paid on the father's insurance rather than the mother's (Department of Social Welfare, 1949).

A proposal in 1951 to increase substantially the maternity grant paid under the social insurance system and to pay a maternity allowance for four weeks in respect of the wives of insured persons was rejected by the then Minister for Health and Social Welfare, Dr Ryan, on the grounds that such an increase would not benefit the self-employed and other uninsured persons (131 *Dáil Debates* 1250 *et seq.*). The Minister stated that he preferred to introduce a means-tested grant which would benefit those not covered by social insurance who were in need of financial assistance on childbirth. Such a grant was established by the Health Act, 1953 and was set at a rate of £4. However, over the subsequent period, the value of the maternity grant was allowed to decline sharply in real terms. The means-tested maternity grant was raised to a level of £8 in the Health Act, 1970 and has never subsequently been increased. The social insurance maternity grant was raised to £8 in 1978 and again was never subsequently increased. It was one of the few social welfare payment to decrease rather than increase in real value from the 1950s.

Maternity allowance　　Although an ILO Convention of 1919 had called for maternity leave of at least twelve weeks with maternity allowance being provided during this period, no maternity allowance existed under the Irish social welfare system until 1953. The Social Welfare Act, 1952 provided for a maternity allowance which was to be paid for six weeks before and six weeks after the date of confinement. Maternity allowance was paid at a flat rate which was the same as the then rate of unemployment and disability benefit paid to men and single women (which was 33 per cent higher than the rate of disability and unemployment benefit then paid to married women). Although this payment appears to have been aimed primarily at women who had to take time off work due to pregnancy, the contribution requirements meant that it could, in fact, be claimed by women who had not worked for some time but who had kept alive their contribution record by gaining credited contributions while claiming unemployment and disability benefit.[1]

In 1973, with the introduction of the pay-related benefit scheme, a pay-related addition was paid with weekly flat rate maternity allowance. No further substantial changes took place in maternity provisions until 1981 when a maternity allowance for women in employment was established. The Maternity (Protection of Employment) Act 1981 provided for a statutory entitlement to maternity leave of fourteen weeks for most employed women. In conjunction with this development, the Social Welfare (Amendment) Act 1981 provided for a new scheme of maternity allowance. Unlike the existing scheme, this applied only to women actually in employment at the time of taking maternity leave and was intended to preserve their income at approximately the level of their take home pay while on leave (327 *Dáil Debates* 77). Payment was made for fourteen weeks at 80 per cent of previous earnings with a minimum payment of £47.50 per week. This payment was confined to those working at least eighteen hours per week and also excluded women on contracts of less than twenty-six weeks or with less than twenty-six weeks left to run.

THE LINK TO EMPLOYMENT (1981–94)

The past decade has seen several important developments in maternity provision. On the one hand, there has been an expansion of the scheme for those in employment to cover part-time workers. On the other hand, the proportion of mothers in employment who actually receive maternity allowance has declined and maternity protection for those not currently in employment has been very much reduced. This has occurred with little public debate and, perhaps surprisingly, with little public dissent.

Maternity grant The social insurance maternity grant, first established in 1911 and renamed under the Social Welfare Act 1952, was abolished in 1983. The Minister for Social Welfare described the payment, which had been frozen at a rate of £8 since 1978, as 'no longer of any real significance in the context of the maternity allowance scheme which was substantially improved two years ago' (340 *Dáil Debates* 2377). There does not seem to have been any great opposition to this move, possibly because of the low level of the grant involved. However, the abolition of this payment was significant in policy terms since it removed the main payment aimed at 'easing the financial difficulties of a family consequent upon the birth of a baby' (131 *Dáil Debates* 1250). The significance of this decision can be seen in the numbers affected. In 1982, 39,055 maternity grants had been paid. In contrast, the maternity allowance, referred to by the Minister, was paid to only 18,670 women in the year from July 1983 to June 1984. Thus many thousands of women ceased to receive assistance with maternity costs under the social insurance system. The abolition of the social insurance maternity grant did not give rise to any increase in the level of the means-tested maternity grant which remained at a level of £8.

Maternity allowance[2] The rate of maternity allowance was reduced to 70 per cent of previous earnings in 1984, apparently on the basis that because of changes in the taxation system the original formula could lead to levels of benefit much higher than originally intended (Joint Committee, 1985, p. 18). The scheme of maternity allowance for women in employment was extended to include insured part-time workers earning over £25 (now £30) per week in 1991. This followed from the general expansion of employment rights to cover part-time workers under the Worker Protection (Regular Part-Time Employees) Act 1991 and the general extension of social insurance to part time workers in that year.

The contribution conditions for the general maternity allowance scheme, which had been introduced in 1952, and which had remained in place after the introduction in 1981 of the scheme for women in employment, were made significantly more onerous in 1987 leading to a sharp drop in those receiving this payment. Those affected by this change were women out of employment. This was justified by the Minister for Social Welfare, Dr Woods, on the grounds that it was reasonable to require maternity benefit to be payable only to persons with a genuine and enduring link with the work force (376 *Dáil Debates* 2377). The Minister said that

> the need for the old scheme has, to a large extent, been superseded by the introduction of the maternity allowance scheme for women in employment and I expect that henceforth the needs of women in the area will be met by this scheme (ibid. 2322).

The change was vigorously opposed by deputies including Monica Barnes who pointed out that it went totally against the proposal by the Joint Committee on Women's Rights for a universal maternity allowance payable to all mothers (ibid. 2376). Payment of pay-related benefit with maternity allowance was restricted and eventually abolished in 1988. Finally, the general maternity allowance payment was abolished with effect from April 1992.

This now means that the only specific maternity provision for women who are not in employment is the means-tested maternity grant of £8 (paid in respect of about 4,000 births in 1992) and payments towards maternity expenses under the exceptional needs payments of the supplementary welfare allowance scheme. However, the Minister for Social Welfare announced that women who were in receipt of unemployment and disability payments would be allowed to continue in receipt of these payments during the maternity period (although they might well not meet the statutory conditions for qualification for such payments) (428 *Dáil Debates* 858 *et seq.*). The position outlined by the Minister represents an administrative practice as there has been no change in the legal position. This is an extremely unsatisfactory way of providing protection in that it leads to a lack of clarity as to both the position in law and in practice: strictly speaking the Minister is not entitled to waive statutory requirements in this way and the administrative practice can change in the future without any public debate. The Minister estimated that only about 100 women a year, who would lose out as a result of the abolition of the general scheme, would not be able to claim an alternative payment.

The contribution conditions for the maternity allowance scheme for women in employment were also made more onerous in 1987. Unfortunately separate figures for those in receipt of the two allowances were not published after 1986. However, the total number in receipt of a maternity allowance in 1986 was 19,881 (or 32 per cent of live births). This declined to 15,240 (28 per cent of live births) in 1988 and it appears that the decline was much sharper in relation to women claiming under the general scheme (i.e. women not in employment). The total numbers subsequently increased again to 16,357 (31 per cent of live births) in 1991 following the extension of social insurance to part time workers but, with the abolition of the general scheme in April 1992, the 1992 figures dropped to 14,876 (29 per cent of live births) before increasing slightly to 15,110 (30.5 per cent) in 1993.

Thus the last decade has seen a decline in the number of people who receive social insurance protection during maternity with the abolition of the maternity grant and the drop in the numbers in receipt of maternity allowance from 32 per cent of live births in 1986 to 30.5 per cent in 1993, despite the extension of the scope of the payment to include part time workers and the general increase in women's participation in the labour force. The maternity allowance scheme was altered, with the introduction of the new scheme in 1981, so that it applies only to those with 'a genuine and enduring link with the work force'. The old general maternity allowance scheme which applied to many more pregnant women has been phased out. Social insurance protection for non-working women has disappeared with the abolition of the maternity grant and the old maternity allowance schemes and there has been no move to fill this gap by the introduction of improved means-tested or universal schemes. Instead the Minister has established an administrative arrangement to allow women who are in receipt of social welfare payments to continue to receive those payments during maternity. Thus, there is no social insurance provision at all for women who are neither in employment nor in receipt of a social welfare payment.

EU DEVELOPMENTS

Several developments under EU law are relevant to this area. First, the Court of Justice has held in the *Dekker* case (case C–177/88 [1990] ECR 3841) that discrimination in employment on grounds of pregnancy can be in breach of EU law on equal treatment of men and women at work. The Irish Labour Court and Equality Officers had already ruled to this effect in several cases. However, these decisions relating to EU employment law are not always directly relevant to the social welfare area, for example it appears unlikely that maternity allowance would be held to fall within the concept of pay for the purposes of Article 119 of the Treaty of Rome (first *Defrenne* case [1971] ECR 445). Therefore, social welfare payments must be considered in the light of EU law on social security.

Secondly, Directive 79/7 on the implementation of the principle of equal treatment of men and women in matters of social security is stated to be 'without prejudice to the provisions relating to the protection of women on the grounds of maternity' (article 4(2)) and allows member states to 'adopt specific provisions for women to remove existing instances of unequal treatment' (preamble to the directive). Given that the directive does not apply to maternity payments, the practical implications of these provisions are unclear (Prechal and Burrows, 1990, p. 177). However, the directive would prevent discrimination against pregnant women applying for payments which are covered by the directive, e.g. unemployment and disability payments. It is unclear if the proposed directive completing the implementation of equal treatment in social security (COM(85) 494 final) will apply to maternity benefits. To interpret the principle of equal treatment so as to apply only in situations directly comparable between men and women, thereby excluding situations such as pregnancy, which apply only to women would be to adopt a very narrow interpretation of the principle of equal treatment (and one which has been rejected by the Court of Justice in the *Dekker* case).

Thirdly, the EU directive on equal treatment in self-employment (86/613) provides that:

> Member States shall undertake to examine whether, and under what conditions, female self-employed workers and the wives of self-employed workers may, during interruptions in their occupational activity owing to pregnancy or motherhood . . . be entitled to cash benefits under a social security scheme or under any other public social protection system.

It appears that no steps have been taken to implement this provision in Ireland. It would seem, in any case, that this provision could not create directly effective legal rights for an individual woman.

Finally, in 1990 the EU Commission proposed a directive on the protection of pregnant women at work which includes provisions on maternity leave and pay (COM(90) 406 final). The original proposal provided for fourteen weeks' maternity leave and 100 per cent of previous pay. However the directive finally adopted by the Council of Ministers on 19 October 1992 (92/85) reduced the level of the payment to that which was normally provided to employees unable to work due to incapacity. The original proposal would have applied to all women in employment but the version finally adopted allows member states to retain qualification conditions for entitlement to benefit. Thus it does not require maternity benefit to be paid to all working women. Minor changes were made to the amount of benefit payable under the Irish scheme in 1994 as a result of the implementation of this directive.

The EU directive also provides some protection for women who are unable to continue in employment due to a pregnancy/maternity related risk to health and safety. In October 1994, the Minister for Social Welfare, in implementation of the directive, introduced a new social insurance payment to be known as health and safety benefit. This is payable to women who are pregnant, have recently given birth or are breast feeding (up to 26 weeks) whose employment gives rise to a risk to health and safety and whose employer cannot remove the risk or move them to alternative work. It also applies to women required to do nightwork during pregnancy or in the 14 weeks after birth where this could be a risk to their health and safety. The qualification conditions are similar to the maternity payment for women in work. This benefit is payable from the fourth week of absence from work with the employer being required to meet the cost of the first three weeks leave. It is to operate on an 'interim basis'.

COMPARISONS AND ASSESSMENT

As we have seen, the scope of the maternity allowance scheme for women in employment has expanded since it was first introduced, although the numbers in receipt of payment have declined both in total and as a percentage of births over the period from 1986 to 1993. The Irish maternity allowance covers a quite limited category of workers. While it has been extended to cover most employees, it still does not cover self-employed workers, who are entitled only to very limited social insurance benefits, nor assisting spouses and relatives who are generally not covered by social insurance at all. This compares unfavourably to some other EU countries such as Denmark (self-employed women and assisting spouses covered), Luxembourg (all women covered) and the UK (self-employed covered).

Secondly, the scheme compares unfavourably to other EU countries both as to the duration of payment (fourteen weeks as against fifteen in Greece, sixteen weeks in Spain, France and Luxembourg, eighteen weeks in the UK, twenty weeks in Italy and twenty-eight weeks in Denmark) and as to the amount of the maternity allowance (70 per cent of previous income as against 75–100 per cent in many other EU countries: MISSOC, 1993). Estimation of a hypothetical replacement ratio for a woman on the average industrial wage shows the Irish allowance in a more favourable light but still below the EU average (European Commission, 1994a).

The position in relation to provisions for non-working women is, however, more critical. As we have seen, these provisions have been almost entirely abolished. There appears to have been little discussion or debate as to the policy (if any) behind these measures. The only remaining provisions in this area are the means-tested maternity grant and exceptional needs payments under the supplementary welfare allowance scheme. The means-tested maternity grant is only paid to those who qualify for a medical card and exceptional needs payments are not paid to persons in full-time work (thirty hours or more per week). Thus many relatively low-paid workers are excluded from any assistance with maternity costs.

Recent research has questioned the extent to which these benefits reach those at whom they are being targeted, i.e. the least well-off. Data from a survey by the Free Legal Advice Centres of 103 households in a Dublin suburb showed that twenty-two households had a child of twelve months or under (Cousins and Charleton, 1991).[3] In seven houses, the head of the household was working. In the remaining fifteen the head of the household was in receipt of a social welfare payment. These households were questioned as to the assistance which they received with maternity costs under the following headings:

• the means-tested maternity grant of £8

• assistance under the SWA scheme with maternity clothes, a buggy and hospital expenses (e.g. clothing)

• free milk.

None of the seven working households received any assistance at all. Of the fifteen social welfare households only five had received the maternity grant, nine had received help with maternity clothes, eleven with the cost of a buggy, four with hospital expenses and four got free milk. The amounts recorded as having been received varied between £20 and £30 for maternity clothes; £30 to £60 for the buggy; and £30 for hospital expenses.

This survey was part of a benefit take-up project and in eight cases claimants were advised to claim the maternity grant and in four cases to apply for exceptional needs payments. In only one case was a claim made for maternity grant. This claim was successful. Several participants said that they were 'deterred from claiming by the extremely low rate of payment and by the fact that they would end up spending as much money travelling around in buses in order to lodge the claim as they would ultimately receive' (ibid, p. 25). Two claims were lodged for exceptional needs payments, one was successful and one was pending at the time of completion of the survey. This low level of take-up of the maternity grant seems to be borne out by the figures available for the total payments made. These have declined from 6,108 in 1984 to 3,963 in 1988. This figure represents about 7 per cent of total births. This appears quite low given that all mothers entitled to a medical card are entitled to the maternity grant and that over 35 per cent of the population is covered by a medical card.

The Irish provisions in this area compare unfavourably with those of several other EU countries. For example, in France 'l'allocation pour jeune enfant' is paid to all mothers for nine months from the fourth month of pregnancy until the child is three months old (Dupeyroux and Prétot, 1989). This payment is at a rate of over £100 per month. Belgium, Luxembourg and Greece also have comparatively large maternity grants.

FUTURE DEVELOPMENTS

Developments in the 1980s and 1990s have seen maternity protection being much more closely linked to participation in the paid labour force and the abolition of both maternity grants and allowances for women who are not in employment. This can be seen as part of the overall government policy of attempting to control the cost of social insurance payments by reinforcing the link with work and cutting the state's contribution to the social insurance fund (see chapter 1). These developments show the weakness of a transient category of persons with little organisational representation (pregnant women who are not in employment) in the formation of social welfare policy and highlight the extent to which trade union priorities involve their own members rather than welfare recipients generally (and particularly women who are not in employment).

It seems likely that the future development of the maternity allowance will be closely linked to the decisions made in reviewing the recent EU directive on the protection of pregnant women (which is to be done in 1997) and also to the extent to which the trade unions make this area a priority for further improvement. The possible transfer of the administration of the maternity allowance scheme to employers or the introduction of a statutory maternity pay scheme must be a possibility given the trends in relation to sickness payments. The expansion of the scope of the scheme to cover self-employed women and assisting spouses may be largely dependent on developments at EU level arising from the implementation of the EU directive on equal treatment in self-employment.

It is more difficult to see any future for the maternity grant. It is obvious that childbirth does give rise to additional costs for mothers and families, although it does not appear that these costs have been accurately calculated in Ireland. Research in the UK in 1985 suggested a figure of ST£250 for necessary purchases for the mother and child (Brown and Small, 1985). The figures available as to the cost of the maternity grant and SWA schemes show that the state pays only a very small percentage of these costs. Successive governments have directed significant resources away from the maternity grant. and there is little indication that this trend will be reversed.

CHAPTER NINE

Social Welfare Adjudication and Appeals

INTRODUCTION

This chapter looks at the development of social welfare adjudication and appeals in the period since the establishment of a structured system of social welfare payments in 1847 to date. Over this period three main trends emerge. The first is the increasing bureaucratisation[1] of decision making, with decision making powers being taken away from (at least partially) democratic bodies such as the Poor Law Unions and the Old Age Pension Committees and concentrated in the hands of civil and public servants. The second is the reliance on wholly 'internal' decision making bodies comprising salaried civil and public servants rather than, as in the UK, opting for a system of 'external' appeal involving lawyers and members of the public or, as in many other EU countries, using the courts as the forum for appeal.[2] This again implies an emphasis on a bureaucratic resolution of decisions rather than a more judicial approach. The third trend is the increasing development of the concept of entitlement to payment and the resultant pressures for a legalisation of the adjudication system so that entitlements can be enforced. Thus persons now have a legally binding right to most main social welfare payments as opposed to the discretionary system existing under the Poor Law scheme. This tendency towards legalisation has led to the development of independent appeal systems within the bureaucracy and to a development of these appeal systems in a quasi-judicial manner rather than simply as an informal review system. However, the bureaucratic tendency is emphasised by the fact that these appeal systems remain part (albeit an 'independent' part) of the bureaucracy and by the fact that jurisdiction has been taken away from courts and from 'external' tribunals. Thus, faced with the tendency towards a greater emphasis on rights, the response of the adjudication system has been to improve the transparency of the operation of the bureaucracy rather than to opt for an alternative (judicial) approach.

Over the period in question, there has been an increasing unification of the various social welfare systems each of which initially had its own adjudication system. There are now, in adjudicative terms, only two main systems: the general social welfare system and the supplementary welfare allowance system (SWA).[3] The general social welfare system has descended from several different schemes including workmen's compensation (1897), old age pension (1908), national health insurance (1911), unemployment insurance (1911), widow's and orphan's pensions (1933) and children's allowance (1944). The SWA system (1975), on the other hand, is directly descended from the Poor Law (1847).

The general social welfare schemes (i.e. those other than the Poor Law) have utilised a variety of methods of initial decision making, including decision making by officials of the state,[4] by state authorised private insurance schemes,[5] by local Pension Committees[6] or by agreement between the parties.[7] In terms of appeals three models can be seen. The first, derived largely from the system established under the Old Age Pension Act 1908, involved appeal to officials within the body responsible for the overall control of the scheme or, where the decision was made by a private body, to officials of an overseeing state appointed body. This model has, to a large extent, influenced the constitution of the current Social Welfare Appeals Office. The second model, initially establish for the unemployment insurance scheme, involved appeal to external tribunals composed of non-civil servants – generally lawyers and representative of employers and employees. This model existed in Ireland in relation to unemployment benefit from 1911 to 1952. It was adopted on an almost universal basis in the UK with its current system of appeal to a three-person Social Security Appeal Tribunal (consisting of a legally qualified chair and two persons representative of the local community) and subsequent appeal to a legally qualified Social Security Commissioner (who has the status of a county court judge). The third model is that of appeal to the general courts. This existed in Ireland in relation to the workmen's compensation scheme until its abolition in 1967. It is common in civil law countries.

When the social welfare system was unified and brought under the authority of the newly established Department of Social Welfare in 1952, the new legislation opted for a system of appeal to departmental Appeals Officers and the system of external tribunals was abolished. The occupational injuries scheme which was introduced in 1967 to replace the workmen's compensation system also opted for the same unified adjudication system and direct appeal to the courts was abolished.

The supplementary welfare allowance system, in contrast, is directly descended from the old Poor Law system which provided the first state system of social welfare in Ireland. Decision making was initially the responsibility of partially elected and partially appointed Boards of Poor Law Guardians. The development of this system will be considered in more detail below. However, we will see that decision making has now become the responsibility of public servants with no direct control from any elected body.

THE DEVELOPMENT OF THE GENERAL SYSTEMS

The old age pension – pension committees   The old age pension was established in the United Kingdom of Great Britain and Ireland in 1908. It appears that the legislators decided to opt for the existing network of local officers attached to the Office of Customs and Excise as the investigation branch of the administration on the basis of their familiarity with local conditions and their financial experience (Carney, 1985). However, an entirely new adjudication system was introduced in the form of local Pension Committees. Each county council and urban and district council with a population of over 10,000 (20,000 in the rest of the UK) was to set up a Pension Committee. The Committee was appointed by the relevant council and could include people other than members of the council. Each committee could set up subcommittees consisting of between 5 and 9 members. It had been argued in the House of Commons that appeal should lie to the courts rather than to a bureaucratic body but this was not accepted by the government which opted instead for an administrative appeal (Carney, 1985, p. 491). The appeal body was initially the Local Government Board for Ireland (from 1922 the Minister for Local Government and Public Health and from 1947 the Minister for Social Welfare).

The system meant that the claimant made a claim to the local post-master who subsequently passed it to the Office of Customs and Excise (from 1922 the Revenue Commissioners). The claim was investigated by a Pensions Officer who reported to the local Old Age Pensions Committee. The Committee then decided whether a pension should be granted and if so the amount of the pension. The Pension Officer could attend meetings of the Pension Committee, but was not obliged to do so even if requested. If the Pensions Officer recommended that no pension or a reduced pension be paid, the claimant was informed and invited to attend the Committee if s/he wished to do so to make his or her case. The Committee could make further investigations if these were felt necessary. Either the claimant or the Pension Officer could appeal. In practice it would appear that, from an early date, the recommendation of the Pension Officer carried much weight with the Pension Committees. If a recommendation was disregarded, the Pension Officer could appeal to the Local Government Department which was reputed to attach little weight to the opinion of the Committee (1 *Dáil Debates* 2127 *et seq.*; 9 *Dáil Debates* 829 *et seq.*).

There was no direct right of appeal to the courts from the decisions of the Committees or of the Local Government Board but decisions were subject to judicial review by the courts and, in fact, several cases came before the Irish courts in the early years of the scheme. In *R. (Cairns) v. Local Government Board* [1911] 2 IR 331 it was argued that the appellant was entitled to an oral hearing before the Board. However, the High Court held that, while the appellant must be notified that an appeal has been brought (by a Pension Officer) and could then apply to be heard by the Board, the Board had a discretion as to whether or not to hear the claimant in person or to hear witnesses. Although Lord O'Brien emphasised that this discretion 'must be a real, *bona fide* and honest exercise of discretion' by the Board, there is little to indicate that the Board (or its successors) held any significant number of oral hearings or informed claimants of its discretion to do so.

A Committee established by the Dáil, which reported in 1926, investigated in some detail the operation of the old age pension administration and adjudication (Committee on Old Age Pension, 1926). The Committee found that the operation of the Pensions Committees which were intended to be the pivot of the adjudication system was a 'serious defect' in the procedure. A 'very large number' of Committees were failing to carry out their duties properly due to apathy which led to irregular attendance and careless investigation of claims. This was contributed to by a feeling that the Pension Committees did not count, were merely figureheads and that whenever a conflict arose between the Pension Officer and the Committee, the Officer almost invariably appealed to the Department which almost invariably upheld his or her view. The Committee investigated the available statistics on claims, decisions and appeals which, while not supporting this view in full, did explain its source. In the year ended 31 March 1924, the Pension Officers recommended 5,633 pensions whereas the Committees awarded 18,570. Of these, the Pension Officers appealed 9,133 (i.e. 71 per cent of decisions not originally recommended by the Officer). There was agreement between the Pension Officer and the Pension Committee in 58 per cent of all claims made. In the same year, the Department of Local Government heard 9,348 appeals. It was estimated that about 97 per cent of these were from Pensions Officers. The Pension Officer's appeal was upheld in 85 per cent of cases. The figures for the following year showed a broadly similar picture with Pension Officer and Committee agreeing on 64 per cent of all claims; the Pension Officer appealing 62 per cent of non-recommended decisions and 73 per cent of Pension Officer appeals being upheld.[8]

The Committee was of the view that the divergence in views between Pension Officers and Committees was contributed to by the lack of attendance of Officers at meetings of the Committees, leading to a lack of any oral communication between the two and consequent misunderstandings. The majority recommended that Pension Officers be obliged to attend Committee meetings and that the 'secret instructions' given to the Officers by the Revenue Commissioners be made available to the Committees. The Committee was of the view that most emphasis should be placed on improving the workings of the Pension Committees and accordingly it did not support a proposal that a regional appeal system be introduced between the Committees and the Department. It recommended that the personnel on the Committees 'should be as representative as possible and include persons from the locality who have leisure to make the business of the committee a special interest, and persons who take an interest in social work'. It also recommended the introduction of an appeal to the High Court on a point of law from the decision of the Department on appeal.

There was, however, little government response to these recommendations and the system appears to have continued without significant changes. In 1947 the Department of Social Welfare took over the responsibility of investigating claims for pensions. The Pensions Committees remained in existence until 1984. These committees were much criticised for contributing to delays in the system (Curry, 1980, p. 253) and for giving unduly favourable decisions. In 1978, a system was introduced whereby a recommendation by a social welfare officer that a pension be paid could be put into effect immediately subject to subsequent confirmation by the Committee. In 1984, the Committees were entirely abolished and their powers transferred to the deciding officers of the Department of Social Welfare.

At that time there were 355 Committees and Sub-Committees. They still operated on a voluntary and part-time basis and sat once a month. Given these facts, it is hardly surprising that the Minister for Social Welfare complained that committees contributed to considerable delays in the application process. He also said that they

> bring the whole adjudication process into disrepute when they award pensions which are not payable or which are clearly higher than those payable under the Acts or Regulations. This is a frequent occurrence which necessitates appeals by social welfare officers against such decisions (348 *Dáil Debates* 2126 *et seq.*)

It appears that the decision to abolish the Committees was broadly welcomed (see, for example, 348 *Dáil Debates* 2150). It is interesting to note that, whereas in the early 1980s, over 4,000 appeals were being made annually in relation to old age and blind pension, this number had dropped to 2,500 by 1986 and to 1,000 by 1993.

External tribunals – unemployment assistance and benefit   On the establishment of the unemployment insurance scheme in 1911, the UK government decided to establish an entirely new administrative system. It appears that the system adopted was largely the work of a Broad of Trade official, Hubert Llewellyn Smith – the Board of Trade being the government body then responsible for unemployment issues (Fulbrook, 1978). It was decided to set up such a system in order to distance the Board of Trade from the day to day operation of the scheme, both from the point of view of the administrative workload involved and also to establish the 'independence' of the machinery. The option of an administrative system of appeal was preferred to appeal to the courts due to the unsatisfactory experience with the courts in relation to adjudication under the workmen's compensation scheme (ibid, p. 139–140).

Initial decisions were made by an Insurance Officer attached to each Labour Exchange. These officers were appointed by the Board of Trade but were legally independent in the performance of their adjudication duties. A claimant could appeal from a decision of the Insurance Officer to a Court of Referees (of which 30 were established in Ireland) consisting of one or more persons chosen to represent employers with an equal number chosen to represent workmen and a chairman appointed by the Board of Trade. The decision of the Court of Referees was binding unless the Insurance Officer appealed to the Umpire who was an independent official appointed by the Crown. Initially this system applied to questions of insurability, i.e. whether and to what extent workers came under the insurance scheme. However, this question was removed from the jurisdiction of the statutory authorities in 1920 and from then on decisions were to be made by the relevant Minister (after 1922 the Minister for Industry and Commerce), subject to an appeal to the High Court. The 1920 legislation also allowed an appeal to the Umpire of behalf of the claimant where this was requested by an association of employed persons of which s/he was a member. This system remained largely unchanged until 1952.

On the establishment of the means-tested unemployment assistance scheme, it was decided to apply the same adjudicative system to the assistance scheme. However, a separate appeal structure was set up in relation to appeals concerning the claimant's means. Initially appeal was to an Unemployment Appeals Committee established by the Minister for Industry and Commerce. This was intended to be 'on somewhat similar lines to the Old Age Pensions Committees' (49 *Dáil Debates* 1654). It was intended that the Committee could request a person to give oral evidence before it where necessary although, in such a case, no other person was allowed to be present except with the permission of the Committee; but it seems that, in contrast to the over three hundred Pensions Committees, only one part-time Unemployment Appeals Committee was established. Not surprisingly, this led to a huge backlog of appeals. Rather than establishing more Committees, the Unemployment Assistance (Amendment) Act 1935 provided that appeal was now to be, in the first instance, to Appeals Officers appointed by the Minister with a subsequent appeal, with the permission of the Appeals Officer, to the Unemployment Appeals Committee.

National health insurance   The administration of the national health insurance scheme was originally the responsibility of a large number of private insurance societies approved by the government-appointed Irish Insurance Commissioners. Initial adjudication on claims was carried out by the societies according to their own rules but subject to an appeal to the Commissioners. Entitlement to the range of medical benefits was generally dependent on medical certification by the claimant's own doctor subject, in some cases, to investigation by sickness visitors and to reexamination by medical referees on behalf of the society. This system led to many complaints, which have continued up to present times, as to overcertification by some doctors and the difficulty of controlling such certifications (Senate Select Committee, 1933; Hughes, 1982; 1988). The Commissioners were authorised to appoint Referees to hear appeals submitted to them. In the case of insurability questions, adjudication was by the Commissioners, subject to appeal on a point of law to the High Court. By 1933, there were 65 approved societies in Ireland with membership ranging from 55 to over 100,00. This led to much duplication of work and high administrative costs and in that year the societies were amalgamated into the National Health Insurance Society. The Society took over the role of the approved societies and the Insurance Commissioners in relation to adjudication and the Minister for Local Government and Public Health became the final authority in relation to appeals. The Minister was given the power to appoint persons to hear, but not decide, appeals. In practice, it appears that claimants could initially apply to have their case referred to an arbitrator who was independent of the Society and was normally a solicitor or barrister. Either party could appeal to the Minister if dissatisfied with the arbitrator's decision. The Minister could decide the case summarily or direct that an oral hearing be heard by an officer of his Department who would then report to the Minister (Department of Social Welfare, 1991).

Deciding officers and referees – Widow's and orphan's pensions and children's allowances The widow's and orphan's pensions established in 1935 provided for both contributory and non-contributory schemes but the same administrative mechanism applied to both. Initial decisions were made by deciding officers appointed by the Minister for Local Government and Public Health, subject to appeal to a Referee (a civil servant appointed by the Minister for Finance). This system was also adopted under the scheme of children's allowances set up in 1944. It was subsequently adopted as the model to apply to most social welfare payments on the amalgamation of the schemes in 1952. The detailed legal provisions concerning the practices of these Referees are almost identical in many cases to those governing the operation of the current Appeals Officers of the Social Welfare Appeals Office. These similarities apply, for example, in relation to the holding of oral hearings and representation at appeals. Unfortunately there is little, if any, material on the operation in practice of this system.

Workmen's compensation The workmen's compensation scheme was introduced in 1897. Unlike the other schemes described here, it was not a state funded scheme but simply involved statutory regulation of the obligations of employers to compensate workmen for accidents or diseases arising out of and in the course of employment. The intention was that disputes between employers and workmen as to compensation would be settled by agreement between the two parties. However, where this was not possible, the legislation initially provided that disputes were to be settled either by arbitration by a committee consisting of representatives of employers and workmen, by a single arbitrator or by a County Court judge sitting as arbitrator. The Courts of Justice Act 1924 transferred jurisdiction for hearing disputes to a judge of the Circuit Court and under the Workmen's Compensation Act 1934 exclusive jurisdiction was granted to the Circuit Court to adjudicate on claims for compensation. Reviews of cases were also to be decided by the court.

An appeal on a point of law lay initially to the Court of Appeal with a further appeal to the House of Lords, although very few such cases went from Ireland. The Courts of Justice Act 1924 transferred this right of appeal to two judges of the High Court with a further right of appeal to the Supreme Court. On the recommendation of a Departmental Committee on Workmen's Compensation, the right of appeal was transferred directly to the Supreme Court under the 1934 Act. This was intended to lead to quicker decisions and greater finality.

Where a dispute arose, either the employer or the workman could apply to the County Registrar to have the case referred to a Medical Referee. One Medical Referee was appointed for each county by the relevant Minister. The opinion of the Referee on any issue referred to him was binding on the court. In hearing a case, the Circuit Court judge could require a Medical Referee either to sit as an assessor or to report to the court and either party could require the judge to do so. However, the Commission on Workmen's Compensation (1962, p. 133) found that the medical referee system 'did not function' to a large extent with referees sitting in less than 10 cases per year on average in the period 1950–59.

Farley reports that in the 1960s there were about 800 cases heard by the Circuit Court annually in addition to 1,000 lump-sum agreements registered with the court out of around 13,500 cases of injury annually (1964, p. 12). A considerable number of cases went to the Supreme Court. Thus the workmen's compensation scheme generated significant litigation. The number of cases going before the courts can be compared with the position under the occupational injuries scheme introduced in 1966 whereby the state took over responsibility for the administration and operation of compensation of occupational accidents. In the early 1980s, there were 14,000 to 15,000 claims for occupational injuries benefits annually but these led to less than 400 appeals per year to the Appeals Officers of the Department of Social Welfare.

A unified adjudication system The Department of Social Welfare was established in 1947 to take over responsibility for the operation of the various social welfare schemes and five years later the Social Welfare Act 1952 amalgamated all the various legislation concerning social insurance payments. This provided for a unified adjudication system of deciding officers and appeals officers. This system was also applied to most social assistance payments. Only the old age pensions system, which retained the local Pension Committees until 1984 (although subject to appeal to an appeals officer), and the workmen's compensation scheme, until its abolition in 1967, retained separate adjudication systems.

The system adopted under the 1952 Act was modelled on the system of deciding officers and referees established for the widow's and orphan's pension scheme. Both the deciding officers and appeals officers were civil servants of the Department of Social Welfare appointed by the Minister. The external tribunals – the Court of Referees and the Umpire – were abolished. There appears to have been little opposition to this approach.

Almost all decisions, including decisions on insurability, came within the remit of the deciding officers. These were relatively junior officers of the Department of Social Welfare and generally had other duties in addition to their adjudication functions. Their role is modelled on that of the insurance officer under the National Insurance Act 1911 and is similar to that played by the adjudication officer under the UK system today. While in theory these officers are independent in the performance on their duties,[9] in practice there has always been a tension between their theoretical status as independent quasi-judicial officers and their relatively junior role within the Department combined with their administrative functions and the fact that the Department regularly issues guidelines for the instruction of these 'independent' officers (see Sainsbury, 1988).

The appeals officers were also officers of the Department of Social Welfare appointed by the Minister. They always operated on a full-time basis as appeals officers with no other functions. Appeals officers have no specific legal training and indeed no formal training in adjudication. A chief appeals officer was appointed who was responsible for overseeing the operation of the appeals system and for reviewing individual appeals decision in the event of an error of fact or of law. However, in practice this was interpreted as analogous to a judicial review process and decisions were only revised when clearly wrong in law or one to which no reasonable appeals officer would have come.

The procedures in relation to appeals were similar to those provided for under the widow's and orphan's pensions scheme. The regulations provided that appeals could be held either by way of oral or summary hearings. The procedure at appeals was quite informal and at the discretion of the appeals officer. In the case of *Kiely v. Minister for Social Welfare* [1977] IR 267, the Supreme Court held that an oral hearing was mandatory unless a decision could fairly be arrived at on the basis of the written submissions. However, in practice, oral hearings tended to be held in specific classes of case, e.g. unemployment assistance and benefit cases (other than decisions on the means test), cases concerning incapacity and disablement.

Although the appeals officers were quasi-judicial officers and were required to be independent in the performance of their functions, appeals were made to the Minister for Social Welfare and, in practice, the administration of appeals was dealt with by the section of the Department being appealed against, i.e. an appeal concerning an old age pension would be submitted to the old age pension section and all correspondence concerning the appeal would be issued from that section. The only direct contact a person would have with an appeals officer would normally be at an oral hearing, if one was held. This undoubtedly led to a perception amongst claimants that appeals officers were merely part of the Departmental system and cast doubts on their perceived independence.

The 1952 Act provided that the Minister could appoint assessors to sit with an appeals officer in any case where this appeared to be of assistance. In practice assessors were appointed in cases where external persons had been involved prior to the unification of the appeals systems, i.e. in relation to unemployment assistance and unemployment benefit appeals. Panels of assessors were appointed consisting of persons nominated by employer organisations and trade unions and one person from each panel was asked to sit with the appeals officer in relation to such appeals. Members of the Court of Referees were appointed initially as assessors (O'Sullivan, 1954). In addition, when the appeals system assumed responsibility for the occupational injuries scheme (which replaced the workmen's compensation system in 1967), a medical assessor was appointed to assist the appeals officer in such appeals where, in some such cases, a medical referee had assisted the Circuit Court judge under the old system.

Decisions of appeals officers were subject to appeal on a point of law to the High Court. However, this was stated to be subject to the exclusion of every question in relation to claims for benefit and it appears that the intention was to allow a quite limited right of appeal in relation to insurability questions only. However, in *Kingham v. Minister for Social Welfare*[10] Lynch J held that 'one must construe the exclusion narrowly so as not to oust the jurisdiction of the High Court save where such ouster is clear.' Appeals decision are in any case subject to judicial review and, in recent years, this has been the more popular channel for challenging decisions (although the number of cases which have ever reached the High Court has been very low). The chief appeals officer had the power to request the Minister for Social Welfare to refer any question to the High Court but there is no reported instance of this power ever having been exercised.

The operation of the new adjudication system came indirectly for review in the context of the report of the Commission on Workmen's Compensation (1962), a body appointed to review the operation of the existing workmen's compensation scheme and to make recommendations for reform of the system. A majority of the Commission recommended a continuation of the existing system with reforms. One member of the Commission, Garret Fitzgerald, agreeing with the majority report, referred to adjudication by the courts as one of the three most desirable features of the existing system (ibid, p. 192). However, the minority report, including representatives of trade unions, stated that 'adjudication by the courts has long been regarded by workers' representatives as one of the most undesirable features of the existing system', referring to the risk of substantial legal costs and expenses for the individual worker (p. 215). The minority were of the opinion that the system of adjudication by deciding officers and appeals officers was 'flexible and impersonal and has worked to the complete satisfaction of the insured population since it was introduced' (p. 203).

However, by the 1970s and 1980s, a degree of dissatisfaction with the existing appeals structure was becoming apparent. This was probably not unrelated to the sharp increase in the numbers of appeals heard over the 1980s as the numbers of social welfare claimants rose. The numbers of appeals increased from around 13,500 in the early 1980s to over 19,000 by 1984. Detailed criticisms of the existing system were outlined by the Coolock Community Law Centre (1980) and others (Clarke, 1978; Whyte and Cousins, 1989). A private members bill calling for the introduction of a Social Welfare Tribunal with jurisdiction to hear appeals both in relation to the general social welfare system, supplementary welfare allowance and other health payments was introduced by Senator Brendan Ryan in 1986. Complaints about the existing system also featured in submissions to the Commission on Social Welfare. The Commission in its Report (1986, p. 186) found that there was

> a perception that the appeals system is not independent of the working of the Department of Social Welfare although the proportion of appeals upheld would indicate that decisions are made on an impartial basis.

The Commission recommended that more information be provided to claimants on the right to appeals and on the grounds on which an unfavourable decision had been given; that an Appeals Office be established as a separate executive office with an independent Chairman who would produce an annual report; that appellants be given the right to an oral hearing and representation at hearings while keeping appeals simple, speedy and informal.

The Irish Congress of Trade Unions (ICTU) had also developed a concern about the operation of the appeal system. In July 1979, following consideration of the *Kiely* decision, the Executive Council of ICTU wrote to the Minister expressing its concern about 'the serious defects in the Social Welfare Appeals Machinery'.[11] ICTU proposed that an Appeals Tribunal similar to the Employment Appeals Tribunal be established to replace the existing system. In 1981, ICTU undertook an examination of the existing system which 'showed up major defects' and called into question 'the fairness and impartiality of the present appeal system'. Arising from the dissatisfaction of the trade unions with this system, a special Social Welfare Tribunal involving representative of employers and trade unions with an independent chair was established in 1982 to hear appeals in relation to disqualification for unemployment assistance or benefit due to participation in a trade dispute. However, this Tribunal did not replace the existing mechanism and simply added an additional layer of appeal in one specific set of circumstances. ICTU also raised the issue of social welfare appeals in the context of negotiating the Programme for National Recovery (an agreement between the government and social partners) and secured a commitment to examine what changes (if any) were required in the social welfare appeals system with particular regard to ensuring that the system was perceived to be fair (Ireland, 1987).

Social Welfare Appeals Office (1990)   Following from the various criticisms outlined above, the Minister for Social Welfare announced a reform of the appeal system in the Social Welfare Act 1990. The changes were essentially a reform of the existing system rather than a radically new approach and were aimed at emphasising the independence of the appeals officers. A Social Welfare Appeals Office (SWAO) was established as an independent executive office with its own separate premises and staff. Appeals are now made to the chief appeals officer rather than to the Minister and communication concerning the appeal is dealt with directly by the SWAO. The chief appeals officer now appoints the assessors and is responsible for producing an annual report. The chief appeals officer also has the power to refer a question to the High Court on a point of law (previously this could only be done with the permission of the Minister). There is a greater emphasis on the provision of information and reasons are to be given for all unsuccessful decisions. However, the personnel of the appeals office remained the same and there was no change in relation to the holding of oral hearings (see generally Cousins, 1992c; Chief Appeals Officer, 1992; 1993).

The chief appeals officer in his first annual report highlighted the importance of high quality decision making at the initial level and the Department of Social Welfare has recently established a Decisions Advisory Office to help improve the standards of decision making.

FROM THE POOR LAW TO SUPPLEMENTARY WELFARE ALLOWANCE

Out-door relief (1847)   The first structured state welfare payments were introduced under the Irish Poor Relief Extension Act 1847. This was a response to the Great Famine and allowed the Poor Law Guardians (established in 1838 to operate the newly established Poor Law system) to pay outdoor relief as the numbers of people in need greatly exceeded their capacity to provide indoor relief in Workhouses as had originally been intended.

The Poor Law system was centrally controlled by the Irish Poor Law Commissioners (from 1872, this function was taken over by the Local Government Board). However, it was administered at a local level by Poor Law Unions, of which there were originally 130, based around the main market towns. These were governed by Boards of Guardians. The membership of the Board of Guardians consisted partially of members elected by the ratepayers and partially of ex-officio members, the local Justices of the Peace. The number of members varied from one Board to another. Initial claims for outdoor relief were made to relieving officers employed by the Unions but the Boards themselves had to authorise all payments (other than in cases of sudden urgent necessity). The relieving officer investigated the circumstances of each claim and brought them before the next weekly meeting of the Board. That this function was not simply nominal or one which could be delegated to the Officer is shown by the case of *R (O'Mahony) v. Ellis* [1898] 2 IR 57. In this case members of the Board of Guardians of the Fermoy Poor Law Union were surcharged by the Poor Law auditor because of their practice of only approving the first weekly payment of relief and of then simply retrospectively sanctioning payments already made by the relieving officer on a weekly basis. The High Court held that the Guardians were obliged in each case to grant authority before payments were made. Retrospective sanction of relief already given was not allowed. Both the auditor and the Court appeared to be impressed by the fact that the practice of the Fermoy Union (which had apparently been in existence for over 20 years) had led to much higher payments of relief than neighbouring Unions.

The 1896 Women's Poor Law Guardian Act allowed women to vote in Poor Law election and to sit as Poor Law Guardians. The Local Government Act, 1898 reformed the system of local government in Ireland providing for the establishment of county councils and borough corporations, urban and rural district councils on a national basis. This Act changed the composition of the Boards. The position of ex-officio guardian was abolished. In rural areas, the members of the newly formed county councils became the Guardians and in urban areas the Guardians were elected in the same way as rural councillors. However, while the 1898 Act did increase the level of democratic control over the Board of Guardians, it did not otherwise lead to significant changes in the adjudication system.

Home assistance (1923) The period both leading up to and after the achievement of independence from the UK in 1922 led to considerable changes in the much hated Poor Law system (although these were arguably more of form than of substance) (Commission on the Relief of the Sick and Destitute, 1927, p. 10). The period of the War of Independence and the subsequent Civil War was one of major chaos in the operation of the Poor Law system. During the

War of Independence, many local authorities transferred their allegiance from the Local Government Board to the Department of Local Government established by the first Dáil (Barrington, 1987). In the years 1920 to 1922, many counties established their own local relief schemes. After the end of the Civil War, the Local Government (Temporary Provisions) Act 1923 gave legal authority for these schemes and authorised local schemes in counties which had not already established any. Many workhouses were closed and the remainder renamed 'County Homes'. The emphasis of the scheme shifted from that of providing indoor relief to providing outdoor relief (now renamed 'home assistance'). A major change in the administration took place with the Boards of Guardians being abolished and their duties transferred to an authority appointed by the county or borough council from amongst their own members.[12] These were generally known as the County Boards of Health and Public Assistance. The overall supervision of these Boards became the responsibility of the Minister for Local Government and Public Health. The Commission on the Relief of the Sick and Destitute including the Insane Poor (1927) found that 'the Boards of Health are as much, if not more, under the rigid control of the Minister for Local Government and Public Health as the Boards of Guardians were under the control of the Local Government Board, and that, therefore, very little initiative or freedom of action rests in the Boards of Health'.

The new Boards consisted of 10 to 30 members (meeting monthly or more often if required) whereas, as the Commission pointed out, previously there were between 150 and 400 Guardians per county (meeting weekly) so that the reform had the effect of reducing drastically the number of elected representatives involved in the administration of Poor Relief. The County Schemes provided for a wide variety of different arrangements for deciding on applications for home assistance. Many of the Schemes abolished the position of relieving officer and were forced to legislate for alternative procedures. Decisions were generally to be made by the Board or a subcommittee of the Board often on the recommendation of a local subcommittee. Initial applications often had to be recommended by an authorised person or persons – for example, a local councillor (Laois, Longford), a member of the relevant subcommittee (Cavan), three 'recognised' persons (clergy, doctor, councillor or brehon) (Clare), or a parish committee consisting of the parish priest and three parish judges or in parishes with a conference of the St. Vincent de Paul the conference might be appointed as the committee (Galway). However the County Board of Health (Assistance) Order 1924 (promulgated by the Minister for Local Government) provided for the appointment of a superintendent assistance officer and various assistance officers. It was their duty to receive and investigate applications for assistance which the superintendent then submitted to the Board for its decision. These officers basically performed the roles previously filled by the relieving officers and continued to be known as relieving officers by claimants in many cases. It would seem likely that they largely replaced the various arrangements set out in the County Schemes although these schemes, renewed on an annual basis, remained in force until 1942.

The Commission on the Relief of the Sick and Destitute had been of the opinion that the 1847 Act placed the Boards under 'a statutory obligation to afford due relief' (1926, p. 4). However, the effect of a Supreme Court decision in the 1930s was to make any such obligation almost unenforceable in practice. In *O'Connor v. Dwyer* [1932] IR 466, several applicants for home assistance applied for declarations that they were legally entitled to relief and a declaration as to the amount due. In the High Court, Meredith J was satisfied that the apparently mandatory language of section 1 of the 1847 Act, which provided that the Guardians 'shall make provision for the due relief' of various classes of destitute poor persons while providing for a discretionary power to assist poor persons not falling within the listed categories, meant that persons who could show that they were disabled by infirmity were in law entitled to due relief. He refused a declaration as to the amount of relief to which the individuals were due but this appeared to be on the basis that he considered the defendants (who were Commissioners appointed by the Minister to replace the Dublin Board of Guardians which had been dissolved in 1923) would grant appropriate relief once their legal obligations were made clear. The defendants appealed to the Supreme Court. Kennedy CJ agreed with the decision of the High Court and in fact said that he would have seriously considered granting a declaration as to the amount of relief due. However, Murnaghan J (with whom Fitzgibbon J agreed) held that as, under the relevant statute and regulation, no relief could be granted unless it had been passed by a resolution of the Board of Guardians, the Court was not entitled to reverse a decision *bona fide* arrived at as to a right to relief or the amount to be granted. The decision would basically allow judicial review of a decision only in cases of *male fides*, a conclusion which to all practical purposes meant that the Boards were not subject to review by the courts. Although the Court expressed no view as to whether or not a legal right to assistance existed, the consequences of its decision meant that in practice any such 'right' was subject an almost unreviewable decision by the Board and was, in effect, discretionary.

Consolidation of public assistance (1939)   In 1939, the various poor relief acts were consolidated into the Public Assistance Act 1939. This Act abolished the existing County Schemes and the Boards of Public Health. The country was divided into public assistance authorities (generally on a county basis as before) and the relevant local authority took on the role of the Board of Assistance. In Dublin, specific Boards of Assistance were appointed including members elected from the local authorities. The Act did not come into force until 1942, by which time a major change had been effected in the management of Irish local government by the passage of the County Management Act 1940. This Act, which applied to the Boards of Assistance, divided the functions of local authorities into *reserved* functions which could only be exercised by the elected members of the authority and *executive* functions which were to be exercised solely by the county manager provided for under the 1940 Act. None of the reserved functions related to decision making in relation to home assistance and, as elected members were specifically forbidden to exercise executive functions, this meant that the county manager now became the final deciding authority in relation to home assistance. The Public Assistance (General Regulations) Order 1942 replaced the 1924 Home Assistance Regulations. These Regulations again provided for assistance and superintendent assistance officers to 'receive, examine and investigate' all applications. Again the superintendent was to submit the application to public assistance authority for decision but whereas, under the 1924 Regulations, such decision was to be authenticated by the Chairman of the Board, the 1942 Regulations reflected the changing power structure by requiring authentication by the *manager*.

Thus in a period of just over 40 years, we have seen a fundamental shift from a position where the members of the Boards of Guardians could be surcharged for not personally authorising each individual application for out-door relief in 1898 to a position following the coming into effect of the County Management Act 1940 whereby elected members of the Board of Assistance were not allowed to have any part in the decision making process in relation to individual claims for home assistance.

The operation of the Boards of Assistance remained subject to the direction and control of the Minister for Local Government and Public Health (from 1947 the Minister for Social Welfare), thus continuing the tradition of strict hierarchical control inherited from the Poor Law Commissioners. Barrington (1975) points out that the setting up of the Boards of Guardians was

> an extensive exercise in democracy for that period, and was, not unreasonably in the circumstances, accompanied by an extraordinarily tight central control over the activities of the Poor Law guardians . . .

While, as he points out, other branches of local government experienced much greater independence, after Independence 'it was the model of the Poor Law branch that was applied to the whole of the local government system' leading to 'a most remarkable degree of central control over local government, perhaps the tightest that exists anywhere in the democratic world'.

In terms of the right to assistance, the 1939 Act did not alter the position from that pertaining under the 1847 legislation. Section 18(1) provided that a poor person who was unable by his own industry or other lawful means to provide the necessities of life 'shall be eligible for home assistance'. Thus no statutory entitlement to assistance was conferred on an individual claimant.

By the time of Ó Cinnéide's study of home assistance in 1968, it is clear that there had been little change in the administrative and adjudicative arrangements surrounding the scheme. However, in practice Ó Cinnéide reports that the superintendent assistance officer 'usually acts for the manager of the authority in making the final decision on the application' (1970, p. 6).

Supplementary welfare allowance (1975) The passing of the Social Welfare (Supplementary Welfare Allowance) Act 1975 (which came into effect in 1977) was hailed as a major reform in the area of social assistance and the final abolition of the last remnants of the Poor Law. The Act provided for the first time that there was to be a legal right to assistance. However, in practice this 'right' remained difficult to enforce in many cases (Independent Poverty Action Movement, 1986; Focus Point, 1988; Combat Poverty Agency, 1991). The administrative arrangements for the new scheme were largely carried over from the old scheme. The eight regional health boards (established in 1971) took over responsibility for the operation of the service, again subject to the overall control of the Minister for Social Welfare. In practice, the elected members of the health boards had little, if any, input into supplementary welfare allowance (SWA) administration and no role in adjudication which remained the function of the board's staff. The assistance officers and superintendent assistance officers were replaced by community welfare officers (CWOs) and superintendent community welfare officers (SCWOs). While the original intention was that such officers should have a much wider role than simply providing financial support, in practice due to the pressures on the scheme and the lack of any serious commitment to providing an alternative approach, the officers' main role was in receiving and investigating claims for SWA. However, in recent years the 'community welfare' aspect of the SWA system has received greater emphasis. Decisions in relation to claims for SWA are made by the superintendent community welfare officers, although in practice it would appear that many routine decisions are made by the CWOs and retrospectively sanctioned by the superintendent community welfare officers. In some cases, approval of the Department of Social Welfare in required before payments over a certain amount can be made (although this currently affects very few decisions).

The 1975 Act provided another innovation in introducing a right of appeal from a decision concerning entitlement to SWA. However, rather than integrating the appeal system into the general social welfare system, the Act provided that appeal would lie to a person appointed by the Minister in each health board area. An amendment requiring that this person not be a staff member of the health board was rejected by the then Minister and, while external persons can be appointed to the position, at present all 8 appeals officers are health board officials. In fact, the Minister has generally appointed the Programme Manager for Community Care as the appeals officer, i.e. the person responsible for the overall supervision of the community welfare service and the immediate superior of the CWOs and SCWOs. In only two health boards have separate appeals officers been appointed and both of these have other health board duties. Recent research by the Free Legal Advice Centre indicates the informal nature of the appeal system with a very low level of successful appeals, no set procedures as to how appeals are to be decided, a lack of fair procedures and of information to appellants, a lack of oral hearings and an unwillingness on the part of appeals officers to challenge directives issued by the Minister (Cousins, 1992c, Charleton, 1993). The Ombudsman has also expressed his 'serious concerns as to the fairness and adequacy' of the existing system (1994, p. 64).

The Minister for Social Welfare has recently announced various reforms of the appeal system including the provision of more information, standardised procedures in all health board areas and greater independence on the part of the appeals officers. In a significant move, he has also stated that the role of the Social Welfare Appeals Office will be expanded to act as a 'court of last appeal'.[13] It may be that this signals a move towards the incorporation of the SWA system into the mainstream social welfare appeal system.

The legal right to SWA proved difficult to enforce in practice given the tradition of discretionary entitlements under the home assistance scheme and the lack of any effective enforcement mechanism. While it was clear that there was a basic right to SWA, the position in relation to weekly additions to cover the cost of rent, heating, diet, etc., proved less clear. The Supreme Court in *State (McLoughlin) v. Eastern Health Board* [1986] IR 416 held that there was legal right to such payments. However, the Minister for Social Welfare and the health boards have basically ignored this decision and continued to pay weekly payments on a discretionary basis. The Social Welfare Act 1992 provided for a legislative reversal of this court decision, although this has yet to come into effect at the time of writing.

AN ANALYSIS OF THE MAIN TRENDS

In summary, we can see three main trends in the development of adjudication systems since 1847. The first is the bureaucratisation of decision making which now rests entirely in the hands of internal appeals officers. The democratic bodies which were strongly involved in decision making at an early stage – such as the Boards of Guardians and the local Pension Committees – have been replaced by bureaucratic structures. The change is exemplified by the contrast between the situation in 1898 when Poor Law Guardians were surcharged if they did not personally authorise all individual payments and the situation after the passing of the County Management Act 1940 when members of the successor body to the Guardians were prohibited from any direct involvement in decisions on individual cases. We have also seen how the participatory method of decision making under the County Schemes was quickly replaced by a bureaucratic system of investigation by assistance officers. Of course, bodies such as the Boards of Guardians were elected from a very restricted electorate (for example, in the 1880s the Guardians were elected by an electorate of half a million people out of a total population of 3.9 million). However, as the electorate grew, rather than expanding the public sphere to include the newly enfranchised classes, political power was withdrawn and remade in a bureaucratic form (Habermas, 1989). This tendency in relation to social welfare adjudication must of course be seen in the context of the general centralisation and bureaucratisation of almost all social services in Ireland leaving Ireland with one of the weakest systems of local government in Europe and a very low level of citizen involvement in any type of government activity (Barrington, 1975; McNamara, 1992).

The second tendency is the reliance on internal rather than external adjudication bodies. Thus appeal to the courts (workmen's compensation) or to tribunals (unemployment assistance and benefit) has been abolished. A position whereby the main social welfare appeals system is entirely internal, with only a tiny minority of appellants having access to the courts, would appear to be unique in Europe and in most common law countries as well. While there has not been a general reluctance in Irish society to entrust adjudication to court or tribunal structures, there has been a noticeable reluctance to provide for appeals from decisions within the civil service to external bodies. Where such bodies have been established, they have tended to be in areas such as taxation or payments to doctors under the General Medical Service rather than in the areas of welfare entitlements. On the other hand, in comparative terms within the Irish context the social welfare appeals system is perhaps the best developed of all such systems of internal adjudication. This is, for example, an almost total lack of any formal appeal structures in relation to payments and services provided by the Department of Health.

Finally, one can see a tendency towards an increased emphasis on entitlements (or rights) and a consequent pressure to improve the mechanisms for enforcing those rights. This echoes a general increase in rights consciousness in advanced capitalist societies. In the Irish context, the obvious example is the fact that the supplementary welfare allowance scheme established a right to assistance in contrast to the preexisting legislation. This led to the consequent establishment of a right of appeal in relation to decisions under the SWA scheme. In the area of the general social welfare payments, this tendency can be seen in the recent reforms of the adjudication system leading to the establishment of the Social Welfare Appeals Office and the Decisions Advisory Office. However, the reforms concentrated on improving the transparency of the operation of the system rather than resorting to an external tribunal to display fairness. The tendency towards 'rights' has been quite weak. While a right to SWA has been established, we have seen that it has been difficult to enforce in practice and the appeals mechanism remains largely ineffective.

Thus the two initial tendencies – concentrating power within the bureaucracy and removing it from democratically elected bodies and from external bodies such as the courts – have been dominant. There has been little effective opposition to the de-democratisation of social welfare adjudication (or indeed of social welfare policy making). The increased emphasis on rights has been managed by reforms of the bureaucracy rather than the adoption of different structures.

The development of social welfare bureaucracy in Ireland supports Max Weber's (1968, p. 70 *et seq.*) view of bureaucracy as an irresistible tendency in modern society: 'Bureaucracy inevitably accompanies *mass democracy* in contrast to the democratic self-government of small homogeneous units'. Weber sees bureaucracy as '*the* means of carrying "community action" over into rationally ordered 'social action'. Therefore bureaucracy is 'a power instrument of the first order and 'amongst the social structures which are hardest to destroy'.

CHAPTER TEN

The Recovery of Social Welfare Overpayments

This chapter considers the operation of one particular aspect of the adminis-tration of Irish social welfare system – that concerning the recovery of overpaid welfare payments. It shows that, prior to 1993, the official practices in relation to recover of overpaid benefits did not coincide with the legal rules in this area, i.e. overpayments were assessed against claimants and repayment of money was sought in cases where, according to the legal rules, there was no legal obligation on the claimant to repay the benefit (and conversely where the authorities had no legal power to demand a repayment). The chapter goes on to consider the implications of this practice in two areas. First, it considers why such a divergence between the legal rules and the official practice can arise in the area of social welfare administration. Secondly, it considers the meaning of 'the law' from a sociological point of view in the light of this case study.

One *caveat* should be entered at this point in that the area of overpayments of social welfare provides only a limited empirical base on which to answer such general questions. Thus this chapter should be seen as a line of argument which would require further (and broader) research in order to lead to more definite conclusions.

THE LEGAL RULES PRIOR TO 1993

As we have seen Irish social welfare payments can be divided into two main categories: social insurance payments (based on contributions previously paid) and social assistance (or means tested) payments. Largely for historical reasons, different rules have applied to the two categories of payments in several areas. One of these is the area of recovery of overpaid welfare. The legal position concerning recovery of overpaid social assistance payments has been extremely unclear and, for that reason, will not be considered further. However, the position in relation to social insurance payments was, prior to 1993, relatively straightforward.[1] Here payments were only repayable in cases of fraud – in the words of the legislation where the overpayment has arisen due to

> any statement or representation (whether written or oral) which was to the knowledge of the person making it false or misleading in a material respect or by reason of the wilful concealment of any material fact.[2]

Thus where an overpayment arose through administrative error or other mistake on the part of the Department of Social Welfare and where there was no question of fraud on the part of the claimant, there was no obligation on the claimant to repay the monies received. This also applied in a case where a claimant might have made a genuine mistake in reporting his or her circumstances to the Department of Social Welfare – again there was no obligation to repay the excess amount received. This interpretation of the legal rules had been confirmed in at least one High Court case (*State (Houlihan) v. Minister for Social Welfare*, High Court, 23 July 1986).

THE OFFICIAL PRACTICE[3]

There are two sources of information in relation to the official practice in this area. The first is from the experience of advice organisations which represent claimants who have had overpayments assessed against them. The second is from a range of government publications.

The experience in practice[4] showed a very varied official response which depended very much on the particular section of the Department of Social Welfare which was dealing with the overpayment.[5] For example, following the High Court case referred to above, the particular section of the Department involved in that case began to issue pre-assessment letters to claimants suspected of fraud outlining briefly the allegations against the claimant and allowing the claimant to comment to the Department on these allegations prior to any decision to assess an overpayment. Other sections of the Department, however, continued to assess overpayments without any pre-assessment hearing and often without any reference to an allegation of fraud. It might have appeared that these sections were not aware of their legal responsibilities but it emerges from a range of official publications that it is their administrative and political masters who were responsible for this practice.

Information on the recovery of overpayments can be obtained from the reports of the Comptroller and Auditor General, from the reports of the Committee on Public Accounts and from responses by the Minister for Social Welfare to Dáil questions. The official practice is perhaps best summarised in two quotes: one from the then and current Minister for Social Welfare, Dr Michael Woods, and one from the Accounting Officer of the Department of Social Welfare. In response to a Dáil question as to whether claimants were liable to repay overpayments arising through Departmental error or because of ignorance of social welfare entitlements, Dr Woods said

> It has always been the practice in my Department to seek recovery of all overpayments of social assistance and social insurance . . . [W]here an overpayment arises through no fault of a social welfare recipient, a very sympathetic attitude is taken towards recovery of the amounts overpaid and all the circumstances of the case are taken into account. Such recoveries are made with the agreement of the recipient and every effort

is made to ensure that hardship is not caused. (*Dáil Debates* 5 June
1991 814–5)

As can be seen, there is no suggestion that non-fraudulent overpayments were
not liable to recovery at all.

The position was echoed by the Accounting Officer of the Department in
his report to the Committee on Public Accounts (1989).[6]

> The Accounting Officer explained that any overpayment, whatever the
> cause, is legally the property of the State and the Department of Social
> Welfare is legally obliged to recover this money.

Both these comments were incorrect statements of the legal position. Yet
there is no indication that either the Dáil or the Committee on Public Accounts
challenged either statement. Indeed, the Committee of Public Account's noted
'the Accounting Officer's assurances that the Department takes a sympathetic
view where these repayments would result in genuine cases of hardship'.

The Comptroller and Auditor General has given considerable attention to
the question of overpayments in recent reports (see for example, 1988, 1989,
1990 and 1991). Each report lists the overpayments recorded for recovery and
the recent reports give a very detailed breakdown of the reasons for the overpayments. The reports make clear that cases of fraud are only a proportion of
the total overpayments recorded for recovery. In the case of social insurance
payments, the reports from 1988 to 1991 show that of the total amount of
social insurance payments 'recorded for recovery' the Department attributed
between 47 per cent and 50 per cent 'to fraud or suspected fraud by claimants'.
In legal terms this means that at least 50 per cent (and almost certainly more)
of social insurance payments recorded for recovery in those years *were not
legally* recoverable under the provisions of the Social Welfare Acts. The
Comptroller makes no reference to the divergence between the official practice
on overpayments and the applicable legislation.

The Committee on Public Accounts in turn reviews the Comptroller's
reports. Again the divergence between the official practice and the legislation
does not appear to have been raised by the Committee. Rather the Committee
noted its concern that 'not enough is being done to prosecute persons who
commit social welfare fraud' (Committee on Public Accounts, 1989).

Thus it is clear that the Minister for Social Welfare and the Department
were operating an official practice in relation to the recovery of overpayments
which was not the same as the legal rules contained in the Social Welfare
Acts. This practice had been noted by the Comptroller and Auditor General,
the Committee on Public Accounts and the Dáil but, although the legal rules
had been interpreted by the High Court, none of these institutions have queried
the difference between the official practice and the relevant legislation.

THE BASIS OF THE OFFICIAL PRACTICE

The question arises as to how and why such a divergence arose between the legal rules which the state was supposed to follow and the rules which it applied in practice.[7] Indeed this is just one of a number of examples of situations where the practice of the Department of Social Welfare diverges from the legal rules set out in the Social Welfare Acts (Whyte and Cousins, 1993). While this divergence often operates to the disadvantage of claimants, in several instances, the Department's practice is more favourable to claimants than the legislation allows.[8] This suggest that there are important influences affecting the Department's operation other than the social welfare legislation.

One explanation of this dichotomy might be based on Mishra's (1977, p. 70) outline of a Marxist view of the role of the welfare system in capitalist society as involving 'system integration or the integration of functions and institutions', i.e. the measures necessary for the continuation, stability and efficient working of the economic system, and 'social integration and social control or the integration of social classes and groups and the maintenance of order'.

Within these broad objectives there are (largely unwritten) objectives for specific welfare programmes. For example, Pennings (1990) in a study of unemployment schemes in four Western European countries shows that the schemes are based on two main principles: subsidiarity (i.e. that the state will only intervene to provide financial support as a last resort) and reintegration (i.e. that unemployment schemes should assist in returning people to paid work). These principles are not legally enforceable rules and must be implemented in practice – both through legislation *and* administrative practices. Similarly, specific objectives exist in other programme areas. For example, a detailed transnational study of disability programmes found that the legal rules as to the definitions of disability were, in practice, overruled by the 'the overall policy that drives the program' (Berkowitz et al., 1987). Thus the detailed theoretical rules as to the assessment of disability in the Netherlands were disregarded in many cases as they were in conflict with the one of the (then) underlying policies of the disability scheme which was to allow people to retire early from the labour force.

An alternative explanation could be that the distinction between the legal rules and the official practice arises from administrative/institutional complexities. Thus the official practice would illustrate the complexities of the policy system with different and perhaps countervailing influences at work at the various levels in the policy system (i.e. policy formulation, legal content, implementation). Indeed this is not inconsistent with a Marxist view of the state operating with relative autonomy to mediate the views of different classes (and different groups within classes) (Poulantzas, 1968; 1974). Either account would however recognise that the role played by the Department of Social Welfare is not simply that of implementing the legal rules but that the implementation itself is affected by political and ideological factors whereby various interest groups (or the dominant interest group) attempt to have their policy objectives implemented.

Thus, while the role of the Department of Social Welfare is, legally, to administer the social welfare system as provided for in the Social Welfare Acts, these Acts themselves are only the formal (and more or less accurate) expression of an underlying, and generally unwritten, range of objectives. The implementation of these objectives rather than the implementation of the legislation (which is only a, frequently imperfect, reflection of the objectives) is arguably the real role of the Department. Generally speaking, there will be a close correspondence between these underlying requirements and the legislation but where there is a divergence between the two, the logic of the operation of the Department will push it to follow the unwritten objectives rather than the legal rules. This is not simply to suggest that there are underlying objectives which *compel* the administration to operate in a certain way despite the legal rules. In practice, of course, a range of social, cultural, ideological and political issues will come into play both in the construction of the system needs, the manner in which they impact on the administrators, and so on.

The role of the Department in administering the social welfare system suggests an analogy with the findings of several studies in relation to the role of the police. Cotterrell (1992, p. 273) summarises these studies as showing 'that, strictly speaking and contrary to general belief, police objectives are not primarily those of law enforcement'. Rather the role of the police is to maintain social order. 'Enforcement of law constitutes a means to the end of order maintenance, rather than an end in itself' (ibid). Again we see the role of a state institution being influenced by the system needs of capitalist society in a way which diverges from the strictly legal role which that institution is supposed to play.

THE CASE OF OVERPAID CLAIMANTS

In the case discussed in this chapter, it is not surprising that overpaid social welfare claimants should be the subjects of unfavourable treatment by the state authorities. Politicians, the media and others who influence the public perception of social groups frequently emphasise 'fraudulent' aspects of welfare claims. For example, the 1991 Report of the Comptroller and Auditor General was reported in the Irish Independent of 10 October 1992 under the headline 'WELFARE SPONGERS CHEATED TAXPAYERS OUT OF £6.8M'. Thus those who receive overpayments of welfare (whether fraudulent or not) are unlikely to be seen in a favourable light. Indeed, unfavourable treatment for such welfare claimants is not unique to Ireland. Lipsky (1991, p. 220) reports that in the US

> The Reagan administration sought to have [social security staff] recover monies from clients who were alleged to have been overpaid without interviewing the clients and without informing them of their right to request a waiver of overpayment recovery.

In the related area of criminal prosecutions for social welfare fraud, Cook (1991) has shown how, in the UK, although tax evasion is on a much larger scale than social security fraud, far more resources are directed towards investigating social security fraud than tax evasion, the enforcement strategies are stricter and the penalties are greater. Cook suggest that these differences are explained by the historical and ideologically more favourable construction of tax payers (as 'givers' to the state and economic successes) as opposed to social security claimants ('takers' from the state, economic failures). It is interesting to note that the European Value Systems Study shows that, on average, Europeans show 'modest' disproval of both tax and social welfare fraud (although the level of disproval of social welfare fraud is higher). In contrast, Irish people show 'high' disproval of social welfare fraud and only 'low' disproval of tax fraud (Fogarty et al. 1984).

An interpretation of the role of the Department of Social Welfare, whereby it is seen as being influenced by the general negative view of welfare claimants, must also take into account the extent to which the Department itself acts as an important body in propagating the prevailing ideological outlook (Althusser, 1976). Thus in reflecting the negative image of overpaid welfare claimants, it reinforces the ideological portrayal of this group of people.

WHAT IS THE LAW?

This case study also raises the question as to the definition of 'the law'? From a legal positivist point of view 'law consists of data – primarily rules – which can be recognised by relatively simple tests or "rules of recognition"' (Cotterrell, 1992, p. 9). The principle test is that the rules have gone through the formal stages of a legislative procedure, i.e. have been properly passed by Parliament or by a subordinate authority. Thus for example one reads that

> Social Welfare Law is a twentieth-century phenomenon and as such is almost exclusively derived from Acts of the Oireachtas and delegated legislation. (Whyte et al., 1994, p. 1)

On this understanding, the law on overpayment of social welfare consists solely of the legal rules outlined previously and the official practice would be considered to have been in breach of the law.

Others however have put forward a much broader view of the law. Ehrlich (1922) for example, sees the law as involving not just the norms created and applied by the state but also including what he calls 'social order', i.e. the rules which are actually followed in social life – the real 'living law'. Cotterrell (1992, p. 43), for the purposes of his study of the sociology of the law, steers a path between these two approaches and refers to law as

> the social rules and related doctrine created, adopted, interpreted and enforced by state agencies as a framework of general regulation within a politically organised society.

The official practice concerning overpayments of social welfare payments could certainly be seen as 'the law' in this sense whereby significant sections of the government and administration of the state had created and adopted a practice which was interpreted by a state agency (the Department of Social Welfare) which was also able to enforce its decisions by deductions from welfare payments to those affected.

The usefulness of definitions depends, of course, on the purpose for which the definitions are required. If one wishes to understand the practical operation of the social welfare system, this study would suggest that a broad definition is more helpful to a practical and theoretical understanding. For example, in one wishes to argue for the development of a welfare rights strategy through the use of the law and the legal system (Alcock, 1988; 1990, see also Hunt 1990), it is as well to be aware that welfare law involves much more than the legal rules contained in the relevant statutes and statutory instruments.

CONCLUSION

This chapter has considered one aspect of the operation of the Irish social welfare system and has shown that a marked divergence existed between the legal rules as set out in the relevant legislation and the actual operation of the system. It has argued that such a divergence is not uncommon in the operation of the social welfare scheme.[9] It is suggested that this divergence is due to the fact that, while the legal role of the Department of Social Welfare is to implement the social welfare legislation, the real role of the Department is to implement a range of largely unwritten objectives both at the macro level, such as the maintenance of social order, and at a programme specific level, such as in the case of unemployment benefits. In the instant case, it is easy to see that the social construction of overpaid welfare claimants did not accord with the relatively liberal approach contained in the legislation leading to the more stringent official practice (and the recent change in the legislation to reflect more closely this practice). However, as we said at the outset, this study provides a relatively limited empirical base for such an interpretation and further research would be necessary, first, to establish how representative the case of welfare overpayments is of a more general pattern of official practices and, secondly, to consider whether there may be other explanations for such a divergence between the law and the practice.

CHAPTER ELEVEN

Backwards into the Future

'A Klee painting named "Angelus Novus" shows an angel looking as though he is about to move away from something he is fixedly contemplating. His eyes are staring, his mouth is open, his wings are spread. This is how one pictures the angel of history. His face is turned towards the past. Where we perceive a chain of events, he sees one single catastrophe which keeps piling wreckage upon wreckage and hurls it in front of his feet. The angel would like to stay, awaken the dead, and make whole what has been smashed. But a storm is plowing from Paradise; it has got caught in his wings with such violence that the angel can no longer close them. This storm irresistibly propels him into the future to which his back is turned, while the pile of debris before him grows skyward. This storm is what we call progress.'

Walter Benjamin, *Theses of the Philosophy of History*, IX.

The Commission on Social Welfare (1986) identified three objectives for the social welfare system, i.e. the abolition of poverty, the redistribution of income different to that generated solely by market forces, and the protection of the standard of living of claimants. However, we have seen in chapters 1 and 2 (and in the specific studies in the other chapters) that the development of the social welfare system in the past has owed much more to economic, political and ideological forces in Irish society than to the achievement of any specific identified social policy goals. It is likely that the future development of the system will continue to be shaped by these forces and so, in the next section of this chapter, we look briefly at some possible future developments in this context. We also consider the demographic trends and their impact on the social welfare system. It is important to emphasise that, while constraints largely external to the social welfare system (such as the political strength of different social classes, the level of economic growth and demographic changes) play an important role in shaping the system, there remains a considerable degree of choice as to the actual policy measures to be adopted.

Because of its role in income replacement, the social welfare system is fundamentally affected by changes in the employment model. We outline some possible future developments in this area and examine how changing employment models may develop in Ireland. We go on to look at three key issues: the growth in atypical work, the role of women and the link between employment and social welfare support (including incentives and disincentives). Finally we consider how these developments may affect the structure of the Irish social welfare system.

Economy and demographics The ESRI (Cantillon et al., 1994) has recently predicted rapid economic growth over the next decade and into the twenty-first century with GNP estimated to grow on average by over 4 per cent per year over that period. If achieved, this would represent a longer period at higher rates of growth than any recent period in Irish economic history. However, the ESRI predict that, without major policy change, long-term unemployment will remain a serious problem with unemployment declining only slightly from its current rate of over 21 per cent of the paid labour force to about 18 per cent by 2000, which would still leave Ireland with one of the highest unemployment rates in the EU. Thus there will be a continued high demand for payments in respect of unemployment compensation although down by at least 15 per cent on current spending (assuming current rates of payment remain the same).

The growth in the proportion of people over the age of 65, rising from 11 per cent of the population in 1991 to an estimated 17 per cent by 2021 and almost 20 per cent in 2031, will call for significant additional expenditure in relation to old age pensions, although the main increases in this area will not be felt for 15 years (National Pensions Board, 1993). This will put significant long-term pressures on the current funding arrangement for pensions.

The number of children under 15 is already dropping sharply, from 29 per cent of the population in 1991 to 24 per cent by 2001 and 18 per cent by 2021. This will lead to a reduction in a range of payments in this area, in particular child benefit and child dependant increases (and also maternity benefit). In the short term, over the next ten years or so, the savings in child payments will more than compensate for the slow rise in old age pension costs (as the schemes are currently structured). However, because of the lower costs of these payments as a proportion of the total social welfare budget, in the longer term the additional pensions costs will far out way savings on payments to children.

On balance, however, the dependency ratio, i.e. the number of people of working age compared to the numbers above and below that age, will drop significantly in the period up to the early twenty-first century before rising again as the population ages. A crucial issue will, of course, be the proportion of those in paid employment compared to those unemployed (including those 'on home duties'). The ESRI predict that in the coming decade, with the rise in the proportion of the population at work, income per head of population will rise, making an important contribution to the convergence in living standards between Ireland and the EU.

These estimates indicate that the next 10 to 15 years will provide an important opportunity to restructure the social welfare system. Over this period, GNP is likely to grow significantly while costs in relation to unemployment and child support will drop. The cost of pensions will grow relatively slowly over this initial period but will increase sharply thereafter, emphasising the importance of restructuring payments now rather than in the more distant future. Income per head of population will rise. However, unemployment is predicted to remain high and it remains to be seen how the overall rise in income will be distributed amongst the population.

Politics If the economic and demographic trends suggest the desirability for an early review of the social welfare system, there is less indication that political trends are likely to favour any major reform in this area. Indeed, the fact that pressures are likely to ease in the short-term may suggest that policy makers are less likely to take immediate action, although this would obviously be unwise in the longer term. While the administration has ensured that the information as to likely trends are available, the administration on its own cannot make important political decisions as to how reforms are to be implemented. For example, in the absence of any major changes or any increased subvention from the state, the rate of employer, self employed and employee contributions to the old age pension scheme will have to increase by 177 per cent in the next 30 years or so. The longer such increases are delayed, the greater the ultimate increase will be (or alternatively the lower the level of pension or the greater the state subvention through additional taxation or borrowing). Yet, despite several recent reports, there is little informed public debate about the future of the social welfare system.

There is also little sign of any radical change in political trends over the next ten years, which would suggest that the existing political balance of power will continue to be reflected in income support policies. This calls into question the possibility of any significant change in redistributive trends.

Ideology The dominant role of the market in providing socio-economic development and the absence of any credible (or credited) alternatives has reached an apex in recent years. However, this very fact, together with the cyclical nature of ideological trends, might suggest that the promised economic boom may represent a last chance for the market to begin to solve Ireland's problems of under-development, emigration and unemployment if alternative ideologies are not to find renewed support in the coming decades. Nonetheless, the important part which the state has played in guiding socioeconomic development in Ireland is reflected in the fact that there has been little enthusiasm for swinging attacks on the state role in providing social services (allied to the fact that the redistributive consequences of this role have favoured many already advantaged classes).

In ideological terms, the role of the Catholic Church has declined markedly in the area of social welfare. Insofar as it retains a direct influence, Catholic groups now support increased social welfare provision (Council on Social Welfare, 1992). Indirectly the continuing importance of the Church in relation to 'moral' issues will continue to affect the social welfare system, for example, through its role in the proposed divorce referendum. Its continued support for the nuclear family and for the view of women as having a more traditional role to play in society will also inhibit a move towards individualisation of benefits (although this is by no means the only factor opposed to such a development).

The dissatisfaction of many Irish women with their existing place in society is likely to continue to grow over the next decades. However, the divisions amongst and within women's organisations as to how their role should be re-interpreted and the lack of any clear counter-hegemonic strategy are palpable (see, for example, the Second Commission on the Status of Women, 1993). No organisation has produced detailed coherent proposals as to how women's independence can be recognised in the context of the Irish social welfare system.

European Union   While Ireland's membership of the EU will be very significant in economic terms, there is little indication that it will have an important direct impact in terms of social policy, although it will, of course, have a major indirect impact in terms of the levels of growth and employment.[1] It is possible that the proposed EU directive to 'complete' the implementation of equal treatment in social security will be agreed within the next decade and legislation may also be adopted in relation to parental leave and atypical workers. However, it is unlikely that member states will agree to anything involving the commitment of major resources and Ireland has, in any case, already taken moves to adopt several of these measures by extending social insurance to part time workers and establishing a survivors pension. The EU recommendations on minimum income and the convergence of social policy objectives adopted in 1992 (Cousins, 1993a) are not legally binding and are unlikely to be of any major importance in the absence of a significant increase in the overall significance of EU social policy. The recently published EU Commission White Paper on Social Policy (1994b) gives little indication that a 'Social Europe' is any closer to becoming more than a cliche.

In economic terms, the EU Commission White Paper on Growth, Competitiveness, Employment (1993b) calls for a reduction in statutory charges on labour (income tax and social insurance contributions) by between one and two per cent of GDP in coming years as part of a strategy to combat unemployment and promote job creation. Possible compensatory measures identified include environmental taxes. Again such proposals have no legal force and, given successive Irish governments' distaste for tax reform, it is difficult to predict whether they will be implemented. However, if economic buoyancy allows a cut in taxation, any such reductions should fall on income tax (which is high compared to other EU countries) rather than social insurance contributions (which, despite constant complaints about this 'tax on jobs', are the third lowest in the EU) (Commission of the EC, 1994a). In the area of funding, there is no current EU funding for social welfare programmes *per se* and no likelihood that such funding will be provided in the short term. However, funding is provided through the Structural Funds for work experience (such as Community Employment) and training measures (such as the Youthstart scheme for young people) and this may increase in the future as the EU seeks to encourage a more active approach to labour market support.

MODELS OF EMPLOYMENT POLICY

The social welfare system was primarily developed to provide income support to those unable to achieve sufficient support through employment and this continues to be its role. Thus the structure of future employment policy will have a crucial bearing on the shape of the social welfare system. The European Commission Green Paper on Social Policy (1993a, p. 16) identifies two possible models for future employment policy:

1) *Dual society* – The Green Paper says that 'there is a high risk that the continued pursuit of present policies will lead ultimately to a "dual" society in which wealth creation is primarily in the hands of a highly qualified labour force, while income is transferred to a growing number of non-active people as a basis for a reasonable level of social justice. Such a society would not only become increasingly less cohesive, it would also run counter to the need for the maximum mobilisation of Europe's human resource wealth in order to remain competitive'.

2) *Active society* – 'The alternative would be to seek to create an "active" society where there is a wider distribution of income, achieved by means other than simply social security transfers, and in which each individual feels able to contribute not only to production (as part of the search for full employment) but also via a more active participation in the development of society as a whole.'

The Green Paper clearly favours the second option. The European Commission White Paper (1993b) on *Growth, Competitiveness, Employment* also appears to envisage an employment model similar to the 'active society' approach with references to the adoption of an active employment model leading to more vocational training (e.g. a guarantee of training for all those leaving school before the age of 18) and the creation of new jobs in areas such as home helps, child care, leisure and cultural facilities with a development of the social economy (p. 19–20). Unfortunately, however, both documents give little detailed indication as to how such a society may be achieved.

3) *American model* – There is of course, at least one further model (and indeed many more permutation and combinations): that which Kennedy (1993) refers to as the American model with the emphasis on creating low wage services employment leading to 'a slower growth in the pretax incomes of workers generally, a need for much wider gaps and greater flexibility in relative wages, and a reduction in welfare benefits'. Variations on or aspects of this model are frequently supported by Irish employer organisations (Madden, 1994). However, leaving to one side the debate as to the merits and demerits of the neoclassical argument that dropping the reservation wage (by cutting social welfare payments) would lead to increased employment, it is likely that in coming years any move to reduce the real level of social welfare payments will be impossible in the context of an otherwise booming economy.

In the Irish context, policy has long been premised on an approach close to that of the dual society: large numbers have been forced to emigrate and married women have been encouraged to stay out of the paid labour force while there has been a consistently high level of unemployment and underemployment amongst those remaining in the paid labour force. This is reflected in the fact that Ireland has had one of the highest ratios of persons not in employment to those in employment in the EU. There is little indication that this trend will change as Ireland struggles to regain anything approaching full employment for the existing paid labour force (which continues to exclude many women). Employees see little benefit in agreeing to drops in wages in exchange for the doubtful benefits of a low wage economy while the unemployed (in common with all other groups) have failed to develop a coherent strategy for large scale employment creation or the significant political support required to implement such a strategy. However, the extent of unemployment may continue to lead to a reallocation of unemployment support from social welfare schemes *per se* in the direction of work experience and community work projects, which have the additional attraction of being eligible for EU funding. While such an approach forms the basis for an active society policy, it is likely that the level of funding will not grow significantly and that these types of project will simply increase the level of atypical working in the Irish employment model.

Thus, in the coming decade, the Irish employment model may continue in its existing three tier approach, i.e. with a proportion of *core* employees, an increasing number of *atypical* workers (including part time, temporary, 'new' self employed and scheme workers: see chapter 3) and a significant number *excluded* from work on a long term basis either through unemployment (particularly the existing long term unemployed, a significant proportion of whom are unskilled manual workers) or by being seen as falling outside the work force (married women, people with disabilities).

THREE KEY ISSUES

The growth in atypical work   The existing social insurance/social assistance scheme is based on a model of full-time (male) employment. As we have seen in chapter 3, there has been a marked growth in the incidence of atypical working in Ireland in recent years. This is likely to continue in the future. Indeed, the one thing that the three models of future employment outlined above have in common is that all three are likely to see a growth in atypical work. The key issue in this regard is whether this type of work is low paid and poorly protected or whether higher levels of social protection can be achieved. This creates difficulties for the existing system which are considered in more detail below.

The role of women   There has been a consistent growth in the numbers of married women in paid employment. This has reflected structural change in the labour market with the working population as a whole (including women) moving from employment (paid or otherwise) in agriculture to paid employment in manufacturing and services. In addition, it reflects the changing ideological construction of women's place in Irish society with a shift away from the notion that women's place is in the home (or on the farm) towards a limited recognition by government and the general public that married women are entitled to participate equally in the paid work force (Fine-Davis, 1983). However, this recognition of formal equality – shown in the removal of the marriage bar in the civil service and the implementation of EU legislation on equal pay and equal treatment in employment and social welfare – has not been accompanied by any serious measures to encourage and support the participation of married women in the paid labour force. Thus the level of child care remains extremely low and the tax and social welfare systems discourage the participation of married women (NESC, 1992). The fact that the exclusion of married women from the paid labour force serves to keep down the recorded unemployment figures suggests that government policy is likely to continue to discourage participation in the foreseeable future. Nonetheless, the number of married women active in the paid labour force appears likely to continue to grow despite these barriers. This creates a conflict in social welfare policy. Existing policy is based on the notion of the male breadwinner supporting his wife and child dependants, with married women's earnings being of secondary importance. This policy is not consistent with actual increases in married women's participation. In the absence of a countervailing policy objective, one would expect to see the system respond to the change in the paid labour market by adapting to the needs of such workers (as it has to a limited extent in extending social insurance to part time workers). However, in this case there is a clear (although unstated) government policy of excluding married women from the labour force in order to keep down the unemployment figures. How this conflict can be resolved remains to be seen.

In addition to the changing role of married women in the paid labour force, the increases in the number of lone parents and in the numbers of separated persons also puts pressure on the existing system and we have seen in chapter 5 how this has led to the introduction of a lone parent's allowance and to the recent adoption by the Department of Social Welfare of a policy of encouraging lone parents to (re)enter the paid labour market.

The links between employment and social welfare   The issue of the link between paid employment and social welfare, including the issue of incentives and disincentives, employment and poverty traps, is one of the most contentious in the Irish debate. It is frequently argued that the system acts as a disincentive to work, with allegedly high rates of social welfare (in comparison to income from employment) in addition to benefits such as the medical card and cheap local authority housing being said to provide disincentives to people taking up low paid employment (the employment trap) or increasing their earnings from employment (the poverty trap). It would, of course, be foolish to deny that the social welfare system can, in some instances, act as a disincentive to people taking up employment or increasing their earnings from employment and we have seen that this is the case in relation to many married women and, at least formerly, lone parents. However, the general arguments in relation to the disincentive effect of the social welfare system are greatly overstated and are not supported by the detailed studies which have been carried out (Blackwell, 1986b; Arthur Andersen 1991; NESC, 1993).

The first point which should be made is that the arguments that the system has a disincentive effect are often based on hypothetical figures based on the calculation of the replacement ratio (i.e. the social welfare income as a percentage of income from employment) in a number of 'typical' cases. The use of typical cases is notoriously unreliable in this context as it is highly sensitive to the actual cases chosen and even a wide range of 'typical' cases is likely to represent only a very small proportion of the actual population. The only recent survey of actual replacement ratios does not support the argument that there is a significant disincentive effect (Arthur Andersen, 1991; see also Callan et al., 1994). Secondly, such arguments often assume full take-up of entitlements. However, the assessment of take-up based on the 1987 ESRI survey would suggest that there is less than full take-up of unemployment payments (Callan et al., 1989) and, therefore, this factor must be taken into account in calculating replacement ratios.

Thirdly, disincentive arguments assume that if the income from social welfare is close to the income from employment then a disincentive effect exists. Empirical research in the UK has shown that a comparison of the level of income from different sources (even if reliable information is available to the individual which it often is not) is *not* the only issue taken into account by people in deciding whether or not to take up employment. A much broader range of issues which vary according to sex, age, qualifications and other factors must be taken into account (McLaughlin et al., 1989; McLaughlin, 1991). Finally, given the lack of employment opportunities in a country with unemployment of around 20 per cent, disincentive effects, insofar as they do exist, simply mean that if one section of the population (for example social welfare recipients with large families in local authority housing) may be affected by social welfare disincentives, there are a large number of other unemployed people available to take up employment to whom no disincentive effects apply.

Given the absence of evidence for the disincentives argument on a general basis, one might suggest that it owes more to the neoclassical argument that the levels of wages are too high and are creating unemployment. It can be argued that social welfare payments act as a floor for wages and prevent wage rates from falling below a certain level. Proposals to cut wages or social welfare payments *per se* have a limited popularity with the electorate. They are perhaps more palatable when dressed up in largely spurious disincentive arguments.

While rejecting much of the current debate about disincentives, it is, of course, important that the social welfare system should generally provide an incentive for people to (re)enter the paid labour force and this must be taken into account in designing the future social welfare system. However, rather than focussing on rates of payment *per se*, much more attention needs to be given to the *structure* of the system with an emphasis on payments which avoid disincentive effects (such as universal child benefit) rather than on payments which tend to increase such effects (such as contingent child dependant increases). This is particularly so in relation to the growing importance of atypical work referred to above.

SOCIAL WELFARE POLICY

It must be noted that, despite the extensive debate in other countries, there is little radical challenge (either from the right or the left) to the existing system in this country (NESF, 1994). Debate has tended to focus on the *level* of benefits with the arguments being that current rates are either inadequate (Commission on Social Welfare, 1986; Combat Poverty Agency, 1993) or that rates are too high and therefore inflating the price of labour above its real level (as well as creating employment and poverty traps) (see OECD, 1994). While there have been occasional proposals that benefits for unemployed people be terminated after 6 months unless they agree to attend full-time training courses (Walsh, 1992), these have attracted little serious support and there has been no serious efforts to dismantle the welfare system to any significant extent.[2] On the other hand, proposals for increased coverage have tended to be incrementalist and have followed the now traditional Irish approach of creating further welfare schemes to cater for people otherwise dependent on supplementary welfare allowance (formerly the Poor Law). Insofar as there has been a shift in the structure of payments it has been away from social insurance and towards a greater reliance on social assistance payments. This has partially been through government policy (with its emphasis on cutting the state subsidy to the Social Insurance Fund and tightening the link between social insurance payments and employment) and partially through the growth in long term unemployment (and the fact that the duration of unemployment benefit has not been increased to reflect the increasing duration of unemployment). There has been a continued commitment to the social insurance scheme with the expansion of insurance to the self employed and part time workers. However, while this has involved a move towards greater universality in coverage, it has not involved comprehensive coverage for all risks with the self-employed being covered for only a limited range of benefits and part time workers also subject to restricted coverage.

Rates of payment   The Irish system has traditionally provided flat rate subsistence benefits and this approach has been endorsed by the Commission on Social Welfare. The rate at which benefits should be paid was discussed in detail by the Commission which opted for a relativist view of poverty. There appears to be a broad consensus around reaching the rates recommended by the Commission. The immediate priority rates were achieved in 1994 and the Programme for Competitiveness and Work agreed by the government, employers and trade unions states that 'further progress towards [the recommended rates] will be an important objective of Government during the period of this Programme' although such progress must have regard to the capacity of the economy to support the increased expenditure (Ireland, 1994, p. 62). The Commission recommended that the rates should be updated in accordance with the Consumer Price Index rather than overall living standards or wages and this approach has generally been followed. However, if one takes the view that social welfare rates should be related to general levels of prosperity in society, one might argue that a linkage to average earnings (or indeed to the growth in GNP) would be more appropriate.[3]

While there has been an official consensus that payments in respect of adult dependants should represent 0.6 of the personal rate (Commission on Social Welfare, 1986; National Pension Board, 1993), there is little, if any, existing research to support such a figure in the Irish context (see chapter 4). In addition, setting the adult dependant rate at this level would actually involve a reduction in the case of several benefits where the adult dependant rate currently varies up to 0.72. Such a reduction would make it more difficult and costly in the future to move towards an individualisation of benefits. An alternative approach would be gradually to float up the level of the adult dependant payment as part of a strategy of moving towards individualisation of benefits. This point will be returned to below as will the question of payments for child dependants.

In terms of income related payments, it would appear that there is little possibility that they will be introduced in the near future. The pay related benefit scheme for short term payments, introduced in 1973, was reduced over the 1980s and eventually abolished in 1994. Only maternity benefit is now linked to earned income. It appears that much of the emphasis behind the removal of the pay related benefit was the desire to reduce replacement ratios. The prospects for pay related pensions looks no more promising. In the late 1970s, it seemed that Ireland would follow the UK in introducing pay related pensions with the publication of a Green Paper in 1976 (Department of Social Welfare, 1976) and a commitment in the 1980 National Understanding to publish a White Paper on the topic. However, while a White Paper was prepared, it was never published and by 1986 the Commission on Social Welfare did not see pay related pensions as a priority. In its Final Report (1993) the National Pensions Board considered the issue of income-related pensions. Given that full pension under a social insurance scheme would become payable at a time when the ratio of contributors to pensioners would be significantly lower than it is at present and given the increased costs of funding even basic pensions (due to the aging of the population), the Board had serious reservations as to whether such a scheme would be sustainable. Accordingly, the Board recommended that the coverage of occupational and personal pensions should continue to be encouraged through tax reliefs and a majority of the Board (with the trade unions dissenting) concluded that it was not appropriate to recommend the introduction of a state earnings-related pension at this time. The employers' organisations were opposed to compulsory earnings related pensions 'under any circumstances' while other members of the majority accepted vaguely that 'it may be appropriate to introduce some provision for compulsory income-related pension at a future date'. Thus, it appears that the

Irish system will continue as a flat rate system for at least the next ten to 15 years.

The structure of payments One of the most fundamental issues facing the Irish social welfare system in the coming decades is the structure of the payment system. At present, the Irish system, like most others, is based on a mixture of social insurance and means tested payments. This system has developed from a period when social welfare payments were intended to cover only part of the population: early social insurance schemes were confined to specific manual employees and early social assistance payments, such as the Poor Law, were intended only for the poorest classes. Over the twentieth century, as we have seen, the Irish social welfare system has expanded to such an extent that there can be very few members of the population who are not affected by it at some stage in their lives, whether through payment of contributions or receipt of benefits. At the same time the tax system, which originally also only applied to a limited category of the population, has been expanded to apply to a much wider segment. This has led to an increased overlap between social welfare and taxation policies. As both policies developed, and continue to develop, largely independently of each other, many anomalies have arisen between the operation of the two and this has led to calls for a greater integration of the tax and social welfare systems.

The social insurance and social assistance schemes are largely based on the notion that the occurrence of one of the contingencies (unemployment, disability, etc.) results in a total (or at least major) loss of income such that compensation through the social welfare system should be provided. However, they are ill adapted to situations involving partial employment and thus have found it difficult to respond to the growth in atypical working patterns and to the increasing numbers of unemployed people whose best chance of finding work may be in some type of atypical employment. This difficulty also arises in relation to categories of claimants such as lone parents and people with disabilities where the earlier notion that such people were outside the work force is beginning to be replaced by a policy of encouraging participation. These difficulties have led to the growth in the last decade of schemes which are intended to provide financial support to people returning to work (Back to Work scheme) or at work on low pay (FIS). However, these types of contingency based and/or means tested schemes have the inevitable consequence that they must be withdrawn or reduced at some stage as employment is taken up or as earned income is increased with the inevitable creation of employment and poverty traps and high marginal tax rates.

Integration of the tax and social welfare systems In the light of these two difficulties, i.e. the *de facto* overlap of the tax and social welfare systems and the change in working patterns, various proposals for radical reform of the social welfare systems have been developed (Clinton et al., 1994). These include the idea of negative income tax whereby existing tax allowances are converted into tax credits and applied to the whole population with persons whose taxable income is below the level of the credit being paid a cash amount to bring their income up to that level (Dilnot et al., 1984, Danzinger et al., 1980). A more far reaching reform, known as basic income (or citizens income), would see the existing tax and social welfare schemes entirely replaced by the payment of a universal tax free amount to all residents with all earned income after that being subject to tax. Indeed there are many variations on this basic income approach (Parker, 1994). Proposals and discussion of negative income tax (NESC, 1978) and basic income (NESC, 1978. Honohan, 1987, 1994) have been put forward in the Irish context but the official response has been less than positive. The idea of a negative income tax has been rejected by the NESC (1978), the Commission on Taxation (1982) and the Commission on Social Welfare, while a shift to basic income has also been rejected by the NESC (1978) and by the Commission on Social Welfare.

The Commission on Social Welfare (1986, chapter 8) considered in some detail and rejected any radical change in the existing structure of social welfare payments, being 'convinced that a comprehensive system of social insurance complemented by social assistance is the appropriate strategy in Ireland at the present time'. Indeed it would seem clear that a shift to a full basic income system (whether desirable or not) is simply not politically realistic in that a system which would pay a basic level of benefit comparable to current social welfare rates would require a very high level of taxation on most incomes – Honohan (1994) and Callan et al. (1994) suggest over 60 per cent – while any scheme involving lower taxation would pay benefits considerably lower than those currently in existence. Thus the question is not whether the Irish system should, in the short term, change its system radically but rather whether such a change might be desirable in the longer term and (whether or not this is the case) how the existing difficulties concerning the link between social welfare and taxation and between social welfare and earned income can be addressed. From this point of view the Commission on Social Welfare can be criticised for asking itself the wrong question.

The NESC has been more nuanced in its approach. While rejecting a radical restructuring of the existing system, it has called for integration of specific aspects of the tax and social welfare systems (1986, 1990, 1993). These have included the taxation of social welfare payments (implemented in 1993 and 1994), the coordination of the levels of social welfare payments and the general tax allowances to avoid a narrowing of the gap between social welfare income and income from employment, the restructuring of social insurance contributions with the abolition of exemptions and the existing income ceiling, and the restructuring of child income support with an emphasis on an increased and taxable child benefit payment (and away from child dependant allowances). However, with the exception of the taxation of short term welfare payments, there has been little movement on any of these issues.

The NESC, however, has given little attention to whether a move towards basic income would be desirable *in the long term* and this must be a crucial issue for the future development of the system. The recently published ESRI analysis of basic income schemes for Ireland (Callan et al., 1994) provides a new opportunity for an informed debate on these issues and one hopes that the Expert Group on the Integration of the Tax and Social Welfare System appointed in 1992 will consider these long-term aspects as well as more immediate reforms (as in its interim report, 1993). The Council of Religious of Ireland have recently published detailed costed proposals for a partial basic income scheme.

Basic income has been supported by a very wide variety of individuals and groups from very divergent political perspectives. Many have argued for the introduction of a basic income as though basic income in itself was an end rather than a means to an end. Walter (1989) has argued that basic income can appeal to almost everybody – from free marketeers to socialists, feminists to upholders of the traditional family. This is true to the extent that all these groups can support *a* basic income (and there are very many variants). However, all these divergent groups would not be able to support *the same specific* basic income were one to be introduced as any specific basic income will reflect a range of other policies (whether they be free market or socialist, feminist or conservative) as to links with the labour market, benefit and tax levels, the unit of assessment, the degree of redistribution and so on. Thus the introduction of a basic income system cannot be seen as a panacea for all problems, nor can it be seen as a policy aim in itself. Rather one must decide on one's overall policies – in relation to employment models, redistribution, etc. – and then consider whether a basic income system will be a more effective policy measure in achieving these ends than the existing system.

Co-ordination rather than integration?   What are the problems with the existing system of social insurance and social assistance? As the NESC has pointed out, many issues concerning the interaction between the tax and social welfare systems can be resolved by coordinating the levels of tax allowances and welfare benefits, by restructuring social insurance contributions in line with the tax system and similar (relatively minor) measures. The existing system can, in principle, cope perfectly adequately with people in permanent secure employment (such as public servants) and those permanently excluded from the work force (such as retired people and those unable to work due to permanent sickness or disability). Questions as to the level of benefits or the ease of qualification for benefit do not affect the system's theoretical ability to cover these situations. The difficulties arise in relation to those in some forms of atypical work (part time and casual employment and insecure self employment) and those who are unemployed and whose best chance of work may be in these types of atypical work. Here the basic issue is how the social welfare system can provide support to such persons without acting as a disincentive to take up employment and without creating employment and poverty traps.

The extension of social insurance to part-time workers has already made a significant contribution to improving the position of atypical workers but further review of the social welfare system is necessary to remove existing barriers to employment. A shift towards a universal child benefit and away from contingency based child dependent allowances would represent a partial solution to this problem and would reduce, to a substantial extent, existing employment and poverty traps. The extension of employment schemes as a partial replacement for unemployment benefit and assistance also allow participants on these schemes to take up additional work where available.

Those who argue that the social welfare system acts as a 'disincentive to work' sometimes appear to assume that there is work for 300,000 unemployed people who are dissuaded from taking up employment because of these alleged disincentives. However, there is no evidence whatsoever to support the view that this scale of employment exists. In practical terms, those likely to be affected by incentives make up a relatively small proportion of the unemployed. Therefore, rather than calling for radical reform of the basis of the social welfare system, the incentive issue requires a solution targeted at those who are likely to be able to benefit from incentives to take up employment, such as an employment package including employment schemes, back to work transitional payments and education/training opportunities (as in Denmark). This would involve a reform and coordination of existing Irish policies rather than any radical reform. The question of providing employment for those who remain on unemployment assistance is not one that the social welfare system can solve and there is little to suggest that active labour market measures can create large scale sustainable employment without displacement effects in the absence of a major employment creation policy for the economy as whole (Commission of the EC, 1994a). There is no evidence to suggest that a shift to a partial basic income system (which would retain a partial means tested system of support) would suddenly 'discover' significant levels of untapped employment. Limited evidence in the Irish context on the operation of the Social Employment Scheme, which allows participants to take up additional work without affecting their scheme payment, showed that only 14 per cent of participants surveyed had taken up additional work (Roynane and Devereux, 1993, p. 35).

A further issue arises in relation to the means testing of couples on a household basis and the loss of dependency increases when the working spouse's income exceeds a set amount (currently £60). If one assumes the three tier model of employment policy outlined above (i.e. core – atypical – excluded) then there is a conflict between resolving this issue and continuing the existing policy of excluding married women from the work force. At a minimal level, a combination of a shift to child benefit, introducing tapered reductions in dependency increases (as recommended by the Commission on the Status of Women and the National Pensions Board) and increasing the earnings disregard as between spouses[4] would at least ensure that marginal tax rates for low income persons whose spouses are unemployed would not exceed 100 per cent (due to social welfare withdrawal). While far from ideal, such a change, combined with reforms in the tax area (NESC, 1992) would be a significant improvement in the present situation and would be in keeping with the policy of extending social insurance to low paid workers.

Individualisation of benefits More radical reforms are not possible without calling into question the traditional exclusion of married women from the labour force and without a move away from long term dependence on social assistance payments. As Esam and Berthoud (1991) show, the introduction of individualised benefits in a system largely based on means tested payments is simply impracticable. It would lead to a massive increase in the number of people undergoing a means test, significant increases in costs with upwards redistribution, and increased disincentives for married women to participate in the paid labour force.[5] The Review Group on the Treatment of Households (1991) show that even a limited move towards individualisation by paying the full rate of means tested payments to both spouses would have significant financial implications while leading to a major increase in the recorded level of unemployment.

Any move towards individualisation needs to overcome the policy of discouraging married women's participation. Were that to be achieved, any major moves towards individualisation would require a shift away from means tested payments and dependency increases towards the payment of benefits to groups who formerly either did not receive benefits at all (e.g. married women whose husbands were working) and to those in respect of whom dependency increases were formerly payable. This could be done either by an expansion of the social insurance scheme with, for example, unemployment benefit being paid on a long term basis (as in Belgium), with periods of caring for children, the elderly or people with disabilities being counted as periods of paid insurance (as is already done in some EU countries)[6] and the introduction of new contingency payments (such as a payment to all parents, see Esam and Berthoud, 1991) or by the introduction of a partial basic income system. The redistributional consequences of such moves in the Irish context would need to be modelled but Esam and Berthoud (1991) in the UK context found that the introduction of either a universal payment for all persons not in employment or a parental care allowance (for non-earning parents) or a parents benefit (for all parents) at a rate of £20 per week underpinned by a means tested payment or a 'basic credits' system (at the same rate and backed up by a means tested system) would all result in a progressive redistribution of resources with low increases in income tax (ranging from an increase in the basic rate of 0.3 to 1.5 pence in the £) while providing an (albeit low) independent income to many married women. In the Irish context, Callan et al. (1994) show that a partial basic income of £21 per week would involve a redistribution of income from high to low incomes, would improve financial incentives for both employees and the unemployed and could be financed by a 1 per cent rise in the standard rate of tax.

It must be borne in mind that it is possible to construct an individualised social welfare system which does not improve the position of women (Ginn and Arber, 1992) and any move towards individualisation needs to be clear as to to the precise goals to be achieved rather than simply seeking payments directly to women. As we have seen in chapters 5 and 6, individual payments to women may simply mirror (or, in the case of the carers allowance, reinforce) rather than challenge the existing construction of women's dependency.

Child support The Irish child support system currently involves a mix of the universal child benefit, child dependency increases payable with social welfare payments, a means tested family income supplement to low income families in employment and limited tax allowances. The existing system can give rise to employment and poverty traps and to high marginal tax rates. In addition, the current levels of child support do not reflect the actual costs of supporting a child. Reports from a range of different organisations, including the Commission on Taxation (1982), the Commission on Social Welfare (1986), the Combat Poverty Agency (Nolan and Farrell, 1990; Carney et al., 1994), the ESRI (Callan, 1991; Callan et al., 1994) and the NESC (1986, 1990, 1993) have called for a shift towards a universal child benefit payment. Indeed this option was accepted as government policy in 1984 (Ireland, 1984). However, in view of the high costs involved in significant increases in child benefit (Blackwell, 1988), successive governments have opted for piecemeal reforms through increasing the levels of child dependency payments and FIS.

Although a significant increase in child benefit is expensive, it is clear that there are affordable options for shifting support away from the existing range of payments and towards a taxable child benefit payment. For example, the Expert Working Group (1993) have calculated that an increase of child benefit to £40 per month with taxation of the benefit and a full clawback of child dependency allowances would cost £48 million in a full year (less than the revenue achieved by the taxation of disability and unemployment benefit) (see also the costings in Callan et al. 1994). While the precise nature of such a reform depends of the particular priorities given to different policy goals (including preventing poverty, removing disincentives, containing exchequer costs), it is clear that such a reform is eminently feasible. The coming decade or more, with a marked reduction in the number of children, will mean that the long term implications of such a reform will not generate significant costs while the fact that at present large numbers of people are already in receipt of child dependency allowances means that the cost of such a reform is less than it otherwise would be (because these people are already in receipt of most or all of the eventual payment). It is, however, clear that the structure of payments is not the only problem and that the level of payments is seriously inadequate, particularly for older children (Carney et al., 1994). This would suggest the need to introduce age related increases in child benefit.

Financing Both the Commission on Taxation (1982) and the Commission on Social Welfare (1986) have recommended that a separate ear-marked social security tax be retained. However, while the Commission on Taxation called for the introduction of a new social security tax payable by employees on earnings and by employers on profits, the Commission on Social Welfare called for more incremental reforms of the system including the abolition of the existing income ceiling. The NESC (1986, 1990, 1993) has tended to support the latter approach rather than the more radical reform proposed by the Commission on Taxation. The idea of a social security tax payable on profits rather than employment would seem to be more logical and would represent a shift of taxation away from labour and towards other factors of production. However, the rate actually proposed by the Commission on Taxation would have led to a significant reduction in the overall contribution by employers to the social insurance fund. Given the ability of employers to avoid other forms of taxation, one can anticipate reluctance on the part of the government to interfere with the existing system despite the theoretical attractions of a social security tax.

About 50 per cent of social welfare expenditure comes from general taxation and the burden of general taxation falls heavily on employees in the absence of significant property and corporation taxation. As we have seen in chapter 2, this tends to lead to most employees being net contributors to the system while farmers at all income levels are net beneficiaries of the transfer system. In the absence of significant change in the overall political system, it is difficult to see any major changes in this area in coming decades. Indeed, the proposals of the Commission on Taxation in relation to income taxes which emphasise a reduction in levels of taxation and an abolition of existing tax reliefs may prove more regressive than the existing system, with higher earners benefiting disproportionately (Callan, 1991).

Administration   We have seen in chapters 1 and 9 that there has been a strong tendency towards the centralisation and bureaucratisation of the administration of social welfare in Ireland. Although there have been recent moves towards regionalisation of services, this has consisted mainly of the relocation of centralised offices or the limited devolution of centrally controlled service delivery functions. There is little, if any, structured involvement of non public servants in the delivery and planning of social welfare services, except by way of the involvement of outside interest groups (such as employers organisations, trade unions and the insurance industry) and 'experts' on government appointed commissions. Even here, the frequent absence of any claimant organisations is noticeable.

The development of the bureaucracy in Irish social welfare administration is not necessarily 'bad'. It may be argued that the present model is more effective and efficient than an alternative such as a more participative model of administration involving a range of interest groups in a structured way in the planning and delivery of services. There is clearly a degree of tension between the desire to apply national standards and the retention of a significant level of local democratic control. However, this approach tends to ignore the wider consequences of opting for bureaucratic rather than alternative models of administration. Thus, in assessing the degree of effectiveness and efficiency of a bureaucratic administration, should we take into account the fact that the constant growth of bureaucracy inevitably disempowers citizens and impedes their ability to play an important role in society? Bagguley (1992) argues that the change in administrative structures of the social security scheme in the

UK from (partial) local democratic control up to the 1930s to the present centralised bureaucracy has meant that it much more difficult for unemployed organisations to have an impact on policy formulation. In the Irish context, it is clear that the Boards of Guardians which administered the Poor Law were an important site for the political struggle between landlords and tenants in the late nineteenth century (Feingold, 1976; 1984). Feingold (1984, p. 178) argues that this had practical implications for the administration of the Poor Law and that Boards dominated by nationalist/tenant guardians were more likely to grant outdoor relief (as opposed to relief in the Workhouse) than landlord dominated Boards.

In Ireland, in recent years, there has been relatively little emphasis on reforming the existing approach and there has been a general consensus around the increased bureaucratisation of social welfare services, as though such decisions were merely technical rather than political. However, the substantive nature of the system is inevitably influenced by the structure of the administrative system. To take just one example, the growth in the use of information technology has had, and will continue to have, profound effects on the way in which people are treated by the social welfare authorities both at the level of direct contact between the two and in terms of the information available to the authorities about individuals. Yet there has been little public debate at any level about how the growth of information technology should be implemented or its implications for claimants.

The potential democratisation of social welfare administration through an increase in the use of participatory structures is one of the most important *possible* future developments in the social welfare system. However, in the absence of any clearly focussed proposals in this area, we are likely to see merely an increased emphasis on consumerism within the existing administrative structures rather than any move towards democratic participation in decision making (Epstein, 1990).

CONCLUSION

In this chapter, we have sketched some of the possible future developments in the social welfare system. Space has not allowed any comprehensive review and it is likely that significant developments may take place in individual programme areas, for example, in the area of pensions in response to the final report of the National Pensions Board and in the area of disability payments which is currently under consideration by the Commission on the Status of People with Disabilities.

In summary, it would seem that reform of the child support aspects of the social welfare system is both logical and timely. Further delay in introducing such reforms only leads to short term increases in FIS and child dependant increases which makes long term reform more difficult. More radical reform is, however, more contested. Accepting the current three tier employment model, difficulties in relation to incentives can be addressed by the provision of an improved employment package to those likely to be affected by existing disincentives and a shift to child benefit while problems in relation to intra-household disincentives can be ameliorated (although not removed) by a shift to child benefit, the introduction of tapered dependency increases and a increase in intra-household disregards (combined with tax reform). None of these reforms call into question the existing structure of payments. However, any challenge to this policy, particularly around the exclusion of women, needs to look at a move away from the existing reliance on means tested payments and dependency increases towards either a radically reformed social insurance scheme or the introduction of a partial basic income.

A challenge to the existing three tier employment model might support an active society in which state policy would be to ensure participation of all members of society with a distribution of income 'by means other than simply social security transfers' (which might involve a basic income scheme providing a basis for such an income distribution) or advocate an approach which recognises that not all people will be in paid employment and provides a generous basic income to allow people to opt out of the paid labour force (Hinrichs et al., 1988; Offe, 1992).

We have argued that economic and demographic trends over the next ten to 15 years are particularly favourable for putting the social welfare system on a sound basis for the twenty first century (when the aging of the population will bring the system under increased pressures). However, it remains to be seen whether the political structures have the capacity to take such a longer term view or whether incremental reforms will remain the order of the day. The restraints imposed on the future development of policy by the existing policy legacies cannot be underestimated. Thus, any future proposals cannot simply look into the future to see what type of system we will need in 2010 but must look constantly backwards at the existing system and at the constraints which it imposes on future possibilities. In this way, the social welfare system indeed resembles the angel in the quote from Walter Benjamin at the top of this chapter, being forced rapidly into the future to which its back is turned by the 'storm called progress'.

Notes

INTRODUCTION

1 Those publications which have considered the social welfare system tend to have done so in the context of an overall examination of the welfare state (Maguire, 1986; O'Connell and Rottman, 1992).
2 Habermas (1987, p. 322) argues that the relationship of clients to the administrators of the welfare state is 'the model case for the colonization of the lifeworld' – the universe of daily social activity – by the economic and administrative systems. For a description of the relationship between claimants and the administration in the Irish context see Combat Poverty Agency (1988; 1991), Cousins and Charleton (1991) and O'Connor et al. (1986).

CHAPTER 1

1 Readers should note that there is often a difference of one year or more between the year in which a measure was adopted by the legislature and that in which it came into effect. The dates given in this book are generally those of the legal adoption of a measure and its implementation may not have occurred for a year or more after that date.
2 It should be borne in mind that the Brehon Laws were not a formal legal system but rather 'a highly idealized picture . . . of what popular practices and habits would be like (or might be like) in terms of law . . .' (O'Faolain, 1969, p. 47).
3 In addition to income support, the Poor Law also provided a range of medical and other social services (Barrington, 1987; Burke, 1987).
4 The workmen's compensation scheme was not a state-funded system of social welfare but provided for a system of compensation of injured employees by their employers.
5 This heavy dependence on farming persisted until the 1960s. In 1961, 36 per cent of the male working population still fell into this category.
6 This clawback was dropped in 1954, although a similar arrangement was subsequently introduced between 1969 and 1974 (Kennedy, 1989).
7 These figures must be treated with some caution as no official estimates were produced before 1938.
8 In addition to over 15,000 person in receipt of pre-retirement allowance and over 30,000 on various employment schemes.
9 Spending as a proportion of GDP declined in 1993 (11.5 per cent) but continued to rise as a proportion of GNP. Given the difficulties with GDP figures, the continued rise in relation to GNP is probably a more accurate reflection of spending patterns.

CHAPTER 2

1 Skocpol (1985) advances an alternative, and in her view complementary, view of states as 'configurations of organization and action that influence the meanings and methods of politics for all groups and classes in society'. It is arguable that this view, is in fact, logically

independent of the 'state as actor' interpretation and that it could be utilised within many other paradigms to explain how developments inspired by social classes/industrialisation/ working class strength (and so on) are operationalised in practice.

2 It should be noted that Whelan et al. (1992) show that 58.5 per cent of all male unskilled workers between the ages of 20 and 64 are unemployed or unable to work due to long term disability.

3 The argument being that higher welfare rates are at least partial compensation for continued high rates of unemployment and an indication of the government's concern for the unemployed. Habermas (1987, p. 346) describes how the political system creates mass loyalty through the provision of social welfare programmes.

4 This does not take into account indirect taxation which as Breen et al. (1990) show again tends to favour farmers as opposed to employees.

5 This is, of course, a generalisation and, since the 1960s, divergent views have become more common within the Catholic Church on social policy matters. The Council of Religious of Ireland (formerly the CMRS) have shown particular interest in the redistributive impact of policy.

6 McLaughlin (1993) describes Ireland as a 'Catholic corporatist' type of welfare state. However, at least in relation to the social welfare system, he perhaps overemphasises the influence of the Church. As Korpi shows, the Church has had relatively little influence on the actual structure of the social welfare system although it has influenced its underlying principles.

7 Including those receiving payments in their own right and those in respect of whom adult dependency payments are made.

8 See, for example, Sandford and Morrisey (1985).

9 Indeed one can see as much variation in the approach of the same party (e.g. Fianna Fáil in its pre– and post–1987 election positions) as between the different parties.

CHAPTER 3

1 See, for example, the series of reports commissioned by the Commission of the European Communities on social protection for atypical workers and for the self-employed in each member state.

2 *Minister for Labour v. PMPA* (1986) 5 JISLL 215.

3 There is a system of pre-entry credits for persons on taking up employment.

CHAPTER 4

1 Millar et al. (1992) estimate that there are approaching 50,00 lone parent families with children up to the age of 18.

2 Under the Poor Relief (Ireland) Act, 1838, husbands were liable to support their wives and children (up to the age of 15), fathers, widows and unmarried mothers were liable to support their children and children were liable to support their parents.

3 Fahey (1993) argues that the Census 'principal economic status' (PES) data in relation to married women are unreliable and understate the level of married women's participation while overstating the apparent increase in participation because the PES measures provide poor coverage of unemployment, part-time work and unpaid farm work. These reservations are not so serious in relation to participation in insurable employment as unpaid farm work is not insurable nor, until recently, was part-time work. Thus the participation of married women in insurable employment has risen sharply over the period in question.

CHAPTER 5

1 This figure includes those in receipt of the means tested disabled persons maintenance allowance (figures provided by the Department of Health) and those receiving invalidity pension and the nominally 'short-term' disability benefit for three years or more.

2 A person is to be regarded as requiring full-time care and attention where s/he is so disabled or invalided as to require (i) continual supervision in order to avoid danger to him/herself, or (ii) continual supervision and frequent assistance throughput the day in connection with normal bodily functions and where the invalidity or disability is such that the person is likely to require such care and attention for at least 12 months – section 163(3) of the Social Welfare (Consolidation) Act 1993.

3 However, social welfare payments are not to be taken into account in assessing what could reasonably be contributed.

4 The Social Welfare (Old Age (Contributory) Pension) Regulations 1994 provide that in future, in order to satisfy the requirement of a minimum yearly average number of contributions for pension, periods spent caring for an incapacitated person will be disregarded in calculating the yearly average. While this is a welcome reform which may assist carers to qualify for pension, it falls some way short of the state paying a full contribution for carers.

CHAPTER 6

1 *Dennehy v. Minister for Social Welfare*, High Court, unreported, 26 July 1984; *Lowth v. Minister for Social Welfare*, High Court, unreported, 16 December 1993.

2 See *Lowth*, supra.

3 When the issue came before the High Court in *Foley v. Moulton* [1989] ILRM 169, Gannon J stated that 'I consider it unwise for the Court to supply a definition when the legislature has refrained from doing so'.

4 *Foley v. Moulton*, supra. See Whyte (1989).

5 The legislators' reasons can only be deduced from their actions as the Dáil and Senate Debates are remarkably silent on these issues.

6 *Kennedy v. Ireland* [1987] IR 587.

7 See *Hyland v. Minister for Social Welfare* [1989] IR 640.

8 *Board of Public Assistance for the South Cork Public Assistance District v. O'Regan* [1949] IR 415. See Whyte (1990) and Cousins (1992b).

9 *Sunday Tribune*, 10 April 1994.

CHAPTER 7

1 Although the rights of women after marriage under the National Health Insurance scheme were already somewhat limited (32 *Dáil Debates* 69 *et seq.*), the government conceded that this amendment limited these rights further.

2 See Fahey's (1993a) reservations on these figures, chapter 4, note 3.

3 Indirect discrimination arises where a provision, which is sex neutral of its face, has a disproportionate impact to the disadvantage of one sex and where the provision cannot be justified on grounds unrelated to sex.

4 *Irish Times*, 13 April 1994; 1 July 1994.

CHAPTER 8

1 However, up to 1973 women were automatically disqualified for maternity allowance on marriage unless they worked for at least 26 weeks after marriage.

2 This payment was renamed maternity benefit in the Social Welfare (Consolidation) Act 1993 but the term allowance is used here throughout to avoid confusion.

3 I would like to thank Brian Charleton who collated this additional information on maternity costs.

CHAPTER 9

1 The term bureaucracy is used frequently in this chapter and is intended in a descriptive rather than a pejorative sense throughout.
2 The term internal and external are used to refer to the position of the adjudication bodies either within the (narrow) concept of the civil and public service or outside that structure. These terms are preferred to the use of term such as 'independent' tribunals for non-civil service bodies as the use of this term begs the question as to the 'independence' of the relevant bodies. Under Irish law, members of such external tribunals may, in fact, be considered to be civil servants in the broad sense in some cases: see *Murphy v. Minister for Social Welfare* [1987] IR 295.
3 One might refer to a third model: that applying to income support payments administered by the Department of Health (such as disabled persons maintenance allowance). In the case of these payments there has been, and is, no formal appeal structure at all.
4 Unemployment assistance and benefit, widow's and orphan's pension, children's allowance.
5 Sickness and maternity benefits under the National Insurance Act, 1911.
6 Old age pension.
7 The workmen's compensation scheme.
8 In these early years, the vast majority of disputes arose in relation to the age of claimants, with the lack of proof of age in many cases leading to protracted disputes.
9 The Supreme Court held that they were quasi-judicial officers who were 'required to be free and unrestricted in discharging their functions': *McLoughlin v. Minister for Social Welfare* [1958] IR 1.
10 High Court, unreported, 25 November 1985.
11 ICTU, Untitled, undated paper, presented at a conference on Social Welfare Appeals, February 1991.
12 This change had previously been recommended by the Report of the Royal Commission on the Poor Laws and Relief of Distress in 1909.
13 *Irish Times* 21 June 1994; 5 September 1994.

CHAPTER 10

1 The law in relation to both social insurance and social assistance has been changed in the Social Welfare Act 1993 to bring the legal rules more into line with the existing official practice and to apply the same rules in relation to both types of payment. The current law is to be found in sections 278 and 279 of the Social Welfare (Consolidation) Act 1993.
2 Section 300(5)(a) of the Social Welfare (Consolidation) Act 1981. This provision was carried over from section 46 of the Social Welfare Act 1952. Unfortunately this section was passed without debate at the Committee stage in Dáil Éireann in 1952 so that no indication was given of the legislators' specific intentions at that time.
3 The term 'official practice' is used since, as will become evident, the practice in this area is not simply a case of a deviant administrative practice within the Department but involves a wide range of state bodies.
4 The account here is based on the author's own experience and that of colleagues rather than on any structured research.
5 The different social welfare payments are dealt with by distinct section of the Department. For example, long term pensions are administered by the Pensions Services Office in Sligo.
6 The discussion arose from a computerised audit which had discovered under payments and overpayments of pensions. These appear to have arisen due to administrative error and there is no suggestion of any fraud.
7 In the absence of any internal information as to the development of this practice within the Department and the other bodies involved, the explanation advanced in this chapter is necessarily at a very general level and no doubt does not take into account specific causative influences.

8 Examples include the payment of unemployment assistance to self-employed persons without requiring the statutory conditions of availability for employment and evidence of genuine efforts to obtain work to be complied with and the payment of deserted wife's payments to legally divorced women who are no longer 'wives' within the meaning of the legislation.
9 It is likely that similar divergences operate in other areas of the administration. See, for example, the granting of extra-statutory concessions in the area of the tax code, the failure in practice to implement the criminal law against homosexuality and so on.

CHAPTER 11

1 For the position of the Irish social welfare system in a European context, see EU Commission (1994a).
2 While supporting the recent OECD (1994) plan for reform of the employment market, which includes proposals to reform unemployment benefit systems to make work more financially attractive, the Irish Minister for Finance, Bertie Ahern, has insisted that this will not lead to welfare cuts in Ireland: cf. *Irish Times*, 8 June 1994.
3 The present policy is in contrast to that adopted in the post-war period up to the late 1970s and early 1980s. Hughes (1985, p. 124) shows that successive governments had implicitly adopted a policy of increasing the main social welfare payments in line with changes in average gross industrial earnings.
4 This is currently set at £45 per week (or less in the case of part time workers) and has not been increased since at least the early 1980s. Had it been increased in line with average hourly earnings in manufacturing industry it would now be at least twice that amount.
5 While these findings are based on a computer model of the UK situation, there is nothing to suggest that similar outcomes would not apply in this country.
6 The Minister for Social Welfare has recently provided that periods spent caring for a child up to the age of six or a person who requires constant care due to disability will be disregarded in calculating the yearly average of contributions for the old age pension. While this is a welcome development, it falls some way short of treating these periods as paid contributions.

References

Adler M., C. Bell, J. Clasen and A. Sinfield eds. (1991) *The Sociology of Social Security*, Edinburgh: Edinburgh University Press

Alcock P. (1988) 'The Future of Welfare Rights'. Conference Paper, Dublin

————— (1990) 'Why citizenship and welfare rights offer new hope for new welfare in Britain' *Critical Social Policy* 32

Althusser L. (1976) 'Idéologie et appareils idéologiques d'État' in *Positions*. Paris: Éditions sociales

Arthur Andersen (1991) *Report to the Industrial Policy Review Group on Reform of the Irish Taxation System from an Industrial Point of View*, Dublin: Stationary Office

Bagguley, P. (1992) 'Protest, acquiescence and the unemployed: a comparative analysis of the 1930s and 1980s' 43 *British Journal of Sociology*

Baldwin, P. (1990) *The Politics of Social Solidarity*, Cambridge: Cambridge University Press

Baldwin, S., G. Parker and R. Walker eds. (1988) *Social Security and Community Care*, Aldershot: Avebury

Barrington R. (1987) *Health, Medicine and Politics in Ireland 1990–1970*, Dublin: Institute of Public Administration

Barrington, T. (1975) *From Big Government to Local Government, the Road to Decentralisation*, Dublin: Institute of Public Administration

Berkowitz, M., D. Dean and P. Mitchell (1987) *Social Security Disability Programs: An International Perspective*, New York: Rehabilitation International/World Rehabilitation Fund

Beveridge, W. (1942) *Social Insurance and Allied Services*, London: HMSO

Bew, P., E. Hazelkorn and H. Patterson (1989) *The Dynamics of Irish Politics*, London: Lawrence and Wishart

Bew, P. and H. Patterson (1982) *Seán Leamass and the making of Modern Ireland 1945–66*, Dublin: Gill and Macmillan

Bieback, K. J. (1992), 'Family Benefits: The New Legal Structures of Subsidising the Family', 2 *Journal of European Social Policy* 239

Blackwell, J. (1986a; 1989a; 1990) *Women in the Labour Force (Supplements)*, Dublin: Employment Equality Agency

————— (1986b) *Unemployment Compensation and Work Incentives*, Dublin: Commission on Social Welfare

————— (1988) 'Family Income Support: Policy Options' in B. Reynolds and S. Healy eds. *Poverty and Family Income Policy*, Dublin: Conference of Major Religious Superiors

————— (1989b) *Family Income Supplement: Report for the Department of Social Welfare*, Report to the Department of Social Welfare

Blackwell, J., E. O'Shea, G. Moane and P. Murray (1992), *Care Provision and Cost Measurement: Dependent Elderly People at Home and in Geriatric Hospitals*, Dublin: Economic and Social Research Institute

Borooah, V. and P. McKee (1992) 'Modelling Intra-Household Income Transfers: an analytical framework with an application to the UK' Conference paper, University of Ulster, Jordanstown

Breen R., D. Hannan, D. Rottman and C. Whelan, (1990) *Understanding Contemporary Ireland*, Dublin: Gill and Macmillan

Brocas, A. M., A. M. Cailloux and V. Oget (1990)*Women and Social Security: Progress towards Equality of Treatment*, Geneva: ILO

Brown, J. (1984) *The Disability Income System*, London: Policy Studies Institute

———— (1989) *In Search of Policy: The Rationale for Social Security Provision for One Parent Families*, London: National Council for One Parent Families

Brown, J. and S. Small (1985) *Maternity Benefits*, London: Policy Studies Institute

Burke, H. (1987) *The People and the Poor Law in 19th Century Ireland*, Littlehampton: WEB

Callan, T. (1991) *Income Tax and Welfare Reforms*, Dublin: Economic and Social Research Institute

Callan, T., B. Nolan. and B. Whelan, D. Hannan, with S. Creighton (1989) *Poverty Income and Welfare in Ireland*, Dublin: Economic and Social Research Institute

Callan, T., C. O'Donoghue and C. O'Neill (1994) *Analysis of Basic Income Schemes for Ireland*, Dublin: Economic and Social Research Institute

Callender, R. (1988) 'Ireland and the Implementation of Directive 79/7/EEC' in Whyte (1988)

Cantillon, S., J. Curtis and J. Fitzgerald (1994) *ESRI Medium Term Review: 1994–2000*, Dublin: Economic and Social Research Institute

Carney C. (1985) 'A Case Study in Social Policy: The Non-Contributory Old Age Pension' 33 *Administration* 483.

Carney, C., E. Fitzgerald, G. Kiely and P. Quinn (1994) *The Cost of a Child*, Dublin: Combat Poverty Agency

Casey, J. (1987) *Constitutional Law in Ireland*, London: Butterworths

Central Statistics Office (1988) *Population and Labour Force Projections 1991–2021*, Dublin: Stationary Office

———— (1989) *Household Budget Survey Vols. 1 and 2*, Dublin: Stationery Office

———— (1991) *Census 86. Vol. 3: Household Composition and Family Units*, Dublin: Stationary Office

———— (1993) *Labour Force Survey 1991*, Dublin: Stationary Office

———— (1994a) *Statistical Release* (24 January), Dublin: Government Information Services

———— (1994b) *Census 1991 Vol. II: Ages and Marital Status*, Dublin: Stationary Office

Charleton, B. (1993) *A Feasibility and Assessment Study of the Supplementary Welfare Allowance Appeals System*, Report to the Combat Poverty Agency

Chief Appeals Officer (1992) *Report 1991*, Dublin: Stationary Office

Chief Appeals Officer (1993) *Annual Report 1992*, Dublin: Stationary Office

Clark, R. (1978) 'Social Welfare Insurance Appeals in the Republic of Ireland' (1978) XIII *Ir. Jur.* (n.s.) 205

———— (1985) 'Law and the Unemployed' 32 *Administration* 413

Clinton, D., M. Yates and D. Kang (1994) *Integrating Taxes and Benefits?* London: Institute for Public Policy Research.

Combat Poverty Agency (1988) *Poverty and the Social Welfare System in Ireland*, Dublin: CPA

———— (1991) *Scheme of Last Resort*, Dublin: CPA

———— (1993) *Building a Fairer Future*, Dublin: CPA

Commission of the EC (1993a) *European Social Policy: Options for the Union*, Luxembourg: Office for Official Publications of the European Communities

———— (1993b) *Growth, Competitiveness, Employment*, Luxembourg: Office for Official Publications of the European Communities

———— (1994a) *Social Protection in Europe*, Luxembourg: Office for Official Publications of the European Communities

———— (1994b) *European Social Policy – A Way Forward for the Union*, Luxembourg: Office for Official Publications of the European Communities

Commission on Social Welfare (1986) *Report*, Dublin: Stationary Office

Commission on Taxation (1982) *First Report*, Dublin: Stationary Office

Commission on the Relief of the Sick and Destitute, including the Insane Poor (1927) *Report*, Dublin: Stationary Office

Commission on the Status of Women (1972), *Report*, Dublin: Stationary Office

Commission on the Status of Women, Second (1993) *Report*, Dublin: Stationary Office

Commission on Vocational Organisation (1943) *Report*, Dublin: Stationary Office
Commission on Workmen's Compensation (1962) *Reports*, Dublin: Stationary Office
Committee of Inquiry into Health Insurance and Medical Services, (1925) *Interim Report*, Dublin: Stationary Office
Committee on Public Accounts (1989) *Report 1989*, Dublin: Stationary Office
Committee on Old Age Pensions (1926) *Report*, Dublin: Stationary Office
Committee on Widow's and Orphan's Pensions (1933) *Report*, Dublin: Stationary Office
Comptroller and Auditor General (1993) *Report 1992*, Dublin: Stationary Office
Cook D. (1991) 'Social injustice: the differential enforcement of tax and social security regulations' in Adler et al. (1991)
Cook, G. (1986) 'Britain's Legacy to the Irish Social Security System' in P. J. Drudy ed. *Ireland and Britain since 1922*, Cambridge: Cambridge University Press
Cook, G. and A. McCashin (1992) 'Inequality, Litigation and Policy Resolution: Gender Dependence in Social Security and Personal Income Tax in the Republic of Ireland' Conference paper, York University
Coolock Community Law Centre (1980) *Social Welfare Appeals*, Dublin: CCLC
Cotterrell, R. (1992) *The Sociology of Law*, London: Butterworths
Council on Social Welfare (1992) *Emerging Trends in the Social Welfare System*, Dublin: CSW
Cousins, M. (1992a), 'Nursing Home Care and Grants', *Irish Social Worker* 11, 1, 21–2
—————— (1992b) 'Liability to Maintain' 86 *Gazette* 387
—————— (1992c) 'Social Welfare Appeals' 10 *Irish Law Times* 114 and 159
—————— (1993a) 'The EC Recommendations on Social Protection: A Case Study in EC Social Policy' 27 *Social Policy and Administration* 286
—————— (1993b) 'Indirect Discrimination in Social Welfare' 11 *Irish Law Times* 147
—————— (1994a) 'The Health (Nursing Homes) Act, 1990' 88 *Gazette* 15
—————— (1994b) 'The Legal Status of Employment and Training Schemes' 12 *Irish Law Times* 43
Cousins, M. and B. Charleton (1991) *Benefit Take Up*, Dublin: Free Legal Advice Centres
Curry, J. (1980; 1993) *The Irish Social Services* (1st and 2nd editions), Dublin: Institute of Public Administration
Curtin, D. (1989) *Irish Employment Equality Law*, Dublin: Round Hall Press
Daly, M. (1989) *Women and Poverty*, Dublin: Attic Press/Combat Poverty Agency
Danzinger, S., R. Haverman, E. Smolensky and K. Taeuber (1980) 'The Urban Impacts of the Program for Better Jobs and Income' in N. Glickman ed. *The Urban Impact of Federal Policies*, Baltimore: John Hopkins University Press
de Beauvoir, S. (1972) *The Second Sex*, Harmondsworth: Penguin
Department of Finance (1958) *Economic Development*, Dublin: Stationary Office
Department of Social Welfare (1949) *Social Security*, Dublin: Stationary Office
—————— (1976) *A National Income Related Pension Scheme*, Dublin: Stationary Office
Department of Social Welfare, Planning Unit (1991) 'The Social Welfare Appeals System – The Legislative Framework' Paper delivered at a seminar on the Social Welfare Appeals System, Dublin
Dignan, J. (1945) *Social Security: Outlines of a Scheme of National Health Insurance*, Sligo
—————— (1950) 'The Government Proposals for Social Security' IV *Christus Rex* 103
Dilnot, A., J. Kay and C. Morris (1984) *The Reform of Social Security*, London: Institute for Fiscal Studies
Dineen, D. (1992) 'Atypical Work Patterns in Ireland: Short-term Adjustments or Fundamental Changes?'' 40 *Administration* 248
Dramin, A. (1986), 'Home Help Services for the Elderly in the Eastern Health Board Area', 34 *Administration* 527
Dupeyroux, J.J. and X. Prétot (1989), *Sécurité sociale*, Paris: Éditions Sirey
Ehrlich E. (1922) 'The Sociology of Law' 36 *Harv L Rev* 130
Epstein, J. (1990) *Public Services: Working for the Consumer*, Dublin: European Foundation for the Improvement of Living and Working Conditions
Esam, P. and R. Berthoud (1991) *Independent Benefits for Men and Women*, London: Policy Studies Institute

Esping-Andersen, G. (1990) *The Three Worlds of Welfare Capitalism*, Cambridge: Polity

European Observatory on Family Policies (1991), *Families and Policies: Evolution and Trends 1989–1990*, Brussels: European Commission

European Observatory on Family Policies (1992), *National Family Policies in EC Countries in 1991*, Brussels: European Commission

Eurostat (1985) *Community Survey on the Structure of Agricultural Holdings, 1979/80*, Luxembourg: Office for Official Publications of the European Communities

Evans, P., D. Rueschemeyer and T. Skocpol (1985) *Bringing the State Back In*, Cambridge: Cambridge University Press

Expert Working Group on the Integration of the Tax and Social Welfare Systems (1993) *Interim Report*, Report to the Department of Social Welfare

Fahey, T. (1992a) 'Catholicism and Industrial Society in Ireland' in Goldthorpe and Whelan (1992)

———— (1992b) 'Housework, the Household Economy and Economic Development in Ireland since the 1920s' 2 *Irish Journal of Sociology* 42

———— (1993) 'Review Article' 24 *Economic and Social Review* 199

Farley, D. (1964) *Social Insurance and Social Assistance in Ireland*, Dublin: Institute of Public Administration

Feingold, W. (1976) 'The Tenant's Movement to Capture the Irish Poor Law Boards 1877–1886' 7 *Albion* 216

———— (1984) *The Revolt of the Tenantry: The Transformation of Local Government in Ireland 1871–1886*, Boston: Northeastern University Press

Fine-Davis, M. (1983) *Women and Work in Ireland*, Dublin: Council for the Status of Women

Focus Point (1988) *At Whose Discretion? a report on the operation of the Supplementary Welfare Allowance Scheme*, Dublin: Focus Point

Fogarty, M., L. Ryan and J. Lee (1984) *Irish Values and Attitudes*, Dublin: Dominican Publications

Foucault, M. (1977) *Discipline and Punish*, Harmondsworth: Penguin

———— (1980) 'The Eye of Power' in *Power/Knowledge*, New York: Harvester Wheatsheaf

———— (1988) 'Social Security' in *Politics, Philosophy, Culture*, London: Routledge

Fulbrook, J., (1978) *Administrative Justice and the Unemployed*, London: Mansell

Fraser, N. and L. Nicholson (1988) 'Social Criticism without Philosophy' 5 *Theory, Culture and Society* 373

Gillion, C. (1991) 'Aging populations: Spreading the costs' 1 *Journal of European Social Policy* 107

Ginn, J. and S. Arber (1992) "Towards women's independence: pension systems in three contrasting European welfare states' 2 *Journal of European Social Policy* 255

Girvin, B. (1989) *Between Two Worlds: Politics and Economy in Independent Ireland*, Dublin: Gill and Macmillan

Glendinning, C. (1990) 'Dependency and Interdependency: the Incomes of Informal Carers and the Impact of Social Security' 19 *Journal of Social Policy* 469

———— (1992) *The Costs of Informal Care: Looking Inside the Household*, London: HMSO

Glendinning C. and E. McLaughlin (1993), *Paying for Care: Lessons from Europe*, London: HMSO

Goldthorpe, J.H., and C.T. Whelan eds. *The Development of Industrial Society in Ireland*, Oxford: Oxford University Press/British Academy

Habermas, J. (1976) *Legitimation Crisis*, Cambridge: Polity

———— (1987) *The Theory of Communicative Action: Volume 2*, Cambridge: Polity

———— (1989) *The Political Transformation of the Public Sphere*, Cambridge: Polity

Hannan, D. and P. Commins (1992) 'The Significance of Small-scale Landholders in Ireland's Socio-economic Transformation' in Goldthorpe and Whelan (1992)

Hardiman, N. (1988) *Pay, Politics and Economic Performance in Ireland 1970– 1987*, Oxford: Clarendon Press

Hensey, B (1979; 1988), The Health Services of Ireland (Third and fourth editions), Dublin: Institute of Public Administration

Hinrichs, K., C. Offe and H. Wiesenthal (1988) 'Time, Money and Welfare-State Capitalism' in Keane (1988)

Honohan, P. (1987) 'A Radical Reform of Social Welfare and Income Tax Evaluated' 35 *Administration* 69

————— (1994) 'Basic Income as a Reform of Tax and Social Welfare' Conference Paper, Dublin

Hughes, G. (1982) *Social Insurance and Absence from Work in Ireland*, Dublin: Economic and Social Research Institute

————— (1985) *Payroll Tax Incidence, the Direct Tax Burden and the Rate of Return on State Pension Contributions in Ireland*, Dublin: Economic and Social Research Institute

————— (1988) *Disability Benefit Reform: Rationalisation or Subsidisation?*, Dublin: Economic and Social Research Institute

————— (1994) *Private Pensions in OECD Countries: Ireland*, Paris: OECD

Humphries, J. (1977), 'Class Struggle and the Persistence of the Working Class Family', 1 *Cambridge Journal of Economics* 241

Hunt A. (1990) 'Rights and Social Movements: Counter-Hegemonic Strategies' 17 *J. Law and Soc.* 309

Independent Poverty Action Movement (1986) *Poor Aid? The Supplementary Welfare Allowance Scheme Ten Years On*, Dublin: IPAM

IPA (1994) *Administration Yearbook and Diary*, Dublin: Institute of Public Administration

Ireland (1958) *Programme for Economic Expansion*, Dublin: Stationary Office

Ireland (1964) *Second Programme for Economic Expansion*, Dublin: Stationary Office

Ireland (1969) *Third Programme for Economic and Social Development*, Dublin: Stationary Office

Ireland (1984) *Building on Reality 1985–1987*, Dublin: Stationary Office

Ireland (1987) *Programme for National Recovery*, Dublin: Stationary Office

Ireland (1991) *Programme for Economic and Social Progress*, Dublin: Stationary Office

Ireland (1994) *Programme for Competitiveness and Work*, Dublin: Stationary Office

Jenkins, S. (1991) 'Poverty Measurement and the Within-Household Distribution: Agenda for Action' 20 *Jnl. Soc. Pol.* 457

Johnson A. and M. Gallagher (1994) 'The Paradox of Irish Economic Development' 22 *Class Struggle* 14

Joint Committee on Women's Rights (1985) *Second Report*, Dublin: Stationary Office

Kaim-Caudle, P. (1967) *Social Policy in the Republic of Ireland*, London: Routledge and Keegan Paul

Kavanagh, J. (1956) *Manual of Social Ethics*, Dublin: Gill

Keane, J. ed. (1988) *Civil Society and the State*, London: Verso

Kelly, F. (1988) *A Guide to Early Irish Law*, Dublin: Dublin Institute for Advanced Studies

Kelly, J. with G. Hogan and G. Whyte (1987) *The Irish Constitution* Supplement to the 2nd ed., Dublin: Jurist Publications

Kennedy, F. (1989) *Family, Economy and Government in Ireland*, Dublin: Economic and Social Research Institute

Kennedy, K. (1993) *The Unemployment Crisis in Ireland*, Cork: Cork University Press

Kennedy, K. and B. Dowling (1975) *Economic Growth in Ireland*, Dublin: Gill and Macmillan

Kerr, C., J. Dunlop, F. Harbison and C. Myers (1964) *Industrialism and Industrial Man*, New York: Oxford University Press

Korpi, W. (1980) 'Social Policy and Distributional Conflicts in the Capitalist Democracies. A Preliminary Comparative Framework.' 3 *Western European Politics* 296

————— (1992) *Welfare State Development in Europe since 1930: Ireland in Comparative Perspective*, Dublin: Economic and Social Research Institute

Lee, J. (1989) *Ireland 1912–1985: Politics and Society*, Cambridge: Cambridge University Press

Lipsky M. (1991) 'The paradox of managing discretionary workers in social welfare policy' in Adler (1991)

Lucey, C. (1943) 'The Beveridge Report and Éire' XXXII *Studies* 36

Luckhaus, L. (1990) 'Changing Rules, Enduring Structures' 53 *Modern Law Review* 655

Luckhaus, L. and L. Dickens (1990) *Social Protection of Atypical Workers in Ireland*, Brussels: Commission of the European Communities

────── (1991) *Social Protection of the Self-Employed in Ireland*, Brussels: Commission of the European Communities

Lyotard, J. F. (1979) *La condition postmoderne*, Paris: Éditions de Minuit

Madden, D. (1994) 'Overview of Green Paper – Irish Perspectives – Employment Issues' Conference Paper, Dublin

Mair, P. (1987) *The Changing Irish Party System*, London: Pinter

Maguire, M. (1984) 'Components of Growth of Income Maintenance Expenditure in Ireland 1951–1979' 15 *Economic and Social Review* 75

────── (1986) 'Ireland' in P. Flora ed., *Growth to Limits: The Western European Welfare States since World War II*, Vol. 2, Berlin: Walter de Gruyter

────── (1987) 'Ireland' in P. Flora ed., *Growth to Limits: The Western European Welfare States since World War IV*, Vol. 2, Berlin: Walter de Gruyter

McCashin, A. (1986) *Income Distribution*, Dublin: Commission on Social Welfare

────── (1993) *Lone Parents in the Republic of Ireland*, Dublin: Economic and Social Research Institute

McCashin, T. (1975–6) 'Rural Dole Payments' 7 *Social Studies* 366

McKee, E. (1986–7) 'Church-state relations and the development of Irish health policy: the mother-and-child scheme, 1944–53' XXV *Ir. Hist. Studies* 159

McLaughlin, Eithne (1991) Work and Welfare Benefits: Social Security, Employment and Unemployment in the 1990s' 20 *Jnl. Soc. Pol.* 484

────── (1992) 'Mixed Blessings? The Invalid Care Allowance and the Carer's Income Needs', Benefits 3, 8–11

McLaughlin, Eithne, J. Millar and K. Cooke (1989) *Work and Welfare Benefits*, Aldershot: Avebury

McLaughlin, Eugene (1993) 'Ireland: Catholic Corporatism' in A. Cochrane and J. Clarke eds. *Comparing Welfare States: Britain in International Context*, London: Sage

McNamara, T. (1992) 'Government without Citizens: The Irish Experience' 40 *Administration* 307

Mangan, G. (1993) 'Social Protection and the Single Market' in S. Ó Cinnéide ed. *Social Europe: EC Social Policy and Ireland*, Dublin: Institute of European Affairs

Millar, J. and C. Glendinning (1989) 'Gender and Poverty' 18 *Jnl. Soc. Pol.* 363

Millar, J., S. Leeper, and C. Davies (1992) *Lone Parents, Poverty and Public Policy in Ireland*, Dublin: Combat Poverty Agency

Mishra R. (1977) *Society and Social Policy: Theoretical Perspectives of Welfare*, London: MacMillan

MISSOC (1993) *Social Protection in the Member States of the Community*, Brussels: Commission of the EC

Mjøset, L. (1993) *The Irish Economy in a Comparative Institutional Perspective*, Dublin: National Economic and Social Council

National Pensions Board (1988) *Report on the Extension of Social Insurance to the Self-Employed*, Dublin: Stationary Office

────── (1993) *Developing the National Pension System*, Dublin: Stationary Office

NESC (1978) *Integrated Approaches to Personal Income Taxes and Transfers*, Dublin: National Economic and Social Council

────── (1986) *A Strategy for Development, 1986–1990*, Dublin: National Economic and Social Council

────── (1987) *Community Care Services: An Overview*, Dublin: National Economic and Social Council

────── (1990) *A Strategy for the Nineties: Economic Stability and Structural Change*, Dublin: NESC

────── (1992) *Women's Participation in the Irish Labour Market*, Dublin: National Economic and Social Council

NESC (1993) *A Strategy for Competitiveness, Growth and Employment*, Dublin: National Economic and Social Council

NESF (1994) *Income Maintenance Strategies*, Dublin: National Economic and Social Forum

Newman, J. (1987) *Puppets of Utopia*, Dublin: Four Courts

Nichols, G. (1856) *A History of the Irish Poor Law*, London: Murray (reprinted 1967 New York: Kelley)

Nolan, B. and B. Farrell (1990) *Child Poverty in Ireland*, Dublin: Combat Poverty Agency

Noonan, M. (1983) *Who Cares about the Carers?*, Dublin: Council for the Status of Women

Ó Cinnéide, S. (1970) *A Law for the Poor*, Dublin: Institute of Public Administration

O'Connell, P., and D. Rottman (1992) 'The Irish Welfare State in Comparative Perspective' in Goldthorpe and Whelan (1992).

O'Connor, J., R. Hearne and K. Walsh (1986) *Social Assistance: Experience and perceptions of first-time applicants*, Dublin: Commission on Social Welfare

O'Connor, J., E. Smyth and B. Whelan (1988), *Caring for the Elderly. Part 1: A Study of Carers at Home and in the Community*, Dublin: National Council for the Aged

O'Connor, J., and H. Ruddle (1988), *Caring for the Elderly Part II: The Caring Process: A Study of Carers in the Home*, Dublin: National Council for the Aged

OECD (1990) *Lone Parent Families: The Economic Challenge*, Paris: OECD

────── (1991) *Shaping Structural Change. The Role of Women*, Paris: OECD

────── (1994) *The OECD Jobs Study: Facts, Analysis, Strategies*, Paris: OECD

O'Faolain, S. (1969) *The Irish*, Harmondsworth: Penguin

Offe, C. (1992) 'A Non-Productivist Design for Social Policies' in P. Van Parjis ed. *Arguing for Basic Income*, London: Verso

Ogus, A., E. Barendt, T. Buck and T. Lynes (1988) *The Law of Social Security* 3rd ed., London: Butterworths

O'Hearn, D. (1993) 'Global Competition, Europe and Irish Peripherality' 24 *Economic and Social Review* 169

Ombudsman (1994) *Annual Report 1993*, Dublin: Stationary Office

O'Sullivan, J.J. (1954) 'The New Social Welfare System' in F. King ed. *Public Administration in Ireland* Vol. III, Dublin: Civics Institute of Ireland

Pahl, J. (1988) 'Earning, Sharing, Spending: Married Couples and Their Money' in R. Walker and G. Parker eds., *Money Matters*, London: Sage

Parker, H. (1994) 'Citizen's Income' 17 *Citizen's Income Bulletin* 4

Pennings F. (1990) *Benefits of Doubt*, Deventer – Boston: Kluwer

Prechal, S. and N. Burrows (1990) *Gender Discrimination Law of the European Community*, Aldershot: Dartmouth

Poulantzas, N. (1968) *Pouvoir politique et classes sociales*, Paris: Maspero

────── (1974) *Les classes sociales dans le capitalisme aujourd'hui*, Paris: Éditions du Seuil

Powell F. (1992) *The Politics of Irish Social Policy 1600–1990*, Lewiston: Edwin Mellen

Revenue Commissioners (1993), *Statistical Report 1992*, Dublin: Stationary Office

Review Group on the Treatment of Households in the Social Welfare Code (1991) *Report*, Dublin: Stationary Office

Ronayne, T. and E. Devereux (1993) *Labour Market Provision for the Long -term Unemployed: The Social Employment Scheme*, Limerick: PAUL Partnership

Rosanvallon, P. (1988) 'The Decline of Social Visibility' in Keane (1988)

Rottman, D. (1994) 'Allocating Money Within Households' in B. Nolan and T. Callan eds. *Poverty and Policy in Ireland*, Dublin: Gill and Macmillan

Rottman, D., D. Hannan and N. Hardiman, M. Wiley (1982) *The Distribution of Income in the Republic of Ireland*, Dublin: Economic and Social Research Institute

Ruddle, H. and J. O'Connor (1993) *Caring Without Limits?* Dublin: Alzheimer Society of Ireland

Sainsbury, R. (1988) 'Deciding Social Security Claims: A Study in the Theory and Practice of Administrative Justice' PhD. thesis, University of Edinburgh

Sandford, C. and O. Morrisey (1985) *The Irish Wealth Tax: A Case Study in Economics and Politics*, Dublin: Economic and Social Research Institute

Senate Select Committee (1933) *Report on the National Insurance Bill, 1933*, Dublin: Stationary Office

Skocpol, T. (1985) 'Bringing the State Back In: Strategies of Analysis in Current Research' in Evans et al. (1985)

Väisänen, I. (1992) 'Conflict and consensus in social policy development: A comparative study of social insurance in 18 OECD countries, 1930–1985' 22 *European Journal of Political Research* 307

Walsh, B. (1974) 'Income Maintenance Payments in Ireland' 5 *Economic and Social Review* 213

———— (1992) 'Appropriate Policy Changes' in A. Gray ed. *Responses to Irish Unemployment*, Dublin: Indecon

Walter, T. (1989) *Basic Income: Freedom from Poverty, Freedom to Work*, London: Marion Boyars

Ward, P. (1989) *The Financial Consequences of Marital Breakdown*, Dublin: Combat Poverty Agency

Watson, P. (1980) *Social Security Law of the European Communities*, London: Mansell

Weber, M. (1968) *On Charisma and Institution Building*, Chicago: University of Chicago Press

Whelan, C., R. Breen and B. Whelan, (1992) 'Industrialisation, Class Formation and Social Mobility in Ireland' in Goldthorpe and Whelan (1992)

Whiteford, P. (1985) *A Family's Need: Equivalence Scales, Poverty and Social Security*, Canberra: Department of Social Security

Whyte, G. (1986) 'Social Welfare Law 1985/1986 – The Year In Review', *Journal of the Irish Society of Labour Law* 5, 135–50

————, ed. (1988) *Sex Equality, Community Rights and Irish Social Welfare Law*, Dublin: Irish Centre for European Law

———— (1989) 'Social Welfare Law – The Cohabitation Rule' 11 *Dublin University Law Journal* 187

———— (1990) 'Enforcing Maintenance Obligations through the Welfare System' 84 *Gazette* 5

———— (1992) 'Report of the Review Group on the Treatment of Households in the Social Welfare Code: A Legal Perspective' 40 *Administration* 134

———— (1995) 'Gender and Equality in the Irish Social Welfare System' in *Yearbook of Human Rights Law* forthcoming

Whyte G., and M. Cousins (1989) 'Reforming the Social Welfare Appeals System' (1989) 7 *Irish Law Times* 198

———— (1993) *A Guide to Supplementary Welfare Allowance*. Dublin: Free Legal Advice Centre

Whyte G., P. Ward and M. Cousins (1994) *Social Welfare Law: Materials for the Professional Course*. Dublin: Incorporated Law Society of Ireland

Whyte, J. (1980) *Church and State in Modern Ireland 1923–1979* (2nd edition), Dublin: Gill and Macmillan

Winslow, A., (1993), 'The Implications of Caregiving for Carers of People with Physical Disabilities', MSocSc thesis, University College Dublin

Index